More Praise For *A Higher Bid*

"Just as Kathy the auctioneer can ignite the passion of an audience, so will she ignite your passion for raising funds and changing the world. If you want to be an effective fundraiser, then read *A Higher Bid* again and again."

Sharon J. Danosky,
President and Founder, Danosky & Associates

"Kathy Kingston has moved mountains for so many non-profits with her impressive auction expertise, event savvy and incredible talent as an auctioneer. In A Higher Bid, she takes special event fundraising to a more meaningful and impactful place, all with an emphasis on mission. Enjoy these words of wisdom from one of the best in the field!"

Hadley Luddy,
Executive Director Big Brothers Big Sisters of Cape Cod and the Islands

"Kathy's book is just like one of her exciting gala auctions: Compelling ideas that you feel good about and want to invest in. It is also easy to read with great take aways to start using for your events right now."

Peter J. Heller
Peter J. Heller Nonprofit Fundraising Consulting

"Kathy's work with us turbocharged our annual auction and enabled us to more than double our live auction proceeds. Her focus on carefully orchestrating the event to communicate the life changing difference Nashoba Learning Group makes for individuals with autism and the clear value of supporting NLG is what made this difference. Kathy's book *A Higher Bid* clearly and engagingly lays out her proven strategies for maximizing the impact of all facets of a charity auction and will empower the reader to create a winning auction."

Liz Martineau,
Founder and President Nashoba Learning Group

"High on my list of books to read is '*A Higher Bid*.' If you run an organization that does any kind of fundraising, you MUST read this book. It will take your organization to a higher level."

Stephen Shapiro,
author, "Best Practices are Stupid.

"Funny, compassionate, and saavy, Kingston demystifies the charity auction so many nonprofits slap together with crazed desperation. She knows exactly how to make people give—and, even better, make them *want* to give."

Jeannette Cooperman, Ph.D.,
author, The St. Louis Woman's Exchange: 130 Years of the Gentle Art of Survival

"If your non-profit or philanthropic organization is looking for ways to raise money, a lot of money, more that you've envisioned, you need to read *A Higher Bid* by Kathy Kingston. Exceptionally successful auctions are more than just asking people to bid. To raise astronomical amounts of money, auctions need to be strategically orchestrated events. *A Higher Bid* provides the roadmap for your next fundraiser. Get it now."

Simma Lieberman,
President, Simma Lieberman Associates

"Kathy Kingston is one of the most respected benefit auctioneers in the business. She truly has the Midas touch—and the good news is that you can, too. Read A Higher Bid and soak in 30 years of wisdom and donor development via benefit auctions."

Connie J. M. Johnson,
BAS, President, Benefit Auction Institute; Kurt Johnson, BAS, President, Kurt Johnson Auctioneering, Inc.

"Are you massively excited about your next auction and fundraising event? Read A Higher Bid and you will be. If you are already excited, read this book to discover tons of amazing ideas to use today and raise more funds than ever."

Karen Eber Davis,
author, 7 Nonprofit Income Streams: Open the Floodgate to Sustainability!

"Going once, going twice, you don't want to miss the opportunity to read Kathy Kingston's inspiring auction story. I'm always amazed at how Kathy creates a bidding frenzy in a crowd of thousands at our Out & Equal Workplace Summit every year. Now you can hear from Kathy how she does it."

Selisse Berry,
Founder and Chief Executive Officer Out & Equal Workplace Advocates

"Here is a new resource book for you—*A Higher Bid!* You will benefit from Kathy's years of experience as an auctioneer and fundraising consultant. She offers specifics to help you plan your benefit auction from start to it financially-successful finish—no detail is left to your imagination. What an unbelievable tool this book is! Kathy is holding your hand throughout. You may have thought you knew about benefit auctions until you read this book."

Sharon Richards Founder, YWCA Alaska

Kathy Kingston is a fundraising genius! I have implemented her strategies in *A Higher Bid* many times in my events that yielded profitable results.

Melissa Davis,
CAI, AARE, BAS, Professional Auctioneer, President, Reppert Auction School

Kathy Kingston's *A Higher Bid* will bring tremendous clarity to all who are charged with the responsibility of raising the bar for their annual fund raising event or onetime gala. Her ability to communicate the challenges with viable solutions will speak to the novice and expert alike. A must read for professional staff as well as volunteers.

Thomas W. Saturley,
CAI President | Tranzon Auction Properties, President,
2014–2015 National Auctioneers Association

"We've benefitted greatly from Kathy Kingston's fundraising strategies. You can too. Read her book *A Higher Bid and* take your benefit auction fundraiser to the next level. Kathy's has been a wonderful addition to our Holiday Auction over the last four years due to her professionalism and high standards. Kathy's focus on connecting our audience with our organization's mission helped us to almost double our auction revenue over the last 4 years—an auction that had already been successful for 13 years at the time. Our Fund The Need in particular went from less than $15,000 to over $60,000. This led to a direct increase in our ability to impact the community we serve."

Joe Hungler,
Executive Director Boys and Girls Club of Greater Lowell

"Kathy Kingston has your key to *A Higher Bid* in her handy-dandy gem of a guide to success of your next (or first!) auction fundraiser. You will say it is worth many times your investment. Kathy is a master teacher and an inspiration and will turn out to be your best friend in the business of fundraising."

Mary Bruemmer,
former Dean of Student Affairs, Saint Louis University

"Kathy Kingston has nailed it! *A Higher Bid* drills down and makes it easy to understand exactly what it takes to make a fundraiser work and what doesn't. A must read for professional fundraisers, auctioneers and anyone managing a philanthropic group, organizing a school fundraiser or overseeing a high profile gala."

Mike Jones,
CAI, GPPA, BAS President | Professional Auctioneer United
Country Auction Services Texas Auction Academy

"What a gem of a book. Kathy Kingston so clearly demonstrates what it means to be strategic as well as practical when it comes to bringing donors closer to the mission and having a successful event. This great resource not only teaches nonprofit administrators, development professionals, board members, volunteers and donors alike how to tell stories that inspire others to give; it provides hands-on advice on production of all aspects of powerful, effective fundraising events and auctions. As she has done throughout her career, Kathy Kingston helps us think more clearly about ways to have the greatest impact we can on making a difference in our community."

Lynn Sobel,
Lynn Sobel & Associates, Full-Circle Philanthropy Development Consulting

"The art and science of "encouraged" charitable giving comes alive in Kathy Kingston's inimitable style in *A Higher Bid*."

Beverly Alter,
Executive Committee Member GALA Choruses

"Kathy Kingston is amazing and so is her book A *Higher Bid.* You'll benefit from her innovative and profitable strategies just like we did. From the first time she worked with our Alaska Native Art Auction, we took our event to a new level. Kathy wasn't just an auctioneer you talk to a couple of times and then shows up at the event. As a strategist, Kathy was there for us every step of the way, guiding us through the planning process and developing our goals. She taught us techniques to get the audience warmed up, engaged and competing over our auction items…in a fun way of course! We quadrupled our revenue the first year and kept using her strategies to grow it from there."

Barbara Donatelli,
Senior Vice President Cook Inlet Region, Inc. (CIRI) Alaska Native Art Auction Executive Committee

"Fundraising veteran Kathy Kingston has documented her many years of successful fundraising and benefit auction knowledge. For non-profits and schools looking to generate more revenue at their fundraising events, *A Higher Bid* is a must have book!

Christie King,
CAI, BAS, AARE, President, C King Benefit Auctions National Auctioneer Association president 2011–2012

"This is required reading for anyone who wants to raise funds for a cause they believe in. *A Higher Bid* connects purpose with people for dramatic results. Kathy is the foremost authority in igniting generosity in others to maximize support for your cause. She shares her expertise in a practical, easy to apply manner that will get you results beyond your wildest dreams. You'll will learn Kathy's secrets in A Higher Bid."

Donna Brighton,
President of Brighton Leadership Group, Leadership: Chicago and Leadership Uncorked

"With competition so tight for the fundraising dollar **A Higher Bid** teaches the event coordinator at any skill level how to rise above the rest, capture more revenue today and into the future."

Jack D. Wilson, Jr.,
President/Chief Executive Officer Northwest Software Technologies, Inc.

"Packed with insight and inspiration, *A Higher Bid* provides you with the essential strategies, creativity and skills you need to make your fundraising auctions truly transformative: for your staff, volunteers, donors and most importantly the population you care about. Let Kathy Kingston's success, meticulous research and passion for making a difference inspire you to exceed your fundraising goals, create lasting relationships with your donors and transform your approach to fundraising."

Kathryn Leavey,
parent and volunteer Tucson Mountain Association

Benefit auctions present unique opportunities as well as pitfalls, and Kathy's comprehensive book helps first-timers and seasoned fundraisers navigate the planning to ensure a successful fundraising event. My advice: read *A Higher Bid* and do exactly as she says!"

Eric Valliere,
Executive Director Symphony NH

"A Higher Bid is an eye opening, heart warming, fun book. Kathy explains sophisticated, advanced strategies with such straightforward simplicity and grace that it took me from knowing *nothing* about auctions to being able to strategically advise my son's Montessori School to raise more money. Kathy Kingston's expertise and skill as an auctioneer, coach, and teacher are remarkable!"

Michele Camacho,
mother of a student at Webster Montessori School, Rochester, NY

"Kathy Kingston's time proven skills, techniques and hints helped us raise 40% more money than the previous year. Kathy's strategic thinking in A Higher Bid will help your non-profit organization reach new heights as well!"

Douglas Lovell,
Director of Parent Relations & Planned Giving,
Cardigan Mountain School

After working with Kathy we experienced firsthand her unique approach that combines theory, strategy, planning, and just the right amount of emotion to create "The Kingston Difference." Kathy's strategies led us to our unprecedented success in our fundraising event. In two short years, we went from $700,000 to over $4 million in the Live Auction and Fund-a-Need Appeal alone! (**Note:** Galvin, Neville, *Wine Scores Big for Charity in 2014:* (Wine Spectator, page 24, April 30, 2015)). *Wine Spectator* named Sonoma Harvest Wine Auction number three in the Top Ten US Charity Wine Auctions for 2014.

Maureen L. Cottingham and Honore Comfort,
Co-Directors, Sonoma Harvest Wine Auction

"Get out your highlighter and sticky notes. *A Higher Bid* is packed with profit-making ideas that you will use immediately. Kathy's book will transform your auction committees from saying "we've always done it this way" to excitement about adopting new strategic approaches for record-breaking success."

Lynne Zink,
Professional Auctioneer & Consultant and International
Auctioneer Champion

A HIGHER BID

How to **Transform**
Special Event
Fundraising
with **Strategic**
Benefit
Auctions

KATHY KINGSTON

WILEY

The AFP Fund Development Series

The AFP Fund Development Series is intended to provide fund-development professionals and volunteers, including board members (and others interested in the nonprofit sector) with top-quality publications that help advance philanthropy as voluntary action for the public good. Our goal is to provide practical, timely guidance and information on fundraising, charitable giving, and related subjects. The Association of Fundraising Professionals (AFP) and John Wiley & Sons, Inc., each bring to this innovative collaboration unique and important resources that result in a whole greater than the sum of its parts. For information on other books in the series, please visit www.afpnet.org.

The Association of Fundraising Professionals

The Association of Fundraising Professionals (AFP) represents over 30,000 members in more than 207 chapters throughout the United States, Canada, Mexico, and China, working to advance philanthropy through advocacy, research, education, and certification programs.

The association fosters development and growth of fundraising professionals and promotes high ethical standards in the fundraising profession. For more information or to join the world's largest association of fundraising professionals, visit www.afpnet.org.

AFP Staff

Jacklyn P. Boice
Publisher and Editor-in-Chief, Advancing Philanthropy

Chris Griffin
Product Development Coordinator

Rhonda Starr
Vice President, Education and Training

Reed Stockman
Content Curator and Internet and Program Associate

2015 AFP Publishing Advisory Committee

Cover image: Christine Simmons, Christine Simmons Portraiture
Cover design: Thomas Nery

This book is printed on acid-free paper.

Published by John Wiley & Sons, Inc., Hoboken, New Jersey
Published simultaneously in Canada

For general information about our other products and services, please contact our Customer Care Department within the United States at (800) 762-2974, outside the United States at (317) 572-3993 or fax (317) 572-4002.

Wiley publishes in a variety of print and electronic formats and by print-on-demand. Some material included with standard print versions of this book may not be included in e-books or in print-on-demand. If this book refers to media such as a CD or DVD that is not included in the version you purchased, you may download this material at http://booksupport.wiley.com. For more information about Wiley products, visit www.wiley.com.

Library of Congress Cataloging-in-Publication Data:

Kingston, Kathy.
  A higher bid : how to transform special event fundraising with strategic auctions / Kathy Kingston.
      pages cm
  Includes bibliographical references and index.
  ISBN 978-1-119-01787-5 (hardback)
1. Benefit auctions. 2. Fund raising. 3. Special events–Planning. I. Title.
  HF5476.K48 2015
  658.15′224–dc23

                                                                    2014046105

Printed in the United States of America

10 9 8 7 6 5 4 3 2 1

*This book is dedicated to
my nephew, Arley,
and nieces Megan, Alysha, Molly,
Brianna, Erin, Lexi, and Lindsey:
with love.*

About the Author

Kathy Kingston is the founder and principal of Kingston Auction Company, which has raised millions of dollars for organizations nationwide. She is the creator of the Philanthropy Model of Fundraising Auctions.

Kathy, who has been a consultant and professional fundraising auctioneer for nearly three decades, has been awarded two of the auction industry's major awards, the 2012 Chuck Cumberlin Memorial Sportsmanship Award and the 2006 Rose Award from the National Auctioneers Association. She holds the Certified Auctioneer Institute (CAI) designation; only three percent of auctioneers worldwide have achieved this status. Kathy was a charter class member and has been an instructor of the Benefit Auctioneer Specialist (BAS) professional designation program.

As a consultant, speaker, and fundraising auction strategist, Kathy conducts benefit auction seminars, tele-seminars, and custom workshops for nonprofit and educational organizations as well as for professional auctioneers. She holds a Master's Degree in Education from Saint Louis University, where in 1986 she was named "Woman of the Year." In 2013, she was inducted into the Million Dollar Consultant™ Hall of Fame.

Join Kathy's community

Join Kathy's community and sign up to receive her complimentary monthly insider secrets e-newsletter BIDhi! You'll be kept up-to-date with complimentary educational fundraising auction videos, tips, podcasts, articles, resources, and more. Learn more and sign up here: http://HowToRaiseMoreMoney.com/. You can reach her at kathy@kingstonauction.com.

Contents

Section III Conducting Strategic Benefit Auctions for Donors and Dollars

Section IV Leveraging Strategic Benefit Auctions

Foreword

MANY OF US ARE IN POSITIONS where fundraising becomes our lifeblood, the marker of our success, and the means to pursue our goals. We run organizations, either professionally or in volunteer positions, where we advance a larger cause and serve a greater mission. Fundraising makes it possible to achieve our mission. Despite its fundamental role in our work, most of us have limited experience or knowledge of the highly specialized strategies that lead to financial success.

This is exactly where Kathy Kingston comes in, and changes everything.

After working with Kathy we experienced firsthand her unique approach that combines theory, strategy, planning, and just the right amount of emotion to create "The Kingston Difference." Kathy's strategies led us to our unprecedented success in our fundraising event. In two short years, we went from $700,000 to over $4 million in the Live Auction and Fund-a-Need Appeal alone!

We first met Kathy Kingston several years ago, as we struggled to take our regional wine auction from a local event to one of the leading charitable wine auctions in the country. Over the phone as we were interviewing her, we quickly recognized that she brought a distinctive perspective and a unique set of skills to the business of fundraising. From our research we had learned that Kathy was one of the country's most successful charity auction consultants; however, it wasn't until we began to work with her that we realized Kathy's true gifts:

Where others take more traditional fundraising approaches in their strategies, Kathy Kingston is a professional coach, a woman with great vision and an ability to inspire, motivate, and drive results.

Where others see tired auction bidders, Kathy sees room to expand the "circle of influence" and generate the expectation to give.

Where others use a single formula across all clients, Kathy sees a community and delves into the culture to inspire meaningful and personal philanthropic giving.

Where others focus on the event, Kathy focuses on the mission and creates a culture of giving that transcends the event for long-term donor and stakeholder support.

We recognize that our newly gained fundraising success also comes with a great responsibility, a duty to use our funds wisely and to work with our donors to make a deep and lasting impact on the children and families in our community. We are making a difference, and we know that this community will be stronger because of the foundation that Kathy helped us build and the spirit of giving that she has inspired.

We will always remember that "the number one rule in fundraising is that people give to people," and Kathy Kingston demonstrates this truth on a daily basis.

Now, through *A Higher Bid*, Kathy is sharing her money-making wisdom with a new audience: you the reader. Make sure to keep a notepad handy. The strategies she shares could be a game-changer for you and your cause.

Maureen L. Cottingham, Executive Director,
Sonoma Valley Vintners & Growers

Honore Comfort, Executive Director,
Sonoma County Vintners

Sonoma Wine Country Weekend and
Sonoma Harvest Wine Auction

Introduction

IT ALL STARTED WITH Mrs. Butterworth.

In St. Louis in 1986, I was the auctioneer for my first antiques auction. Near the end of the auction, I heard loud outbursts as two men engaged in heated disagreement over an old, empty Mrs. Butterworth's maple syrup bottle. This was not a valuable item—it had been included as part of a box lot that sold for less than a dollar.

What am I doing? I wondered. There's got to be a better way to conduct auctions. At the time, I had a job as the director of the Saint Louis University Recreation Center. I had just used all my vacation to attend auction school and to set up for that antiques auction. I knew I absolutely loved being an auctioneer, but two men fighting over an empty maple syrup bottle? Really?

I've been raising money for good causes since I was eight years old, when I set up a penny carnival in my backyard to support Easter Seals. I enlisted my friends and invited the whole neighborhood, and we raised a whopping $38! What sticks with me to this day was the handwritten letter I got from the director telling me what a difference the money I'd raised would make to those inner-city kids who would now be able to go to Easter Seals summer camp. When I read her warm letter and, later, saw a photo of happy kids splashing in their lake—I was hooked.

The week after the Mrs. Butterworth's fiasco, I received a phone call from a local school that needed help with a fundraising auction. Here was the chance to do two things I loved: be an auctioneer and help a worthy organization raise money. I jumped at the opportunity.

That was nearly 30 years ago. Since then, I've conducted thousands of auctions and raised millions of dollars all across the country for amazing causes. I know and feel the power of the auction method of fundraising. It's not about selling exotic trips and fancy dinners. It's about communicating the impact of a donor's gift for a cause he or she believes in and loves. It's about engaging supporters to become dedicated donors, now and in the future.

That's why I wrote *A Higher Bid*. I wanted to share my strategies, insights, methods, and, most of all, my passion for using auction fundraisers as a catalyst to create a community of champions for your cause—all the while maximizing fundraising, having fun, and inspiring a culture of philanthropy.

I wrote this book for nonprofit and educational organizations, charities, associations, boards of directors, volunteers, sponsors, kids, executives, auctioneers, event planners, caterers, librarians, development professionals, fundraising consultants, students in nonprofit management and philanthropy programs—and, of course, our generous donors, bidders, and guests. It's also for anybody who commonly uses auctions and events to raise funds, advance a cause, and engage donors.

If that seems like just about everyone, well, actually, it is.

You see, for 29 years I've conducted my own mini-survey whenever I meet someone new. When they ask me what I do, I tell them, "I ignite generosity as a fundraising auctioneer and consultant."

So far, about 70 percent of new people that I meet have been involved in some kind of auction fundraiser—from a complete stranger on a plane who serves on several boards to the owner of a wild bird specialty shop who donates auction items to a new neighbor who volunteers at her kid's school auction.

My next mini-survey question is: How did your fundraiser go?

Without hesitation, people launch into a litany of problems: too much work, burnout, the program was boring, the auctioneer dragged on and on, low bids, people were embarrassed to bid, there were too many items, no one could hear, guests left early, and we didn't make much money. Sometimes I hear confessions: This was not any fun. I hate auctions. I hate events.

Yet auction fundraising is thriving. Billions of dollars are raised annually at charity auctions. In fact, the National Auctioneers Association research shows that over $16.3 billion is raised at benefit auctions annually.[1] Unfortunately, I've heard these same challenges over and over for almost three decades, and not just from auction newcomers. Veteran auction chairpersons and guests make the same remarks. That's because so many organizations are using old tools when they should upgrade to new and innovative approaches that are far more strategic. The old methods leave money in the room and fail to employ a long-term donor engagement strategy.

The truth is, organizations can strategically raise billions *more* every year with a new approach that focuses first and foremost on connecting people to your cause. When designed and conducted strategically, benefit auctions are one of the most powerful ways to raise significantly more charitable dollars annually. Strategic benefit auctions are catalysts for donors to make long-term impacts on causes that impassion them.

It's not what people *get*; it's how much people *give* that makes a difference. That's my core message to charity auction clients and audiences. (Hint: That's how I sold a tangy tangerine for $2,500 in an audience of 37 people. See Chapter 3 for the full story.)

Sadly, many organizers unknowingly misunderstand the power and potential of fundraisers and benefit auctions to be more than just one-time event parties. As a result, they leave untold thousands and thousands of dollars in the room every year. Worse yet, many donors are never invited to stay connected with the organization after the doors close. After the event, they simply leave, taking their energy and dollars elsewhere.

When you fail to deeply engage donors and maximize fundraising, the impact is immense. This is a shame, because your auction proceeds matter deeply. The money raised at these events goes to feed hungry kids their only meals for the day, save injured and abandoned animals, perform lifesaving cancer research, use technology to open communication for people with autism, prevent child abuse and neglect, stimulate downtown small business development, teach third graders to read, enrich communities through music and theater, stand steadfast by our wounded warrior veterans, restore hope and homes for tornado and flood victims, and much, much more.

A Higher Bid draws on my 30 years of experience in fundraising, marketing, and consulting experience in benefit charity auctions and special events. I'll share my proven strategies and, most important, I'll be introducing my strategic benefit auction philanthropy model, which uses auctions as catalysts for greater fundraising and long-term donor engagement.

Let me explain how the book is laid out. In Section I, I invite you to consider a powerful mindset shift that will turn your benefit auctions into an ongoing, inspiring culture of giving. Included here is information about how to determine if auction fundraising is right for you. I'll show you how your stakeholders and auctioneer can serve in new, dynamic leadership roles.

In Section II, I discuss intentional strategic design for your auction events. The idea is to create a unique blueprint for your audience development, show flow, high profit auction items, donor-centered marketing, measurement of impact, and use of technology.

In Section III, I talk about profitable strategies you can use to conduct your auctions and fundraising events. These strategies include robust new income streams, turbocharged strategies for live and silent auctions, and inspirational approaches for fund-a-need special appeals.

In Section IV, I tell you how to bring together all of these strategies so you know where to go from here.

In A Final Call, I share some ways to inspire others and yourself.

With my strategic approach, you can use benefit auctions to create catalysts that create an entire community of champions around your cause. You can create a powerful group of energized supporters who will give to your cause year after year. I've included success stories about some of my clients who have significantly benefited from my experience. You can benefit, too.

I'm delighted that you're reading my book. I hope the dynamic strategies I've collected here will help significantly transform the causes for which you care so deeply. I wish you unprecedented success. I'm here to help you create your own philanthropy. Please feel free to join my community for complimentary resources, newsletters, tips, and videos at http://www.HowToRaiseMoreMoney.com. Please feel free to write to me and share your ideas at kathy@kingstonauction.com.

Kathy Kingston, CAI, BAS

Note

1. Morpace, "Auction Industry Holds Strong in 2008 with $268.5 Billion in Sales," Auction industry survey, 2008. Retrieved from www.exclusivelyauctions.com/pdfs/naa-2008.pdf.

Section I

Strategic Benefit Auctions: The New Catalyst for Philanthropy

1

The Shift: Event Transaction to Philanthropic Transformation

THE BALLROOM PLUNGED INTO DARKNESS. You could hear a pin drop. The silence stilled the guests. Suddenly, a spotlight on stage framed a young man's face.

"I live in a very fast world. That's because I'm a professional race car driver and my car reaches 150 miles an hour with a singular goal—crossing the finish line first. But the first time I saw my brother Jack in the intensive care unit, my life slowed to almost a stop. He was so small—born with Down syndrome—and faced so many challenges, but I saw a light in him. I knew that he would be a great little brother.

"I was right about Jack, because that tiny baby is now the happiest kid I've ever met. There is something about him that just lights up your day. As we have grown up together, I've seen how much Jack's time at the STAR Rubino Family Center has helped him. His speech has improved so much, and he's learned how to swim, even underwater.

"STAR is so important to Jack and countless other children that they are now my racing team's designated charity. So every mile I drive builds awareness and raises funds to help kids like Jack cross their own finish lines and realize their dreams of victory. My name is Justin Piscitell. And STAR is leading the way for my brother Jack."

The house lights went up, illuminating the guests.

"This is only one of the hundreds of success stories you make possible because of your generosity," remarked STAR's board president. "Lives are changed every day because of the dedicated professionals at STAR, and they cannot continue their work without your support. We are here tonight to raise as much money as we can. Your high bidding in our live auction will make a world of difference to our STAR participants. And here to help us raise as much money as we can, please welcome our auctioneer, Kathy Kingston."

As STAR's professional auctioneer, this was my cue. "Together, we are about to do something amazing tonight," I said. "It's really not about what you get, it's about how much you can give to change a person's life, at STAR, just like Justin's brother Jack."

"And now it's fundraising time," I continued. "Live auction item number one is so special. Our STAR participants will create and personally deliver a beautiful flower arrangement to you once a month for an entire year. Remember, the last bid card in the air wins! Let's go. If you believe that your gift can make a difference to help someone like Justin's brother, Jack, raise your bid card for $1 to start."

Every single guest raised their bid card. Quickly, bidding blew past $100; then, $500. Bidding was already over value, and the excitement mounted with each beat of the benefit auction chant. Bid cards were waving at $1,500, $2,000, and $2,500. Suddenly, the bidding jumped to $4,000, and then $5,000.

Two gentlemen fervent to win stood and faced each other with huge smiles. Guests cheered them ever onward. They bid higher and higher, from $5,000 to $6,000, to $6,500, to $7,000! Finally the bidding hit $8,000—for flowers delivered once a month from our STAR participants! Going, going...and they kept on going. The crowd went wild. These two battled back and forth, the audience members on their feet along with the bidders. At the crescendo, the bids reached $8,500. Finally, the second bidder conceded with a grin. I sold the flowers for $8,500!

The board president called out, "We can double this auction item. Sell two, Kathy."

"Sold! Sold!" A live auction item valued at only $380 had just raised $17,000—in only two minutes.

But what happened next was a stunning example of an inspirational surprise that propelled guest emotion and engagement even deeper.

I ran over to the winning bidder and said, "Thank you for your generous bidding for STAR. I'm sure that your wife and family will love these beautiful flowers." The winning bidder leaned into the microphone, "Yes, we really did want to make a significant contribution tonight to STAR. As far as the flowers go, we're going to be giving them to our neighbor who has been having a tough time with her cancer treatments."

This story exemplifies the power of benefit auctions to create a dynamic culture of philanthropy in action. Fundraising is not about items. It's about having the right people in your audience who have the capacity and passion, and then communicating the impact of their high bidding.

What an unforgettable, magical moment.

You can create magic just as STAR, Inc., does at each annual benefit auction. How can you make this magic happen consistently? It requires strategy and preparation and, most of all, it requires a shift in thinking. To show you how you can make this important mind shift for your organization, I'd like to share two models that I created and teach, the Five Pillars of Strategic Benefit Auctions and the Philanthropy Model of Strategic Benefit Auctions.

Benefit auctions are one of the most powerful catalysts for identifying new donors, engaging audiences, raising funds, having fun, and increasing supporter participation across many levels, to ensure long-term giving.

Most importantly, your benefit auction event is an untapped, golden opportunity to connect your supporters meaningfully and deeply to what they love and care about most—by showing them how their gifts will positively impact the cause that impassions them.

Volunteers, board members, development professionals, auctioneers, caterers, and event planners *already hold this golden key in their hands.* The strategies in this book will teach you how to use this key to unlock the ability to raise more money and more deeply engage your donors.

I talked about this vital concept with Jack Wilson, founder and CEO of Northwest Software Technologies, Inc. "Event and auction fundraising is the most effective method of fundraising, designed to engage individuals and businesses that might not otherwise give to your organization," he agreed. "This results in the expansion of your pool of potential long-term financial contributors."[1]

Let's review the five core principles of strategic benefit auctions. We'll look at each pillar and then show how STAR, Inc., leveraged each one to achieve breakthrough success for their fundraising and donor development.

> Five Pillars of Strategic Benefit Auctions
> 1. Find out what matters most to your supporters.
> 2. Invite your supporters in.
> 3. Inspire your supporters to fall in love with you.
> 4. Give them reasons to stay in love with you forever.
> 5. Invest in what counts; ignore the rest.

Pillar 1: Find Out What Matters Most to Your Supporters

"People do not give to needy organizations. They give to lofty causes that can make a difference," says Sharon Danosky, president of Danosky and Associates. Design your event around this core idea, and you will have great success. Why do donors give? In *What Do Donors Want,* Dr. Daniel Oppenheimer, a professor at Princeton University, summarized the research of several prominent social scientists on the determinants of giving behavior. Oppenheimer found that no matter what objective information is available to donors, the majority of donors will give as a result of emotional or relational factors.[2]

In strategic audience development, the personal "ask," which connects people to something they care about, is absolutely critical. It also underscores the importance of developing your audience one guest at a time. Treat your donors as donors and let them be vested in your mission.

At STAR, Inc., board, staff, and volunteers all get to know—personally—the guests who attend their auction. They understand how and why their services and programs matter to each guest. Furthermore, STAR's gala committee members strategically hand-select auction items to match the interests of their audience.

Pillar 2: Invite Your Supporters In

Benefit auctions are one of the most powerful catalysts for identifying new donors. Research by Blackbaud, provider of nonprofit software and services, shows that special events were rated the most effective donor recruitment method in the United States and Europe.[3] The goal of audience development is to not only invite people who care about your cause, but also to inspire power bidders and the other supporters attending your fundraising event and excite them to wave those bid cards higher.

Developing and cultivating an audience filled with guests who are committed to promoting your mission is best achieved through personal and targeted outreach, as well as careful creation of a guest list. In the case of STAR, long-time board member Rob Cioffi brought his friend Matt Glass, whom he wanted to introduce to STAR's services. Prior to the auction they both decided to help raise more money and to have fun doing it by going head-to-head to bid for the flowers. This resulted in $17,000 in funds raised in just a few short minutes.

Pillar 3: Inspire Your Supporters to Fall in Love with You

In his newsletter article "Why Gifts Matter," Thomas Ahern wrote,

> Making a gift is a purchase decision. I expect something in return. What? Just a feeling really, the feeling that by making a gift, I've made a difference. If you don't convey that feeling regularly in your communications, don't expect me to continue giving. Fundraising communicators know the business you're in. You are into making all donors feel very, very good. Too often donors are served a steady diet of how great the agency is when they should receive, instead, heaping helpings of how great the donors are and how much good gifts do.[4]

This wonderful statement underscores the need to communicate the impact of your supporters' gifts at your benefit auctions. We'll be covering this in-depth in the chapters on marketing and measuring impact.

STAR intentionally showcases true stories—for example, Justin, the race car driver, and how STAR changed his brother Jack's life and other kids just like Jack. Each year, the auction's organizers strategically select, write, and rehearse emotionally inspiring stories. Those stories are told in the first person to illustrate their impact on their clients and to deeply engage the audience. A very high percentage of guests return each year, and they tell me that as far as they're concerned, hearing the stories is one of the highlights.

Pillar 4: Give your supporters reasons to stay in love with you forever

Leverage your benefit auction to build long-term relationships and engage your wonderful supporters year-round, before, during, and after your benefit auction event.

My philosophy on fundraising auctions is to maximize the proceeds, of course, but also to create a dynamic climate for giving that transcends the benefit auction event. In other words, you create a culture of giving that begins with pre-action planning, is highly visible at the auction, and continues long after your event ends. In this culture, you can actually make the most money *after* the event, when the doors are closed.

Effective follow-up after the benefit auction event is critical, and many organizations miss this vital process altogether. Successful organizations create strategic plans to deepen relationships with donors and bidders after their benefit auction events. We'll discuss how to build strong relationships after the doors close.

STAR's board and staff understand that their event is not transactional, it's relational. And relationships are built over time. That's why they create a strategic year-round cultivation plan of personally contacting and thanking every guest, inviting them to become more involved with STAR throughout the year. Don't underestimate the power of strategic benefit auctions to deeply activate a new culture of giving. As you'll recall, in the auction the winning bidder gave away the flowers to a friend with cancer, further illustrating a truly generous spirit of giving.

Pillar 5: Invest in What Counts; Ignore the Rest

Spend your valuable time and resources on what raises money and retains donors. This is one of the most overlooked areas of event fundraising. Many volunteers and organizers get wrapped up in aspects of the event that have little or no impact on fundraising or donor loyalty. Let go of things that do not raise money, such as the color of the table napkins, how tall your centerpieces are, the type of dessert served, the band, the dance floor size, even the silent auction. Concentrate on major income producers like live auctions and the fund-a-need appeal, as well as sponsorships and donor engagement and cultivation.

While STAR ensures that all the logistics, including the meal and day-of-event details, are handled professionally and guests have an outstanding and fun experience, the core focus is to more deeply engage guests about the cause and to raise funds for the long term.

Revitalized Leadership Roles for Board Members and Auctioneers

Board members play a pivotal role in the success of a benefit auction event. Benefit auction fundraisers offer a natural way for board members to become more engaged in fundraising and guest cultivation. These events provide a unique forum for people to support your cause. This is the opposite of what most people think. A charity auction event is *not* just a way to raise funds for your charity. It is also a rare opportunity to help board members understand how to fundraise.

The revitalized leadership role of the auctioneer is to serve as a quarterback and also a coach (learn more in Chapter 4), by providing expert fundraising and auction consulting for months prior to the event and months afterward. He also is the strategic quarterback for your entire fundraising event and serves as the ambassador for your cause on and off stage. We'll be discussing this pivotal role in the chapter on auctioneers. The auctioneer works during the pre-auction meetings, during the cocktail hour and silent auction, and before the live auction even begins. You'll want the auctioneer to mingle during the silent auction, meeting and getting to know guests and asking key questions such as: How are guests connected to the organization? Next comes the even more crucial question: What specifically do guests love about the cause and why? By the time the auctioneer gets to the stage for the live auction, he or she will have met nearly all of your guests by interacting with them during the cocktail hour and silent auction, and people will be accustomed to hearing the auctioneer's friendly and knowledgeable voice.

Philanthropy Model versus Transaction Model of Auction Fundraising

Let's look at what's been happening in the past at fundraiser auctions, as well as a new opportunity to take your special event fundraising to the next level with my Philanthropy Model (see Figure 1.1).

The Merriam-Webster dictionary defines *transaction* as "a business deal, an occurrence in which goods, services, or money is passed from one person, account etc., to another."[5] Philanthropy is defined as "the practice of giving money and time to help make life better for other people."[6]

The strategic benefit auction philanthropy model uses benefit auctions as catalysts for greater fundraising and long-term donor engagement (see Figure 1.2). The emphasis is on leveraging the auction event itself as a powerful entry for new and existing supporters to learn about and to become more deeply engaged in the organization. The focus is on higher-level fundraising such as live auctions and fund-a-need appeals. Board members and stakeholders take an active role in guest cultivation and fundraising.

Figure 1.1   The Philanthropy Model of Fundraising Auctions

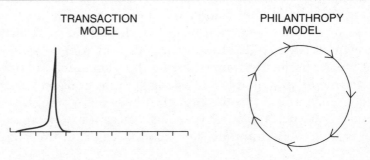

TRANSACTION
MODEL

PHILANTHROPY
MODEL

In contrast, the transaction model uses benefit auctions as a one-time event, a short-term approach (see Figure 1.3). In this transaction model, people often look at the approach as broken. It's very much focused on event-planning transactions, with people simply exchanging money for goods. This is more of a shopping mentality—guests are looking for a bargain. In the transaction model, the audience's motivation to attend is social, and many times there is little emphasis on the mission of the organization.

Simply said, if you want to raise a lot more money and keep your donors, shift from a friend-raiser mind-set to a philanthropic giving mindset. Change your one-time event mind-set to one in which you leverage your auction as a gateway to long-term donor development. And instead of simply "doing" an auction and crossing your fingers, adapt a strategic philanthropy model mind-set.

As nonprofits and schools are challenged for greater income and resources to support their missions, sustainable solutions are required. This paradigm shift advances organizations from the limited view of the transactional model of single-event planning to a long-term view philanthropy model. You get this by creating a culture of giving that has a lasting impact for your entire organization, clients, and community. A strategic approach means that your auction fundraiser has a greater purpose. It goes beyond raising money that night at your event. It has the power to unite people to generate enthusiasm and action—not only to raise money, but also to deepen their relationships to you and your great cause. With this approach, you unite people with fun and energy and purpose.

Figure 1.2   Philanthropy Model Word Cloud

Figure 1.3   Transaction Model Word Cloud

Long boring speeches **Getting**
One-time event No attention to lighting Theme-focused invitations   Donor recognition program
Thank you for attending   Event guests **Friend-raiser mindset** Have a good time
Basic data to measure impact   Auction items found by committee
Amateur auctioneer Focus on party
Use of statistics to show impact   No attention to sound   **Buffet**
Food focus**Transaction Model**Silent auction
Facts to drive giving   Board members, staff, volunteers tell what the organization does
Describe what organization does

Committees sometimes think of a benefit auction or another special fundraising auction event as a one-day business or a stand-alone fundraiser. But fundraising auction events are year-long opportunities, not one-day events. A strong philanthropic program brings people into your organization and strategically ensures that you retain all of those donors, many of whom will upgrade their gifts over time until they give their ultimate gift.

The number-one problem for many nonprofit organizations in this country is that they are not retaining their donors. Donor attrition may be as high as 40 to 70 percent for a typical nonprofit.[7] If you were running a business and lost 60 percent of your customers every year, you'd be out of business. It is as critical for a nonprofit to develop a pool of donors who upgrade their gifts as it is for a business to build steady customers. If you only look at your fundraising auction event as a silo, you are losing the opportunity to cultivate your donors and make sure that they stay by your side over time. Instead, create a dynamic climate for giving that transcends your benefit auction event. It's far more than a party. It's a cultivation event. It's a point of entry for long-term supporters. You must demonstrate fantastic hospitality and set a positive, upbeat inspirational energy that encourages giving. This is critical.

Have you ever been to a school auction where the first-grade cookie jar containing every child's thumbprint sold for thousands of dollars? I have actually sold that exact item for over $10,000! Why? Because this unique handmade cookie jar connects families with the school, their kids, and the ways that education will impact their lives and families.

The Giving Gap

The Giving Gap at benefit auction and fundraising events is the difference between what organizations are raising now and what they could be raising if they designed and conducted their fundraiser events with the Philanthropy Model mind-set. The gap represents the funds organizations are failing to raise with the old Transaction Model approach. This gap also highlights the loss of donor support, not only at the event but also over time. The Giving Gap represents the staggering amount of money that organizations are losing by using an old transaction model instead of a new philanthropy model (see Figure 1.4). Projecting this financial and donor loss over five and ten years, you quickly see the staggering negative consequences. The proven strategies and tips that I've developed will show you how to catapult over the Giving Gap, transforming special events to maximize fundraising and to engage more donors now and into the future.

Figure 1.4   The Giving Gap

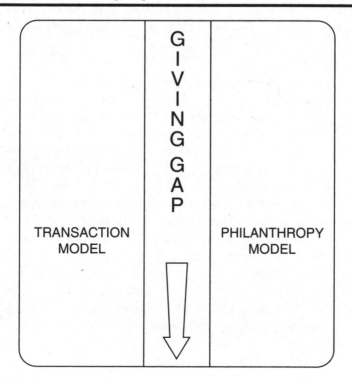

Using the Philanthropy Model and the strategies in this book will help you focus on keeping and treasuring every donor. You will ultimately help your supporters become the philanthropists they all can be. Remember that the fundraising auction event is a terrific opportunity to build relationships. A top predictor of success is how well the organization integrates all aspects of their auction fundraising and donor cultivation into their overall advancement plan.

People do *not* give to needy organizations. They give to lofty causes that can make a difference. In the benefit auction world, we are not in the auction business, nor are we in the event or party business. We are in the relationship business. This is a paradigm shift that moves us from a mentality of "people are just coming to our auction to buy some items" to "our guests are really getting involved by coming to an amazing event where they become more greatly invested in our mission and wish to stay connected to us as a charity of choice."

Transformational Benefits of a Strategic Auction Fundraiser
- Adds an upbeat, exciting dimension to your fundraising capabilities
- Maximizes your staff and volunteer effort
- Creates pride and momentum within your organization
- Generates increased awareness in your community
- Educates the public about your cause
- Encourages businesses to become part of your constituency
- Helps merchants attract new customers, as a result of exposure at your auction
- Binds members and volunteers to your organization
- Offers attendees double the fun: buy at auction *and* support a great cause
- Continues to bring in money long after the event is over
- Broadens your financial base by attracting new donor sources
- Makes everyone a winner: donors, purchasers, your organization, and the clients it serves

Conclusion

Fundraising auctions, when strategically designed and properly conducted, can be a highly effective solution for donor retention, audience engagement, board empowerment, supporter cultivation, mission-focused marketing, and maximum fundraising.

Using the Five Pillars of Strategic Benefit Auctions and the strategic benefit auction Philanthropy Model, organizations can strongly position their fundraiser, auction, or charity benefit to serve as a *powerful catalyst* that can be integrated into a sustainable long-term successful development plan.

Notes

STAR, Inc., Lighting the Way, in partnership with the families and communities we serve, is an innovative leader in providing opportunities for a meaningful life to individuals with disabilities through personal development and participation in the community.

1. Jack Wilson, personal communication, October 28, 2014.
2. C. Gibson and W. M. Dietel, "What Do Donors Want?" *Nonprofit Quarterly*, September 22, 2010. Retrieved from https://nonprofitquarterly.org/index.php?option=com_content&view=article&id=5866:what-d.
3. Blackbaud, *The 2012 State of the Non-Profit Sector Report.* Charleston, SC: Blackbaud, 2012.
4. T. Ahern, "Why Gifts Matter: They Buy Impact and Self Esteem," *Ahern Donor Communications.* Retrieved from http://aherncomm.com/ss_plugins/content/content.php?content.5069.
5. *Merriam Webster Online.* Retrieved October 28, 2014, from www.merriam-webster.com/dictionary/transaction.
6. *Merriam Webster Online.* Retrieved October 28, 2014, from www.merriam-webster.com/dictionary/philanthropy.
7. Association of Fundraising Professionals and the Urban Institute, "2013 Fundraising Effectiveness Survey Report", Fundraising Effectiveness Project, 2013. www.urban.org/uploadedpdf/412906-2013-fundraising-effectiveness-survey-report.pdf.

2

Bid High and Prosper: Are Auctions Right for You?

IN LATE 2010, CHERYLANN GENGLE CONTACTED ME. She was a grieving mother reaching out for fundraising suggestions. Her college-age daughter, Brittany, had been killed in the Haiti earthquake earlier that year. CherylAnn's family wanted to build an orphanage to honor her daughter, while being respectful to the over 250,000 Haitians who had lost their lives. Her goal was to raise enough money to build an orphanage in a developing country.

I remember thinking: Auctions are *a lot* of work. What advice can I possibly give CherylAnn in this tragic moment? She needed more than a fundraising auction event. Raising millions of dollars requires a multipronged strategic fundraising approach.

I advised her about the labor-intensive nature of auctions, especially if the goal is to raise millions of dollars for a building. I also let her know that by choosing a charity auction, she could generate great awareness and new donor support.

In fact, the family did hold an online auction, and it was so successful, it's now an annual gala. CherylAnn's grassroots efforts flourished, growing into a successful fundraising strategy that supports a thriving nonprofit called *Be Like Brit*. Their orphanage houses over 60 children, a school, and a water purification plant for the community—and they're expanding rapidly. "We never looked at this as fundraising. We wanted to honor our daughter Brittany," CherylAnn told me. "We learned that people have to believe in what you are doing and see where the money is going. We're not in the nonprofit world—this is our journey."[1]

A beloved maternity nurse at a regional hospital in Maine was diagnosed with stage IV cancer. Laura was facing huge medical bills. The local community was in grief. A fellow nurse and Laura's friend, Patty, asked me if an auction might be the right way to help Laura. Patty immediately spearheaded a small dedicated group of Laura's friends and colleagues in producing a one-time special charity auction that resulted in an outpouring of love, support, and donations. Laura's bucket wish was to be able to go to Ireland with her husband and two sons. This fundraising auction raised enough money for both the trip and to pay off Laura's medical bills. As their auctioneer and consultant, I too was swept away from the power of their community involvement and a strategic benefit auction—a winning combination![2]

Hundreds of thousands of organizations rely on annual benefit auctions and fundraising events as a staple in their development plans. Well-executed fundraising and charity auctions have proven to be highly successful fundraisers for nonprofits, associations, and schools of all stripes.

Fundraising events and auctions come in all shapes and sizes. Sometimes they meet your immediate needs, as in the case of Laura. Sometimes they are annual events that are part of a development plan (as we see nationally). And sometimes they inspire giving that takes your cause far beyond your dreams (as *Be Like Brit* did for CherylAnn).

That is the point of this book. Are fundraisers, charity galas, and benefit auctions right for you? In most cases, the answer is a resounding yes. Designed and executed strategically, these events can be your gateway to significant fundraising and long-term donor engagement.

However, special events are undoubtedly one of the most labor-intensive, detail-ridden, volunteer- and staff-intensive ways to raise money. Far too many organizations rely heavily on special event fundraising as a key source of income. Bouncing from event to event is a surefire recipe for board burnout, staff stress, and the demise of your donor base—it's inherently shortsighted and unsustainable.

In some cases, an ongoing auction is absolutely the right fundraising move for an organization. In others, it's not. And, for some organizations, a one-time fundraising auction is the correct answer. Let's look at the questions you should ask to determine the right strategy for your organization.

Critical Factors for First-Time Benefit Auctions and Every Year, Really ...

The most important factor in launching a first-time benefit auction is to have the organization's board of directors buy into the labor-intensive, long-term planning required for a successful fundraising event. A benefit auction event has to fit into the organization's overall fundraising plan. In addition to special event fundraising, there are many other aspects of strategic fundraising that must be in place such as annual giving, major gifts, planned giving, and other special initiatives.

If board members agree to move forward, the next step is to plan out the benefit auction event in detail. Create a budget. Figure out how much it will cost to put on the event. Estimate how much money you can realistically make from this event. Will that justify the time and effort required?

To be successful, you'll need strong leadership on your auction teams. I recommend having co-chairs for the event, and for each team. There are five essential teams needed to carry out the work before, during, and after your benefit auction event:

Audience development: To get the right people to your benefit auction event.

Acquisition: To procure high-yield auction items.

Communications and marketing: To promote the event and, most important, to communicate the impact of your mission.

Logistics: To take care of all of the practical details, including food, sound, lighting, volunteers, check-in, checkout, and the venue.

Sponsorship: To solicit and engage corporate and business sponsors.

There's a high degree of correlation between successful fundraising auctions and board involvement. Benefit auction events that do *not* do well typically have board members who are hands-off and don't attend the event. Get your board members involved and engaged—serving on committees and as liaisons, soliciting auction items, and promoting the event in the community.

Is an Auction the Right Answer for Your Organization?
- Will the auction complement your ongoing fundraising program?
- Will your guests/volunteers/staff feel pleased to take part?
- Do you have the capability to undertake the event?
- Will it make enough money to warrant the effort?
- Can it accomplish objectives beyond raising funds?
- Does it have a good track record within your organization?
- Can the auction compete successfully?
- Do you have full commitment from your board or committee?

Each year, revisit your benefit auction event. Don't just blindly start a new event without figuring out what worked and what needs improvement based on the prior year's event. Take the time to capture this feedback in writing. For example, if your team members need better training, create a strategic plan to put that in place.

Decide What Kind of Auction You Want

The best way to predict the future is to invent it.
—ALAN KAY

Determine Why You Need a Benefit Auction

Fundraising auctions are profitable, fun, and rewarding. Organizing an auction is also one of the most difficult and time-consuming ways to produce income. It requires a strong set of dedicated volunteers. Work closely with your organization's development professionals and board of directors when making this decision.

Define Your Fundraising Goal

Your first meeting agenda's top discussion item should be to determine how much money you need to raise and how those funds will be used. This discussion lays the foundation to critical strategic auction planning. It will guide your planning and excite donors, sponsors, and guests to participate generously.

Understand the Purpose of Your Auction

A successful auction starts with clarifying the vital mix of goals. Raise money. Host a social event. Increase awareness. Develop friends. The auction committee and board must decide what goals are most important. Is the emphasis on revenue generation? Throwing a fabulous party? Showcasing your mission and programs? Or cultivating relationships with current and potential supporters? The outcome is a unique blend of all of these purposes. Figure 2.1 shows a model that I use when consulting with my clients, to help clarify the purpose of the fundraising event and auction.

Figure 2.1   Four Facets of Fundraising Auctions

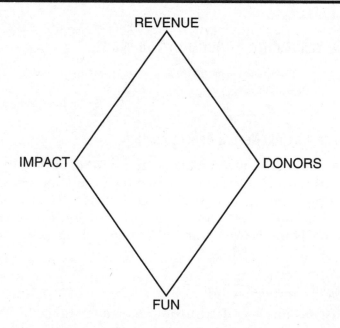

There are four core benefits of a fundraising auction.

1. Raising Revenue
2. Developing Donors
3. Communicating Impact
4. Creating a Fun Social Event

Choose Your Specific Mix of Fundraising Goals

As you strategize about your fundraising auction goals at your planning session, invite each team member to discuss the relative emphasis of each of the four goals and estimate how much emphasis to assign to each one. Group consensus early in the process will build a strong team foundation. For example, an auction with a focus on net profit is designed very differently from an auction at a "social party" event with low emphasis on raising money. Using the Four Facets of Fundraising Auctions model will help to clarify your short-term strategies as well as integrate the auction into long-term development strategies.

Consider These Questions for a First-Time Auction

Why do you want to have an auction? Is there another way to raise funds? Will you raise sufficient funds to warrant the effort? Do you have the needed leadership? A large active auction committee? Enough staff and volunteer support? Ample time? What are your auction goals? How do these fit with your annual fundraising plan? Do you have the full commitment of the board and organization? Revisit these questions each year prior to planning the next auction.

What Kind of Auction Fundraiser Event?

Whether you are holding a fundraiser auction for the first time or the fortieth, it's vital to know what type of event you are planning. This is where your strategic auction design will be paramount, because each auction type requires unique strategies.

- Classic dinner auction, with a sit-down dinner
- Gala with auction and other activities, such as dancing and entertainment
- Food stations event, followed by a fundraising auction and program
- School auction
- Auction at a professional conference
- Specialty auction
- Golf
- Wine
- Art
- Fund-a-need special appeal only

Across the country, volunteers often base their fundraising benefit auctions on ideas they have seen at other benefit fundraisers. This can be a mistake, because many of those ideas date from the old one-time event fundraising mentality of bake sales and bingo. Benefit auctions are labor-intensive, and success depends on the hard work and dedication of volunteers who often strive too hard to use strategies that are not relevant to today's audiences. By learning and using the fundraising auction strategies and techniques presented in this book, your team can work strategically to produce record-breaking fundraising success.

How Do You Spell Success in Fundraising Benefit Auctions?

A: retain an experienced Auctioneer

U: select Unique auction items

C: Cultivate auction guests

T: get your Timing right

I : Inspire your guests to action

O: achieve Outcomes

N: make sure No bidder is left behind

S: orchestrate your Sounds and lights

A: The Role of the Professional Benefit Auctioneer

Retaining a professional benefit auctioneer is the magic ingredient in any auction, taking the risk out of fundraising. Most volunteers across the country work hard year-round to maximize fundraising efforts. When the day of the event arrives, too many organizations turn the auction over to someone who does not have the training, passion, dedication, or relevant knowledge to be your auctioneer. The mayor, a media personality, or even a celebrity will not raise nearly as much money as a professional fundraising auctioneer. This common pitfall means that well-deserving organizations lose hundreds and thousands of dollars of potential fundraising each year.

This is what I call *tripping over a thousand-dollar bill to pick up pennies.* Typically, a VIP or celebrity auctioneer may have the allure of bringing local prestige to an event. They most often volunteer their time or request only a small honorarium. However, the savings realized on the front end almost always result in a loss of proceeds for the organization in the end. If you're interested in multiplying your organization's proceeds by hundreds or thousands of dollars, the most potent way to maximize fundraising efforts is to retain a professional benefit auctioneer.

In 2010, the National Auctioneer's Association found that auctioneers with a Benefit Auctioneer Specialist (BAS) professional designation raise *twice* as much for organizations as auctioneers who do not have a BAS professional certification. Further, BAS auctioneers also earn double the profits for their own auction businesses.[3]

Your organization will benefit greatly by retaining someone who understands fundraising, who will be dedicated to your cause, and who is a specialist in benefit auctions. Remember, people who attend fundraising auctions are now giving very deliberately, choosing organizations that touch their hearts and minds. BAS-certified auctioneers are trained to promote philanthropic giving in a professional and strategic way that will maximize proceeds and strengthen connections to your cause.

So how do you find a good professional auctioneer? There is a strong network of professional benefit auctioneers across the United States. Finding one that is right for your organization will take a little bit of research. I've included several resources in the Resources section at the back of this book.

Pop Quiz: What Generates the Most Revenue?

Which of the following live auction features generates revenue?

- An auctioneer who is specialized in fundraising
- Composition of audience
- Food style choices
- Live auction items
- Brief inspirational remarks
- Timing
- Sound
- Lights

If you answered yes to all of these, you're right! This is what you and your volunteers need to keep in the forefront of your thinking and planning. Other aspects of benefit auction fundraisers, which are often the focus of most committees, do not have the ability to increase your fundraising efforts. Invitation design, tablecloths, and entertainment are important but not essential to raising funds or promoting your cause.

U: One-of-a-Kind Items Make Your Event Unique

Soliciting and procuring the best auction items for your auction can make the difference in reaching your fundraising goal. Maximizing your fundraising efforts requires you to think strategically and to carefully identify specific items you will want volunteers to solicit *before* they start asking for donations. The best auction items are the ones that sell for more than their value. The best-selling items are the ones that are unique and match your audience:

one-of-a-kind items such as specialty trips, dinners, and other items that guests can find only at *your* auction.

Finding items that match your audience's desires and purchasing power will dramatically increase your charity auction proceeds. For example, if your audience is arts and culture focused, unique items that your guests would enjoy might be a package tour in Hollywood, a sold-out concert in your area, or perhaps a New York Broadway show package. If you have an audience that loves sports, consider tickets right behind home plate on the 100th anniversary of your wonderful stadium, or a meet-and-greet with players or coaches.

A great example comes from the grand opening fundraising gala for the Katharine Hepburn Cultural Arts Center in Connecticut. With my consultation, the gala committee created a live auction item to match the audience's interest in Katharine Hepburn. They contacted the current owner of her estate, who agreed to donate his home for a dinner party. The committee then procured Chef Jacques Pépin. They put together a dinner for 12 at Katharine Hepburn's estate prepared by Chef Pépin and served in Katharine Hepburn's dining room. This item was so successful that it sold for over $8,000—twice!

There are two ways to determine how to match items to your audience. The first is to review and study records from previous auctions to determine what items were the most and least desirable and the most and least profitable. Make a list of the top 20 best-selling and worst-selling items that your team can use to solicit and procure best-selling auction items.

The second way is to match items to your organization's cause. For example, a dog rescue group knows that their audience will include dog owners and dog lovers. A perfect auction item for this audience might be a VIP package to the Westminster Dog Show, including airfare, hotel, and VIP access to the event. This unique item would have dog lovers practically drooling.

In both cases, matching items to your audience and your cause requires a thoughtful approach to solicitation, which needs to start long *before* any volunteers begin asking for donations. Remember, the best auction items are the ones that sell, and the best-selling items are the ones that are unique and match your audience's interests.

C: Cultivate Auction Guests

Developing your audience is a critical aspect of a successful auction. Having a competitive crowd means attracting people who have the capacity to bid high in your auction. Why? You need attendees who have the ability to support you financially. That means you'll need to put power bidders in the room.

To do this, create a special team which focuses *only* on getting the right people in the room. This is called audience development, and it's the most vital aspect of a successful benefit auction. So, form an audience development team, not a ticket or invitation committee.

An audience development team builds a competitive audience by getting high bidders in the room. If possible, include people who represent different areas of your community, so they can conduct significant outreach to people who can and will bid high.

An audience with the capacity to give generously will drive bidding *over* 100 percent of the value of items for two main reasons: They have the financial capacity to bid high, and they connect to your cause. Past performance is the best indicator of future performance, so identify your top 10 bidders from past events, and have the audience development team do everything possible to get them to attend again. We'll discuss audience development in more detail in Chapter 5.

T: Timing Is Everything

Timing is one of the most overlooked areas in auction planning. Effective timing means putting all of the elements in your program in the best order to support your fundraising goals.

Timing is mainly based on food style choices. So, the very first thing you have to decide is what style of food you will have at your benefit fundraising event: a sit-down dinner or food stations. (Note: Buffets don't work for benefit auctions under any circumstances. If you are considering a buffet, let me be blunt: Don't.) We'll discuss this in more detail in Chapter 7.

The number of items you auction will also impact timing. For example, school auctions tend to have a lot more items, which requires starting the meal service earlier. Gala-style auctions typically have just a handful of items, meaning the auction can start later. In any case, time your auction with a stopwatch.

At a recent golf auction for Big Brothers and Big Sisters on Cape Cod, I recommended that the auction team close the silent auction 15 minutes earlier than originally planned, seat golfers immediately, skip the salad, serve dinner with a plated meal, and begin the fundraising auction during dinner. With these minor modifications to the sequencing and pacing of the event, the organization doubled their money. Why? They were able to capture golfers' attention and dollars right away. They also held the awards ceremony *after* the dinner and the fundraising auction, which meant that the audience stayed for the entire event.

I: Inspiration for Impact

Your top priority is to showcase your organization's mission and *inspire people to action*. This means encouraging generous bidding—and giving that transcends the benefit auction fundraiser. It does not really matter, says fundraising consultant Tom Ahern, if people think about your cause. What matters most is that the audience is "moved enough to lend a hand and make a gift."[4]

In a two-year study of over 100 Super Bowl advertisements, John Hopkins University researchers Keith Quesenberry and Michael Coolsen found that the most successful ads told stories.[5] Neuroeconomist Paul Zak says that stories evoke a strong neurological response.[6] So, inspire your audience with stories, not statistics. Million-dollar consultant Alan Weiss says, logic makes us think, emotion makes us act.[7]

It's not about how many meals you serve or how many people come to your event. Tell the stories to inspire your audience to action. The best stories are ones that emotionally communicate the impact of the donor's gift.

When do stories work best to inspire your audience to action? First, when you welcome your guests, simply put your hand on your heart and make brief inspirational remarks about the impact of the sponsoring organization. This can be one sentence. Brevity and authenticity are key.

Second, use my proven *59-second story* to share a first-person testimonial immediately prior to the fund-a-need as a way for the audience to understand the power and the impact of their giving. Finally, right before the fundraising auction is a perfect time to engage and inspire the audience.

A quick note. Long, boring speeches do *not* inspire. In fact, I'd like you to remove the word "speech" from your benefit auction fundraising vocabulary. If you want to inspire, make *brief inspirational remarks.* These are a montage of short, well-crafted, authentic, and heartfelt statements about how the organization has changed someone's life. Think strategically about your stories and storytellers and select the stories and storytellers that inspire you. If you are inspired, chances are your audience will have the same response. An inspiring story connected to your organization's cause will move your audience to take action, bid high, and truly engage with your mission.

O: Outcomes

The desired outcome of benefit auctions is to raise as much money as you can for your cause and to engage your audience for long-term support. Achieving outcomes is easy because auctions are formulaic. They are based on past data, simple math, and strategic thinking and planning. See more on how to measure impact in Chapter 9.

Because auctions are formulaic, you can actually predict how much money you're going to make. It's simple math. Who are your top bidders? Who are your supporters? Who are your sponsors? How much did they give previously? What's your return on investment?

The ratio to measure is the value of an auction item to a high bid. For example, if you have a $100 gift certificate to the new great restaurant Mama Kingstoni, which a guest buys for $50, you have only achieved 50 percent of value. If a guest buys the gift certificate for $115, however, you've received 115 percent of the item's value.

Know this ratio for every single item—in aggregate for fundraising, in aggregate for the silent auction, and for each individual category (e.g., beauty, travel). Why? It makes it easy to think about how to reduce the number of items and actually increase revenue. How much money do you think you leave in the room? How much are the speeches costing you?

Every auction has revenue-producing activities and non-revenue-producing activities. When thinking strategically about your auction, identify the activities that produce revenue and those that do not. Your goal is to change the outcome by focusing on those that do.

How much focus are you putting on non-revenue-producing activities? What are those activities? Dancing? Standing around talking? Speeches?

A common mistake is for a board president or event chairperson to take time allocated for the fundraising auction to give a speech. Ten minutes taken for what should have been a one-minute speech means a loss of five items sold on behalf of your cause. Think strategically about how to control the amount of time and the positioning of your speeches.

N: No Bidder Left Behind: The Fund-a-Need

I've learned over the years that people *do* want to give to organizations they support. However, if you want them to give to your cause, you have to ask. The way to ensure that every bidder has the opportunity to give at a level that is meaningful to them is to structure your event in a way that allows every guest to participate at that level.

The fund-a-need is the winning way to engage every single guest in your audience. Also called a special appeal, it's a powerful technique you can use at any fundraising event. Guests want to support you, but they may not want or need a silent or live auction item. A fund-a-need gives them the opportunity to raise their bid cards and give cash at various levels—essential to a modern fundraising auction. We don't want any bidders to feel left out or to not have the opportunity to give meaningfully to your organization. While the silent and fundraising auctions are competitive bidding, the fund-a-need is collaborative giving. That's why it's an absolute must for every single auction without exception.

Imagine sitting in the audience at a Labrador retriever rescue fundraising auction when out from behind the curtains comes Sailor, a three-legged yellow Labrador. This was the culminating moment for a brilliantly crafted fund-a-need. The founder and a volunteer veterinarian pieced together the tragic story of Sailor, the first dog the rescue group had ever rescued. They revealed that Sailor had been run over by a driver, and the veterinarian shared how he and his team volunteered to bring Sailor back to life. The audience was glued. You could hear the silence and feel the emotion in the room. When Sailor came out, there was no doubt how important giving was to this group.

At the end of the story, the group literally illuminated the inspiring significance of their mission. They passed out over 300 battery-operated tealight candles that the audience turned on all at once. This represented the number of dogs the group had rescued since its inception, with Sailor as the first rescue. Donors felt the impact of their gift and consequently the organization raised over $50,000 in just 10 minutes.

A well-executed fund-a-need can significantly increase revenue and dramatically deepen donors' connections to a cause. We'll discuss this in more detail in Chapter 13.

S: Sound, Lights, Action!

Often, committees skimp, forget, or just avoid using professional sound and lighting, but they are critical. Here's a basic truth: If the audience cannot hear you, they will not bid. A benefit auction has a very specific design, and there are two components that matter. First, insist that professional audio and visual specialists take care of the sound and lights. Never, ever use the speakers in the ceiling of a venue—they are designed to make one announcement or maybe play a little background music during dinner. They are inadequate for auctions, and if you use them, you will have miserable fundraising results.

Speakers on stands that surround the audience will help guests hear every single word, which keeps them engaged. Whether at the $5,000 level or at the $50 level, you want to make sure that your guests are inspired to action. An auction-quality sound system is important for fundraising, and also for a silent auction when the room is the noisiest.

Lighting matters too! Make sure that you light your silent auction items so that guests can see the items, read the descriptions easily, and bid high. During the fundraising auction, the house lights should be turned up. Please do not have subdued or romantic lighting, because you want to light the real stars of the event: your guests. We'll discuss sound and lighting in more detail in Chapter 7.

Conclusion

There is nothing more important to your organization than fulfilling its mission. Benefit auction fundraising can help raise funds to position your mission in the community, support your cause, and impact your community. Fundraising auctions have the greatest potential for raising the most revenue. Use the proven strategies and techniques in this book to ensure record-breaking fundraising and donor engagement! How do you spell success? A-U-C-T-I-O-N-S!

Notes

1. CherylAnn Gengle, personal communication, October 7, 2014.
2. Patricia V. Mosher, personal communication, October 31, 2014.
3. N. Saffer and K. A. Kingston, *Trends in Fundraising for the Benefit Auctioneer*. Session presented at the International Auctioneer Conference & Show, Orlando, FL, June 2011.
4. T. Ahern, "The Brain According to Me: Neuroscience Is the Most Important Force at Work in Fundraising Today. Or It Should Be," *Ahern Donor Communications* 12.03 (2012).

Retrieved from http://aherncomm.com/ss_plugins/content
/content.php?content.5093.

5. H. Monarth, "The Irresistible Power of Storytelling as a
Strategic Business Tool," *Harvard Business Review*, March 11,
2014. Retrieved from, www.pauljzak.com/images/documents
/The%20Irresistible%20Power%20of%20Storytelling%20as
%20a%20Strategic%20Business%20Tool%20-%20Harrison
%20Monarth%20-%20Harvard%20Business%20Review.pdf.

6. R. Ayyar, "Why a Good Story Is the Most Important Thing You
Will Ever Sell," *Fast Company*, October 24, 2014. Retrieved from
www.pauljzak.com/images/documents/fastcompany.com
-Why_A_Good_Story_Is_The_Most_Important_Thing_Youll
_Ever_Sell.pdf.

7. Alan Weiss blog, May 27, 2013, Issue #192. www.contrarian
consulting.com/alan's-monday-morning-memo—52713.

3

Energize and Empower Your Board and Team

*Never doubt that a small group of thoughtful, committed
citizens can change the world. Indeed, it's the only thing
that ever has.*
—MARGARET MEAD

LIONS, TIGERS, AND BEARS, OH MY! How do you keep everyone happy
in the auction zoo?

Start by calling the groups who work together on your event
teams, as opposed to committees. When you have a team, members are working toward a common goal. In contrast, when you
organize a committee, each member may come with his or her
own goal, many of which, while well-intentioned, do not match
the goal of the event.

Engaging your board of directors in the benefit auction is
vital to the success of your fundraising efforts. In this chapter,
we'll focus on creating roles and using fundraising strategies to
motivate and focus your volunteers and board of directors. That's
how you achieve maximum fundraising auction results—and
minimum distractions.

Boards play an important role in raising money, especially
when it comes to a fundraising auction or a special event. Whether
it's a golf tournament, an auction, or a walk-a-thon, an event
provides a very natural and safe environment to train board
members, other volunteers, and even donors to help you to raise
more money.

Engaging your board of directors in the benefit auction is vital to your success. I'm often asked about the role of board members in fundraising. Why aren't boards excited about raising money? Why is it so hard to interest board members in fundraising? Shouldn't board members be eager to raise money? To engage your board members, you have to understand fundraising from a typical board member's perspective, and you have to know exactly what it will take to get that individual fully engaged in your fundraising efforts.

Engaging Board Members

To understand the primary reason why board members are not excited about raising money, first picture yourself as a member of the board. You go to a board meeting and you're asked for the names of five people you're going to contact in the next six months. Then you're told to ask each of them for a minimum of a thousand dollars. Most board members quake and want to run for the hills when told they need to ask for money.

Board members *are* eager to help the nonprofit they support, but most of them don't feel comfortable raising money. In fact, most people would rather talk about *anything* else to avoid having to ask somebody for money. Board members usually realize that their most important role is helping to raise money. However, they often feel totally unequipped, afraid, and skeptical about their ability to do this.

How to Get Them Engaged

Board members may give you the names of colleagues they believe are interested in your cause, but that doesn't mean they know how to approach those folks. Tell your board, "We have an event coming up. Invite John to be your guest at the event, and then we can talk to him after the event." When you do speak to this individual after the event, share a moving story, your mission, and the focus of your fundraising auction event. It's easy to do, and he will then understand what your nonprofit is all about.

Start with a Discussion

Fundraising is a dialogue about something people care about. It's about values, and it's about philanthropy. Raising funds for your charity involves much more than money. Philanthropy gets at the core of what is value-driven in all of us. So instead of talking about the money needed for the benefit auction event itself, board members should talk to potential sponsors in different terms. If they're at a meeting, on the golf course, or out to dinner with friends, it's easy for them to say, "I was just at my favorite nonprofit this morning. I learned the most important thing about this nonprofit organization (or about the people they are serving, or about an upcoming activity they're doing in the community)...."

They can talk about why they're on the board, what the board means to them, and the things that they're doing. The other person will likely say, "Oh, I'd love to learn more about that!"

"Terrific! Why don't you join me at the fundraising auction event we are having next month? Come as my guest."

This exchange flows much more naturally than the awkward, "Would you do this for me?" It lets board members share something that means a lot to them and hear what others think. It's a shift from the typical "fundraising ask" to a conversation about the vision, mission, and core purpose of the nonprofit they serve.

How do you help board members begin a dialogue about fundraising? The first step is to identify friends and colleagues who might be interested in the organization. Second, they should spend at least three minutes in the next six months talking with these individuals about something special that happens at the organization. They can do this in the course of their social life: when they are out to dinner, at a gathering of friends, in any kind of a social setting. The key is to have the conversation for at least three minutes. It's about setting an expectation.

Some board members worry about asking for money from people who have already paid for a ticket to the event or become a sponsor. None of us has the right to assume what someone else wants to do. In a fund-a-need, you'll be amazed who raises their hands. No one twists anyone's arm to give, but people everywhere are waiting to be asked to make a difference. Many have come to that event prepared to do so.

Today's donors are far, far different than they were even a few years ago. Donors want to come to an event where they are moved. They want a cathartic experience; they want to feel their actions will have an impact. As you communicate with board members and design your fundraiser, be sure to provide an experience that engages your donors in meaningful ways. Don't shortchange your guests by not allowing them to become the philanthropists they want to be. Finding out what impassions your supporters in a simple dialogue can make a powerful difference. Everyone who is engaged in a conversation should be paying attention to generational differences in people's motivation for attending the event.

Kick Off Your Benefit Auction Event

The kick-off is a mini-event in itself, designed to motivate, inspire, and recruit team members for your main benefit auction event. You'll want to invite as many people as you can. Make sure your board attends, especially the key individuals who are going to lead each team. This is a great way to generate enthusiasm. People want to have fun!

To build attendance, send out an e-mail blast encouraging people to come to the kick-off event. Explain that this is an opportunity to learn how an event is planned. Serve hors d'oeuvres and adult beverages to create a party-like atmosphere. Make sure that everyone is socializing and having a good time, but also offer a program as strong and inspirational as your main auction event.

Consultant Sharon Danosky recalls a fun and engaging kick-off party:

> One year, I remember doing a kick-off party for an organization that had just finished a video. We had decided we were going to preview this fabulous video at the kick-off party, but we didn't want people going around and talking about the video, because we wanted to show it at the benefit auction event itself. We set up a whole mock security thing. We had a couple of guys dressed up like the Blues Brothers with dark suits and

glasses, perched at each side of the stage looking out at the audience to make sure no one was pirating it or going to spoil it.

We had a lot of fun with this. The video was so powerful and moving that when we asked, "Who wants to get involved and who wants to serve on a committee for the actual benefit auction event?" The answer was "I do!" People were motivated. We touched their hearts and, if you touch someone's heart, he or she will want to give. In this case, they wanted to give their time to volunteer to help with the benefit auction event.

Danosky had the whole room decorated with Monopoly money as part of the fundraising theme. Board members were greeters, and the atmosphere was warm and inviting. A kick-off party is a terrific way to jump-start your benefit auction event.

Don't Underestimate the Potential for Fundraising

In my experience, a common mistake many board members make is to underestimate both the audience and the potential for donations. I was the speaker consultant for a special kick-off party for Ability Beyond. Board members, both honorees, other volunteers, and staff attended. There were 37 people—a very nice turnout on a snowy evening. We enjoyed delicious appetizers and wine and showcased a heartwarming success story about a client. As part of my consulting role, I was asked to conduct an interactive presentation to the nonprofit's leaders about how they could make a greater impact for fundraising and donor development. I always enjoy warming up the group by auctioning off something. However, I forgot to bring a small gift to sell. When the executive director asked me, "Kathy, what are you doing to auction off?" I drew a blank. Then I reached into my purse and exclaimed, "This tangy tangerine can change someone's life. Who will make a difference tonight?"

The next thing I knew, the bids went up and up: five dollars, 10 dollars, a hundred dollars, two hundred,...finally the winning bidder paid $2,500 for the tangerine, and we all cheered him. Then, I pulled out a second tangerine and said, "Would the next bidder like this one?" Everyone's mouth was on the floor. We sold two tangy tangerines for $5,000. People want to donate and make a difference. They're just waiting to be asked.

Kathy's Magic Question

How can event guests at your benefit auction really make a difference? The first rule of fundraising is that people give to people first. They're motivated by causes they really care about. How do you engage your board members and volunteers to make that happen?

After conducting fundraising auctions and all types of events for almost 30 years, I have found my Magic Question to be one of the most effective and quickest ways to more deeply engage leaders and donors around an organization's mission. And better yet, it allows you to share a quick personal conversation about the impact of the organization for them. I designed and tested my Magic Question as an auctioneer during cocktail hours and silent auctions, because I wanted to quickly and meaningfully engage as many guests as I could.

It's simple; just ask, "How are you connected to (fill in the name of your organization)?"

Set the Tone—Invite Conversation

At your cocktail reception, invite your leaders to strategically walk around and personally engage at least three guests each that they don't already know. Have them ask my Magic Question, "How are you connected to (fill in the name of your organization)?"

That simple question will engage and guide your leaders, and it's the fastest, most compelling way to inspire your guests and solidify their relationship with the organization. The stories shared in those 30-second exchanges are powerful. And that power is multiplied exponentially when your board members and volunteers bring this information back, so that you can incorporate the stories into your messaging. This also actively prepares your audience to become more personally connected to your cause. Now, during your reception and silent auction, everyone will be talking about your organization and its mission, not their new shoes or where they're going on their next vacation. When they are ready to bid at your live auction, the auctioneer will say, "It's not really about taking a trip to Tuscany or going on a fishing trip. It's really about making a difference for the organization." Your guests will understand your impact at a deeper level, because they've engaged in this 30-second warm-up about your organization's cause.

There is a second important part to the Magic Question. Ask everyone to memorize what guests share with them at your event. You'll want to have a debrief to capture all the interaction from these rich conversations. Further, like many of my clients, you may find new volunteers, board members, auction item donors, and even major donors by using this simple yet powerful donor engagement strategy.

Use this strategy as a discussion point during board and stakeholder meetings, then invite your board to practice at your next auction.

Never Too Many Thank Yous

Nonprofits often take a fragmented approach to benefit auction events. There are certain things you must do after the event to make your fundraising year a blowout success. For example, there's nothing more powerful than an executive director or chief development officer calling volunteers the next day. This is a great opportunity to rehash the night, but the main purpose is to say, "Thank you" and, "By the way, we raised this much money, and we could not have done it without you."

Volunteers absolutely love these phone calls, and they don't want to wait a week wondering how successful the event was. They want to know how much money they raised—not how much money raised by the organization, but how much money *they* raised for you. Call team chairs, thank everyone, and also be sure to follow the IRS regulations in terms of thanking people. That means a "thank you" has to go out, stating how much the person gave, and whether or not any goods or services were received. This is a legal compliance matter. But you'll also want board members to pick up the phone and personally call people who gave. It's a great way to get them involved. All they have to do is say thank you.

A board Thank-a-Thon the week after the benefit auction event is a great way to do this. Board members get together, pick up their phones, and call people. If they reach people live, that's great. If not, they can leave a heartfelt voicemail. This is another training opportunity for board members, because they'll get to hear how excited people were to be able to give. They thank you for the privilege, and that's important for board members to hear.

For a thank-a-thon, include people who chose to give during the fund-a-need, even if they donated at the lower levels. There's no reason not to! And don't stop saying thank you at the thousand dollar level. You can easily call a couple of hundred people in an evening with five or six board members. That is not a hard thing to do, and it means so much to your donors. When you make the effort to say thank you in a meaningful way, it can brighten someone's day. By thanking someone for a contribution, you show great kindness to that donor.

Keep the Energy Going after Your Auctions

The process doesn't end the night of the auction. Engage your board and stakeholders. Keep in touch with your donors. Let them know how the income from the fund has been used. Remember, when a guest is the winning bidder or makes a gift to you at the event, that's only the start of an ongoing relationship. Your leadership team can be involved in a meaningful way by staying in contact with donors and guests and by involving them in your organization after the auction.

After the thank you calls, hold a review of the event with board members and leaders. Then, start planning how you can reach even more people's hearts next year.

Start Now for Next Year

How soon after the benefit auction event do you begin forming your teams and starting over again for the next event? This depends on the benefit auction event and the organization. If you're doing a good job on development, you will be communicating with donors all year long. If you hold a very large-scale event with 500 to 2,000 people and you are raising hundreds of thousands of dollars, you will probably need the full 12 months to plan an event and get things going. For smaller nonprofit organizations, it's difficult to sustain that level of engagement for a solid year. Get your audience development, item procurement, and logistics nailed down six to nine months in advance, and start engaging your team during the same time period. That will let you build enough momentum and keep your board's enthusiasm high.

Personalize Your Benefit Auction Volunteer Recognition

Recently I had an exciting opportunity to volunteer at the Provincetown International Film Festival. What a great way to support this fantastic event! Their volunteer training and recognition were impressive. I loved my volunteer jobs: counting and ripping tickets, greeting film aficionados, and my favorite—sweeping up popcorn off the theater floor. Really. Why? It's simple—there was a beginning, a middle, and an end!

In my case, I was thrilled to help out with simple duties where I didn't have to organize, fundraise, or be in charge of an event—things I do all the time. When I lived in Anchorage, Alaska, my volunteer work for the Iditarod Sled Dog Race entailed shoveling snow *back* into the street so mushers had plenty of white stuff on the ground during the ceremonial start.

So here's my first big tip for working with volunteers. Engage each volunteer personally. Ask each person what *they* would like to do before each event. Don't randomly assign tasks or assume they would like to do the same volunteer job each time. Sometimes a volunteer would like to perform or learn a new task that is completely different than what she does in her regular life.

Secondly, ask your leaders to engage volunteers. During the Provincetown film festival, I was impressed that board members, filmmakers, and producers made a point to thank me personally for lending a hand—even when that hand only held a broom! From the volunteer side, it meant the world to me. What a great reminder for me about the power of personal acknowledgments for auction volunteers, too.

So keep up the enthusiasm throughout the many months of auction planning. Give lots of recognition, say thank you, and feed your volunteers plenty of healthy, delicious food!

Vendors Are Part of the Team, Too

To create a culture of philanthropy, you'll want to take a strategic look at teams, by getting *all* the key players involved, including auction co-chairs, a board liaison, sponsors, honorees, event planners, venue managers, caterers and their staffs, bartenders, audio visual professionals…and of course your auctioneer.

Why? Even though event planners, caterers, and audio-visual professionals have outstanding expertise in planning and serving events, their skills and experience may *not* include those considerations that are unique to fundraising auctions and benefits. You're moving away from the old transactional method, focused primarily on party planning, to a new model of fundraising and donor engagement. You'll want to intentionally involve all the key players, making sure they understand that your auction fundraiser needs to be designed quite differently than a party or wedding. Naturally, you want to focus on a high quality guest experience with food, beverages, and atmosphere; however, some event planners and caterers can unknowingly destroy your ability to raise money.

Here are a few examples. I've seen molten lava cake served right in the middle of an inspiring, emotional fund-a-need story—causing the entire audience to dive into liquid chocolate and stop giving. I've seen a caterer feature a glistening ice carving of a group's logo in the center of a silent auction room, surrounded by tables filled with mounds of delectable appetizers, where almost all of the guests gathered. The new wine pull raffle was relegated to the corner, where it drew scant attention. I've seen a venue place the bar right inside the door to an event, causing a log-jam before guests even caught a glimpse of the silent auction items. I've seen audio-visual teams set up two big speakers at the front of the venue and, in order for guests in the back to hear, crank the volume so high that the VIPs, honoree, and sponsors plugged their ears and left early—without bidding in the live auction or giving to the fund-a-need.

That's why you need a team approach!

Event planners and venue/hotel managers bring expertise in creating themes, designing and tracking event details, creating event budgets and timelines, coordinating logistics, navigating and negotiating with vendors and suppliers, planning meals and themes, and managing food, beverages, entertainment, and safety.

Caterers provide professional expertise in food and beverage planning, creating unique and distinctive menus and presentations. They think of every minute detail, from glasses and dishes to the proper ratio of food and beverages to the number of guests. Caterers provide professional wait staff and bartenders, and, of course, they set up before and clean up after your event.

Audio-visual professionals provide expertise, equipment, and technical ability for events and production, including sound, lighting, video, staging, and special effects. They can also design and manage the event production.

A professional fundraising auctioneer can consult with your organization, using specialized expertise to help you focus on things that make you money and engage donors. Be sure to retain and involve your auctioneer first. An auctioneer who specializes in fundraising will give you expert advice on how to design your timeline, lay out the venue, and handle sound and lighting design. This valuable strategic consultation can return from thousands to millions more dollars for your organization. Use your auctioneer's event-planning perspective and insights to help you avoid costly pitfalls and maximize your fundraising from the start.

Engage Your Volunteers, Too

From a strategic perspective, you'll want to make it as easy as possible for your volunteers to stay enthusiastic and involved. My favorite organizing secret is to advise teams to take time at their first meeting to set the meeting schedule for the entire year. Find a time then and there that everyone actually agrees to and places on their calendars. Ask everyone to lock in these meetings and conference calls. Publish this information for volunteers and send out regular reminders. This tip alone will make you super-productive!

To energize volunteers, focus your dedicated volunteers on tasks that really matter for fundraising and donor engagement.

Don't waste the precious resource of volunteer time on decor, dessert, and dancing. Concentrate on getting the right people in the room, on getting high-performance live auction items, and, especially, on adding to the quality of the donor's experience.

The key to energizing your board members and event and auction teams is to serve great nutritious food at all of your meetings. (No, this is not subs and pizza!) Be sure to serve salads and protein, like chicken or steak tips. Also, be sensitive to special needs, such as gluten-free, dairy-free, vegetarian, kosher, or halal. It's easy to secure a food sponsor to make your volunteers feel appreciated and keep that energy flowing.

Volunteers Give More Than You Think

Here's a fact that might surprise you. Research shows that 79 percent of volunteers donate money to charity, compared to 40 percent of non-volunteers.[1] Be sure to recognize this amazing fact. Your volunteers are donors, too. Treat them as donors, and ask for their generous support beyond volunteering their time.

Recognize Those Volunteers

Here's a checklist of meaningful volunteer recognition ideas.

- ✓ Designate a great volunteer coordinator
- ✓ Deliver excellent volunteer training with written handouts
- ✓ Smile!
- ✓ Provide name tags and T-shirts
- ✓ Create opportunities for volunteers to get to know each other
- ✓ Ask the board and staff to talk personally with volunteers
- ✓ Send handwritten thank you notes
- ✓ Call each of your volunteers personally and ask for their insights and ideas
- ✓ Invite them to participate in other ways with your organization

✓ Serve nourishing food during meetings, set-up, and auction nights
✓ Solicit sponsors to provide all the volunteer meals
✓ List each volunteer in the auction catalog
✓ Hold a special thank you reception with great food
✓ Include special awards and prize drawings
✓ Be creative
✓ Have fun!

Thank your volunteers early and often. The spirit of recognition and appreciation creates a dynamic climate for future participations and giving.

Leverage Board Contacts for Sponsorships

The person who chooses the sponsorship team is typically a business executive who doesn't want to have a lot of meetings. She might get together with the team once, and the team members then divide up the names of all the potential corporate sponsors in the area and make phone calls. They ask restaurant owners for sponsorships when they're out at lunch or dinner.

Do not tell a board member to get 20 sponsorships. Ask him to get two or three. One can be his own business, and then all he has to do is close one or two more. That's how to use the team structure to engage your board members. Make sure that every board member has some kind of a role on the event team, because this allows them to get excited and convinces them to attend. They will bring friends to the event, and in the process, they will begin to see that raising money isn't all that hard.

Conclusion

Not only do you want to invite your board members to your fundraising auction event, you also want to engage them more deeply at the team level. Successful benefit auction events have successful teams behind them, and successful teams place the right board members in the right roles. Invite your board members to take a leadership role for your event, gala, or auction team, and ask them to selectively choose which team they'd like to serve. Ensure success with a highly inspired and engaged board and members.

Note

1. Giving USA Foundation, *The Annual Report on Philanthropy for the Year 2013* (Indianapolis: Indiana University Lilly Family School of Philanthropy, 2014).

4

Make Your Auctioneer
Your Quarterback

Can just anyone conduct a fundraising auction? Are auctioneers
even necessary anymore?

Can a football team win a game without a quarterback? A quarterback is indispensable because he knows the unique game plan
well enough to execute it in real-time leading the team to score
while rousing fans. *Touchdown!* Similarly, a benefit auctioneer is
vital because she has specialized fundraising expertise needed to
strategically conduct a charity auction in real-time to maximize revenue and inspire donors. *Sold!* In both cases, that's how records
are broken!

Some people think that anybody with a strong voice and a
sense of humor can lead a successful benefit auction. Yet the
modern auctioneer is part psychologist, business manager,
fundraising expert, event planner, marketer, motivator, communi-
cator, expert salesperson, consultant, audience engagement strategist, and more. A professional auctioneer, especially one who
specializes in fundraising, can make a huge difference to the
success and tempo of your special fundraising event. Using a
"free" celebrity, media personality, parent, or friend as a volunteer
auctioneer may actually be the biggest expense of your entire
fundraising event—resulting in a loss of many thousands of
dollars! While you may reach your fundraising goal without a
professional fundraising auctioneer, it's highly unlikely that you'll
achieve your true potential.

Why? Both volunteer auctioneers and professional commercial auctioneers who don't specialize in fundraising often leave

money on the table. Because volunteer auctioneers don't have the background or training of professional benefit auctioneers, they make three critical mistakes. First, they don't maximize revenue for auction items. Second, they don't focus on the organization's mission, which is essential for both raising funds and cultivating a donor base for long-term giving. Finally, without a trained eye and specific fundraising skills, many amateurs and volunteers miss bidders, which is an additional loss of revenue. This chapter provides an in-depth look at how professional fundraising auctioneers maximize revenue, engage guests, and advocate for your mission.

The most valuable thing a professional benefit auctioneer can bring to an organization is expertise and ability in strategic consultation. A pro will give you fresh, profitable ways to take your auction to the next level.

Catapult Your ROI: Increase Your Profit by 20 Percent or More

Many event organizers who won't hesitate to pay for entertainment, food, beverages, a band, or even decorations are unwilling to hire a professional fundraising auctioneer. However, retaining a professional benefit auctioneer is an investment that will net *far* more revenue for organizations than any other aspect of an event.

It's the experience of a professional benefit auctioneer that can help you shift your benefit auction event and donor base from a transaction model to a philanthropy model. This is how you achieve your maximum return on auctioneer (ROA). A professional benefit auctioneer creates an entertaining and profitable event to which guests eagerly return year after year—a key to vital donor retention. A pro can help take the risk out of fundraising by generating more profit, awareness, and excitement for your organizations. This is what I mean by ROA.

Trained professional benefit auctioneers use innovative, proven strategies that help you maximize your full potential—not only in raising money, but also in engaging your donors. For example, a professional knows how to design and conduct an inspirational and profitable fund-a-need special appeal. This is the gold standard of fundraising at events. A successful fund-a-need can and often does yield more money than the live auction. We'll discuss this further in Chapter 13.

All Auctioneers Are Not the Same

What's the difference between a benefit auctioneer, a commercial auctioneer, and a volunteer auctioneer? A benefit auctioneer is a licensed professional with unique training, and he or she is dedicated to serving nonprofits, schools, and associations. Also called fundraising auctioneers, many benefit auctioneers offer consulting and other services to support fundraising. A commercial auctioneer is also a licensed professional; however, his or her focus is often in a specialty such as automobiles, antiques, real estate, industrial, livestock, or art. A volunteer is an organizational leader, celebrity, or media personality.

Audience Motivation

At a charity auction, the goal is to inspire your guests to bid *over* the value of the auction item. I've named this "Philanthropic Bidding!" *It's not what you get; it's how much you give.* This is a paradigm shift. Unfortunately, many people see benefit auctions as places to find the next bargain. That's the transaction approach. In the philanthropy model, the emphasis is on giving to a cause. A professional benefit auctioneer makes this happen in spades.

Benefit auctions have multiple goals: to raise funds, to communicate the impact of donors' bids and contributions, to create awareness of the cause, to have an exciting, fun social environment, and to create amazing opportunities for the long-term cultivation of guests, turning bidders into major donors. Both the nature of the audience and the motivation of its members are very different from what you'll see at a commercial auction. Guests at a benefit auction are donors and sponsors who may not even know much about the organization yet, but have come for a wonderful evening.

This means that the auctioneer has to help guests understand where the money goes and, more important, how their gifts can help transform the life of an individual, a family, or a community. The items at a benefit auction are typically different than a commercial auction, too. At a commercial auction, typical items are antiques, collectibles, intellectual property, or cars. At a benefit auction, the items may include travel and dining packages or exclusive experiences.

Lead Time

Benefit auctions have a very long lead time—6 to 11 months in some cases. Many benefit auction teams start planning next year's event the day after the post-auction evaluation meeting. This is because in the philanthropic model, benefit auctions are golden entry points for donor identification and cultivation. A professional fundraising auctioneer offers invaluable pre-event consultation to help organizations turn a laser focus on year-round donor cultivation.

The Style of Selling: The Chant (That Thing Auctioneers Do)

You're probably familiar with that quick rhythmic chant that auctioneers use to keep the bidding going and raise money. It's named bid calling. The chant for benefit auctions is markedly different than that for commercial auctions. For a benefit event, the selling chant is much slower and clearer. Sometimes, depending on the audience, a good fundraising auctioneer communicates the bids without any chant at all. The ability to be flexible and match your unique audience is an important skill.

Automobile auctioneers, for example, sell one car approximately every 45 to 60 seconds. An antique auctioneer might sell 100 to 150 items an hour. In contrast, the benefit auctioneer sells fundraising auction items at a pace of two to two and a half minutes *per item*. This includes describing the item, thanking the donor, selling the item, and allowing for applause to acknowledge the winning bidder. This slower pace is for good reason. Auction guests at a fundraising event need to understand clearly how their bidding will benefit the cause, and they also need to know the details of the auction item descriptions. Most importantly, the benefit auctioneer will need to adopt a pace where the audience can clearly follow the increments and bidding action.

Benefit auctioneers also inspire higher bidding because they incorporate the organization's mission message into their chants to remind guests continually and warmly that their contributions makes a difference for the organization. Why? Because the event is, in essence, the gateway to more deeply engaging your donors. This underscores the value that a professional benefit auctioneer brings. She can change the mindset of the audience from a transaction model to the philanthropy model of giving.

Showmanship and Fun

According to the National Auctioneers Association (NAA), 92 percent of people report "fun" as the number one reason they attend auctions.[1] The unspoken mandate at fundraising auction events is that guests must have a fun, entertaining experience and feel a connection to the cause. A fundraising auctioneer has the advanced education and skill to keep up the excitement and momentum. Benefit auctioneers are really in the entertainment business. They know that when guests come to benefit auction events, they like to have fun. Professional benefit auctioneers have the skills to design and lead interactive and revenue-producing activities that get the audience excited and engaged.

When it's time for the mission moment story in the fund-a-need, fundraising auctioneers have unique training, insights, and experience. That means they're better able to hold the emotion, inviting guests to give generously by communicating the impact their gifts will have.

Advantages of a Professional Fundraising Auctioneer

A professional fundraising auctioneer will help you comprehend what sells best. They will provide you with sound advice based on their experience of what raises the most funds at benefit auctions. They will also help you understand which items are not selling well.

Often, nonprofits ask me, "How can you tell if an item should go in the live or silent auction?" A professional benefit auctioneer can consult with nonprofits to bring more value, ideas, and revenue-generating activities to the market for his clients.

Fundraising auctioneers know the best order in which to auction items to create the optimal flow and the greatest excitement. They're able to squeeze more money out of an event by maximizing bidding. Today, we can no longer rely on an auctioneer who just sells items. A successful benefit auctioneer sells the mission of your organization. That's what makes a professional auctioneer's fund-a-need so inspiring and compelling.

Your Magic Formula: Return on Auctioneer (ROA)

There are gifted benefit auctioneers who have dedicated themselves to working with nonprofits because this is their passion and their life's work. Many of them have highly specialized training, expertise, and commitment. There are outstanding fundraising auctioneers across the country available for you to hire.

Hiring a professional benefit auctioneer is not a cost. It's an investment. How much of a return on that investment can you reasonably expect? Ask this question: "How much money do you leave in the room without the hand of an experienced, professionally trained auctioneer, especially someone who considers this to be her life's work?"

This is a paradigm shift from thinking about the cost of an auctioneer to understanding the return on the investment that comes when you retain a professional fundraising auctioneer who will net more funds for your organization. A professional fundraising auction specialist is a distinct asset to your core leadership team, not a liability expense on a spreadsheet.

It makes me scratch my head when an organization tells me they will be using a VIP, a celebrity, a media personality, or even a commercial auctioneer for their charity auction because it's cheaper. This short-sighted approach is a common misconception and represents an easy way to leave money in the room and lose long-term connections to your donors.

A Unique Financial Advantage

What's better than free? Something that makes you money!

Look at this from a financial perspective. Make a list of expenses for a benefit auction. This will likely include food, mailing, linens, tables, wait staff, sound system, and beverage costs, to name a few line items. Add a line for a professional auctioneer.

Review the entire list of expenses. What is the one item that actually *makes* money before, during, and after your auction? The professional benefit auctioneer! Can the band make you money? No. Can the food make you money? No. That's why it never costs you to have a professional auctioneer. This can only make you more money. Free is an expense. A professional fundraising auctioneer specialist is an asset.

What Do Organizations Want?

Several years ago, I conducted qualitative research analysis from over eight years of events. Hundreds of nonprofits from all over the United States answered the question, "What can benefit auctioneers do to raise more money?" There are seven core competencies that nonprofits expect from their auctioneers:

1. Be an ambassador for the mission
2. Offer consulting and pre-auction planning
3. Generate momentum and excitement
4. Engage and match the audience
5. Exhibit polished professionalism
6. Be adept in advanced fundraising auction techniques
7. Exude fun and showmanship

Let's look at each of these individually.

Your Auctioneer is Your Mission's Ambassador

The number one competency that nonprofits want from a benefit auctioneer is to act as an ambassador who brands their mission. This helps raise more money and engages guests in long-term giving. In most cases, the majority of benefit auction guests know at least something about the organization, but some people may know virtually nothing because they've come as a guest of a friend. This is a fantastic opportunity to showcase your organization—not only what you do, but how you transform individuals, families, and the community.

A benefit auctioneer really understands what makes nonprofits and schools tick. The pros are well-versed in fundraising, special events, capital campaigns, major gifts, annual giving or direct mail, and the various vehicles for generating revenue. For a nonprofit, these are important areas to discuss with your benefit auctioneer so that he or she understands the full picture of your development activities and schedule. A tremendous benefit of hiring someone who specializes in benefit auctions is that you will have someone working with you who understands your mission and truly cares about your work.

To help brand the mission and communicate impact, it's important for benefit auctioneers to know who are the top supporters, guests, and sponsors. Have a handler from the organization introduce the auctioneer to all the top guests during the silent auction and thank the VIPs for being there as part of the team. Provide the benefit auctioneer with a bulleted list of outcomes and impacts from the organization's perspective that he or she can weave into the bid calling and announcements.

Consulting and Pre-Auction Planning

Pre-auction consulting may make the difference between having a nominally successful event and triumphantly setting a new fundraising record. Pre-auction planning helps nonprofits increase their revenues by ensuring time efficiency and saving volunteers and development staff from burnout.

One of the most important aspects of consulting is the positive long-term relationship between a nonprofit organization and a benefit auctioneer. Year after year, you can work together as a team to continue to create great signature events and break fundraising records.

Professional benefit auctioneers can consult on goal-setting, budgeting, branding the mission, creating master calendars, procuring high-yield items, knowing what sells best, and creating the optimal selling sequence.

A professional benefit auctioneer can also guide your audience development and cultivation, lighting and sound, silent auction displays, stage layout, catalog ideas, marketing, fund-a-needs, show flow, and motivating and training volunteers. He or she can help you coordinate the spotters and organize professional auction bid assistants, as well as design and lead interactive revenue activities. Today's professional benefit auctioneers should also be knowledgeable and skilled with technology.

Generate Momentum and Excitement

Being in charge *graciously* is another vital skill that organizations should expect from benefit auctioneers. Many auctioneers provide consulting months ahead of the auction to help their nonprofit and school clients build an exciting timeline and inspiring program. One vital consulting area is designing a momentum-building show flow timeline. Work collaboratively with your auctioneer to create and follow a written, agreed upon timeline. Your auctioneer is the key person to "call the plays" before and during your event and drive your auction toward its goal. Many professional benefit auctioneers also serve as your emcee. In addition to your auctioneer, it's also a great idea to assign a key volunteer or staff person from your organization to keep everybody on track. Create a volunteer stage manager position responsible for sticking to the timeline and working with volunteers. Conducting a benefit auction is more than just standing on the stage and selling auction items. An organization and its auctioneer must also be adamant about the quality of sound and lighting. These are often overlooked, causing huge losses, up to thousands of dollars. Have contingency plans and talk about them ahead of time.

Engage and Match the Audience

A professional benefit auctioneer will consult with the organization months ahead to leverage trends in philanthropy and bidder psychology. The auctioneer will then begin to choreograph myriad logistical details so you can maximize fundraising and engage donors. Uniquely trained, the benefit auctioneer understands the performance aspect of the job. He or she is there to capture the attention of the guests, tell success stories, and create momentum and excitement. Benefit auctioneers understand the philanthropy model, so they can orchestrate strategically planned and sequenced events that maximize fundraising, audience engagement, energy, and fun. At an auction, he or she is the most important person on your team, because it's his or her job to engage your guests at the highest level.

"Engagement is being driven by the common experience connections," says Lesa Ukman, Chief Insights Officer at IEG, LLC. "It's being part of a tribe and wanting to join. And when you create this energy, people can bypass their brain and tap right into their powerful feelings, self-image, aspirations, and dreams."

That's what a great professional benefit auctioneer can do for your organization. He or she creates an exciting philanthropic atmosphere in which everyone feels great about giving and becomes more deeply connected to your cause.

Polished Professionalism

Your professional auctioneer should treat guests well and appreciate the diversity of multicultural audiences. Although it goes without saying, auctioneers are working at auctions and gala events and should *not* be drinking while they are working. It's also important that they refrain from potentially offensive jokes and topics. They should always have tip-top manners and proper attire.

Match the Audience

There are different species of fundraising auctions, such as wine auctions, golf auctions, school auctions, art auctions, the classic dinner auction, and gala auctions. The auctioneer should work closely with the organization to understand the goals of the event, know who is in the audience, and adapt his or her style accordingly.

Be Adept in Advanced Fundraising Techniques

Benefit auctioneers have to be experts in designing and leading fund-a-need activities. They should know the top ways to transform silent auctions. They need fresh, fun, and interesting revenue activities that bring in significant dollars. Benefit auctioneers should have at least 12 to 15 activities in their arsenals, and each year they should sprinkle in new ones to keep things fresh.

Exude Fun and Showmanship

If you think that auctioning fancy dinners and exotic vacations is all your auctioneer needs to do raise money—think again. The new fundraising auctioneer must go beyond bid calling, developing expertise in conducting all sorts of money-making games and generating just the right amount of fun and inspiration. (See Chapter 14 for an in-depth discussion of strategic auction income streams that add fun.) Additionally, the modern benefit auctioneer needs to understand how to work on the floor within the audience, not stuck behind a podium reading the item description. Further, while working with producers and sound professionals, some benefit auctioneers have the understanding and skills to carefully integrate music, dance and theatrical elements into the auction for added pizzazz.

Guests expect an enjoyable, meaningful and fun event. The key distinction here is that a fundraising auctioneer should be entertaining, not the entertainer. A benefit auctioneer has a rare opportunity to showcase his or her style and personality while spicing up the live auction, but while doing so, he or she should be delivering compelling remarks about the organization's impact.

How Nonprofits Benefit: What's in It for You

Benefit auctioneers are excellent at asking for money, because that's their primary function. From a nonprofit perspective, is there anyone better suited to represent your mission and graciously ask your guests to become more involved and give more generously? This is a distinct skill set that very few celebrities, volunteers, or local TV weathercasters have. When you're considering who to hire, this is the primary skill you need to evaluate. Graciously asking for money and inviting guests to be generous on behalf of an organization is a part of the unique skill set of auctioneers who specialize in fundraising. Remember, it's not how much money a professional benefit auctioneer costs, it's how much more money that auctioneer will raise for your great cause.

Other Services Fundraising Auctioneers Offer

Professional benefit auctioneers can offer additional services, including consulting and pre-auction planning, training, conducting seminars, and staffing auction check-in and checkout services. Many auctioneers represent several different fundraising-auction software and credit card processing companies. Some auctioneers offer innovative auction technology, including hand-held bidding devices and online auction programs. Other services include registration and cashiering services, bidding assistance, additional auctioneers, and additional auction staffing. Some benefit auctioneers have access to consignment items. They can provide benefit auction supplies, such as bid numbers, bid forms for the silent and live auctions and the fund-a-need, spotter flashlights, written guides and supplemental materials, and stage numbers. When you talk to benefit auctioneers, ask them what services and supplies they offer.

The Auction Team: Professional Auctioneer Bid Assistants

Bid assistants help the auctioneer spot bids and create audience excitement and engagement. There's so much riding on the success of a benefit auction. Big audiences require more management, and professional benefit auctioneers have to keep the audience covered. Professional auctioneer bid assistants ensure accurate bid spotting and communicate with both the lead auctioneer and auction guests what's happening during the live auction and fund-a- need.

Professional benefit auctioneers also bring other team members along. For example, they might bring a manager from their auction company. They could also bring a person to serve as a liaison to different volunteer groups. Some benefit auctioneers have registration, cashiering, and technology services as well.

How to Retain a Great Auctioneer

Retaining the right professional benefit auctioneer is one of the most important steps you can take to maximize fundraising and create an exciting, fun event. Here are eight steps to help you match the best professional auctioneer with your great cause:

1. Interview your top prospective auctioneers via phone or in person.
2. Visit their websites and blogs. Watch videos. Check out their resources.
3. Check references.
4. Insist on a written proposal and agreement (a law in many states).
5. Ask for their client lists—and call a few organizations not on the reference list.
6. If possible, attend a similar benefit auction that each auctioneer is conducting.
7. Ask how much experience each auctioneer has with fundraising auctions.
8. Learn as much as you can about their styles, mannerisms, and attitudes.

How to Interview an Auctioneer

When hiring a professional benefit auctioneer, you'll want to find out how much experience he or she has with fundraising auctions. You'll want to learn as much as you can about his or her style, mannerisms, and experience in fundraising and working with your type of donors and guests. It is critical to match the benefit auctioneer with your specific audience.

19 Key Questions to Ask Your Potential Benefit Auctioneer

1. Tell us about your experience in nonprofit fundraising auctions.
2. How many fundraising auctions have you conducted?
3. What percentage of your business is fundraising auctions?
4. Do you have the BAS (Benefit Auctioneer Specialist) professional designation?
5. What are the highest and lowest grossing live auctions you've conducted?
6. Give us a sample of your bid-calling technique.
7. Explain one of the toughest situations you've encountered as an auctioneer and how you solved it.
8. Here's a situation we had at a past auction. How might you have addressed this situation?
9. What's your experience conducting fund-a-need appeals?
10. Describe your style and how you would interact with and engage our guests.
11. How can we observe you conducting a benefit auction?
12. Do you provide consulting or other services?
13. When do you arrive at an auction? When do you leave?
14. Do you have access to any auction items?
15. What is your compensation structure?
16. Why should we retain you—what value do you bring to our organization?
17. Is there anything else you'd like to add about your services and approach to working with nonprofits and schools?
18. May we have a list of your references and client list?
19. Why do you believe you are a great fit for our organization?

Don't be afraid to ask in-depth questions. One of my favorite questions is, "What is the toughest situation you've ever encountered as an auctioneer and how did you solve it on stage?" That tells you how someone thinks on his or her feet.

One reason people bring in a professional benefit auctioneer is that challenging and even dangerous situations can arise.

Here are some true stories. One time the entire backdrop, scaffolding and sound speaker set crashed down behind me as I was auctioning the premier live auction item. I literally jumped off the stage hand-in-hand with two volunteers—probably saving all three of our lives. When my feet hit the floor, I immediately continued selling that live auction item with the last bid of $1,000, asked for $1,500, and sold it for $10,000 without any interruptions to a generous appreciative audience. It was my first time as a Families First auctioneer and that item alone fetched more than their last entire live auction net proceeds! I've experienced a table centerpiece catch fire. While selling, I just poured a pitcher of beer on the flames and kept up the auction bidding at a heated pace. I've had a sound system go completely dead and used my Division I Saint Louis University volleyball coach voice to capture the audience to continue to bid high.

Anyone can be great on autopilot, be sure to find out how a prospective benefit auctioneer will handle unexpected and tough situations. Ask him or her to share a true story from a previous benefit auction. You can also prepare a challenging case from one of your previous auctions and ask your prospective auctioneer how he or she would address it for you.

Competencies of a Benefit Auctioneer

It's really important to expect a benefit auctioneer to know your mission and be able to articulate it with passion and conviction. They need to have clear and understandable bid calling. An exceptional benefit auctioneer will be able to include your organization's cause and talking points in the bid calling in a way that is not a fast-selling auctioneer style, but one that helps the audience become authentically engaged in the mission.

Your auctioneer needs to tell guests why it's important to participate generously. He should recognize donors and sponsors. In terms of showmanship and fun, each benefit auctioneer has his or her own personality. Make sure it's a match for your specific audience. Manners and smiling are critical. Benefit auctioneers should be punctual and arrive early to train the live-auction volunteers, do the sound and light check, and go over any final details. When the benefit auctioneer greets guests during the silent auction and thanks them for their generous bidding at the end of the night, it can make a huge difference. Fundraising is friend-raising, and creating relationships with guests will have positive long-term implications for your nonprofit. A professional benefit auctioneer's style, positive attitude, pacing, attire, showmanship, and ability to engage the audience around the mission are critical.

Auctioneer Compensation

There's a wide variety of compensation structures for benefit auctioneers. Many professional benefit auctioneers create a customized services package for each client based on the specific needs of each auction and the value of the project. Sometimes auctioneers will combine all of their services into one fee. Other times they break their services out in a menu format, which enables clients to look at itemized costs. A professional benefit auctioneer can be compensated in numerous ways: flat fee, combination of flat fee and commission, commission[2], flat fee and bonus, and a services premium. Other options include fees based on a scale and fees for specific services. Another compensation structure is known as a buyer or services premium, where guests pay a small percentage on top of their purchases to cover the costs of services such as an auctioneer, as well as for other services. With this method, the organization retains the full amount of the auction profit of items sold at the auction. Fees can also be based on the size of the benefit auction or the additional services provided by the auctioneer.

To serve the broad constituency of nonprofits, schools, charities, and organizations, benefit auctioneers provide a wide scope of compensation structures in comparison to commercial auctioneers, who most typically are compensated on a commission basis.

Professional fundraising auctioneers also provide various levels of consulting and professional services. Consulting fees may be included with other professional auction services or may be presented as a separate project. Consulting fees are based on the value of the professional guidance to the overall project.

A federal law prohibits auctioneers from talking to each other about fee structures, which prevents price fixing. This means that each nonprofit should have this conversation directly with each benefit auctioneer.

Your Mission Ambassador

Organizations should expect benefit auctioneers to communicate the impact of their causes and engage the audiences in their missions. This is what I call being an auction ambassador. In this role, the benefit auctioneer promotes the mission of the organization by highlighting the organization's unique outcomes and services. She also showcases the brand and tells transformational stories right before the fund-a-need. The benefit auctioneer is the spokesperson or ambassador for the nonprofit's cause, focusing on how programs and services transform individuals, animals, families, or communities. This is critical because it motivates guests in a new positive way and effectively communicates the mission. Through the rapt attention of the audience, the benefit auctioneer is involving as many people as possible. Make sure your benefit auctioneer knows exactly where the funds from the benefit auction will go. Set up a meeting to review this. Provide your auctioneer with a bulleted list so he or she can give the audience members specifics about how their gifts will make a difference. The bullet points are critical.

Working with a Professional Auctioneer

- Meet with your auctioneer many months before your event.
- Look to your auctioneer for consulting and expert advice.
- Give your auctioneer all of your organization materials to study.
- Expect your auctioneer to meet guests during the cocktail hour and silent auction.
- Expect your auctioneer to be an advocate of your cause from the stage, not just sell items.
- Expect your auctioneer to thank bidders, donors, and guests during the auction and afterward.

The Fundraising Auctioneer—Your New Philanthropic Partner

Months prior to your auction, retain your auctioneer as a vital member of your executive event team. Since great auctioneers are booked sometimes a year or two in advance, it's wise to call your auctioneer first before you commit to a date and auction venue. A professional fundraising auctioneer is an expert advisor and consultant. He or she will communicate the impact of the donor's gift, serve as an ambassador for your mission, and be uniquely positioned to engage donors at the event.

Services Provided by Professional Fundraising Auctioneers

- Professional auctioneering
- A professional auctioneer bid assistant team
- Consulting and planning
- Registration and cashiering
- Benefit auction event staff
- Emceeing and announcing
- Providing auction supplies
- Coordinating AV vendors for a professional sound system
- Conducting seminars, tele-seminars, and webinars; giving lectures and providing books and educational materials
- Working with technology companies for software, online auctions, and mobile bidding

Your Auctioneer Can Be Your Coach Too

How will you catapult your fundraising to the next level?

Learn from the pros. Hire a coach.

A benefit auction consultant is an invaluable advisor who helps you design an exciting and memorable fundraising event to boost your bottom line and to drive donor engagement. As early as possible, months prior to the event, a skilled and savvy auction consultant can provide expert advice on powerful revenue ideas, capitalizing on new trends, leveraging donor and bidding psychology, energizing your program, communicating the impact of your mission, and adding fun and pizazz.

If you're lucky enough to find a seasoned fundraising auctioneer who can also serve in a consulting role, you'll be surprised by what a difference his or her counsel can make. Fundraising auction consulting topics can range from basic auction logistics to advanced donor cultivation strategies. The following is a sample list of ways a benefit auction consultant can provide expert advice to nonprofits, associations, schools, and charities.

Fundraising Auction Consulting Topics

- Live auctions
- Silent auctions
- Fund-a-need special appeals
- Innovative money making games
- Auction item acquisition methods
- Selection of best-selling silent and live items
- Proper sequencing of live auction items and bid increments
- Benefit auction design, budgeting, and planning
- Designing timelines, event structure
- Benefit auction logistics, forms, and procedures
- Streamlined registration and cashiering
- Pre-bidding and absentee bidding
- Technology: benefit auction software, mobile bidding, online auctions
- Audio-visual specifications
- Tour venue, recommend floor plan, and set up
- Adding music, entertainment, and fun
- Audience development and engagement
- Donor cultivation and retention
- Sponsorship engagement and benefits
- Volunteer, board, and staff training
- Auction committee motivation and training
- Fundraising storytelling at auctions
- Coaching speakers and fund-a-need storytelling
- Maximum impact marketing and messaging
- Advice on scripts and program design
- Review of marketing materials and auction catalog

- Strategic analysis of auction revenues and procedures
- Pre- and post-auction evaluation
- Custom live workshops, teleseminars, and webinars

Note: this list is just a sample of benefit auction consulting areas, so be sure to ask your auctioneer about other topics and services he or she provides.

The following example showcases the value of retaining an auctioneer who specializes in fundraising auction consulting. AIDS Resource of Wisconsin initially contracted with Kurt Johnson Auctioneering for professional auctioneering and consulting services.

Kurt Johnson's professional consultation focused on three vital areas: first, Kurt provided advice to ensure that live auction packages matched the financial and emotional demographics of the audience; second, he taught them how to leverage leadership gifts for fund-a-need to maximize the untapped large donor potential already in the room; third, he helped them design an inspiring speaking program and timeline to meld the complexities of a major live auction and fund-a-need with large-scale production elements such as sound, lighting, music, video, and talent.

Dan Mueller, Vice President & Chief Development Officer at AIDS Resource Center of Milwaukee, Wisconsin describes their results. "We contracted with Kurt Johnson Auctioneering in 2010 when we sensed that, left to our own devices, our live auction was not as successful as it ought to be. In the five years that we have been working with Kurt Johnson Auctioneering, our auction revenue has increased 46 percent and our fund a need has increased 96%. Learning from the pros pays real dividends."[3]

Additionally, a fundraising auction consultant can be a powerful philanthropic partner even when you already have secured your auctioneer. For example, in 2013, the Sonoma Harvest Wine Auction retained me as their auction consultant, even though the executives already had retained their auctioneer. As a consultant, my core strategy was to intensify audience development and cultivation that targeted vintners, stakeholders, big bidders, and major donors. Further, I advised the Sonoma executives and board to create an inspiring mission messaging campaign that engendered community pride for the outpouring (pun intended) of charitable generosity at their auction.

Designing the centerpiece of fundraising and donor engagement, I provided advanced strategies to design a riveting fund the future appeal to support literacy in Sonoma. My consulting included choreographing an emotional success story, personally coaching the program speakers, and showcasing the powerful impact of reading to the audience. The result—records were shattered: from $700,000 in the live auction and fund-a-need in 2012 to $1.4 million in 2013 to over $4 million in 2014. However, numbers tell only one side of the story, as other valuable benefits included building capacity and intensifying fundraising leadership for the key stakeholders and boards as well as energizing the entire community to continue to create and celebrate a world-class fundraising auction in Sonoma.

Your auctioneer is your fundraiser event's quarterback, but an auctioneer who offers consulting can also be your strategic coach, year-round. He or she can be by your side between seasons to keep you motivated, refine your skills, point out weak spots in your strategy, and help you overcome every obstacle. A benefit auction consultant can strengthen your organization's team and take your fundraising and organization to the next level.

Learn from the pros. That's the playbook for success.

Conclusion

Thriving in today's fundraising environment requires new, advanced skills from auctioneers. An experienced fundraising auctioneer is an invaluable philanthropic partner who can help organizations cultivate guests, make sure they have a fantastic time, and engage them in generous bidding. Furthermore, the benefit auctioneer acts as a spokesperson for the organization's cause, focusing on how to communicate the impact of donors' gifts. A fundraising auctioneer is uniquely positioned to motivate guests in a new, positive way and involve the entire audience. First and foremost, he or she will create a climate of giving in which all the donors feel great about their gifts and are excited to be present. They'll say, "I love the auction. I'm so happy to donate. I cannot wait to come back next year to bring my colleagues and friends and become more involved in this great cause!"

Notes

1. Morpace, "Auction Industry Holds Strong in 2008 with $268.5 Billion in Sales," auction industry survey, 2008. www.exclusivelyauctions.com/pdfs/naa-2008.pdf.
2. The Association of Fundraising Professionals (AFP) Code of Ethical Standards does not approve of commissions in certain circumstances where revenues are raised for straight donations. For more information about the AFP and their Code of Ethical Standards please visit: http://www.afpnet .org/files/ContentDocuments/CodeofEthics.pdf
3. Personal conversation on January 21, 2015 with Kurt Johnson, president and owner, Kurt Johnson Auctioneering and Co-Founder of Benefit Auction Institute.

Section II

Designing Strategic Benefit Auctions

5

Attract the Right People First

Never treat your audience as customers, always as partners.
—JIMMY STEWART

ONE OF THE MOST COMMON QUESTIONS I'm asked is, "How can I get more big bidders and donors to come to my fundraiser event?"

Would it surprise you to know that special events are recognized as the top way to identify donors in North America and Europe? Your fundraiser event, gala, or benefit auction is the golden gateway to finding and engaging your supporters in your cause. However, your event is just the beginning.

Obsess on Strategic Audience Development

How do you attract the right guests to your fundraiser and auction? Many of your key supporters are already attending your event, and they're just waiting to be asked for their help. They are eager to give and happy to help you engage other supporters long after your event is over.

However, you'll need to consider a new approach. Audience development is a strategic and focused effort to ensure that you invite and engage your audience year-round. Stop thinking of your gala or auction as a one-time event; this is the limiting transactional approach we talked about in Chapter 1. Instead, be more strategic. Know that your event can be inspiring enough to transform its guests into dedicated donors.

To take advantage of this opportunity, you'll want to design a targeted campaign by identifying, inviting, and cultivating major donors, prospects, and influential leaders. You'll need to know what impassions your guests and why they're connected to your cause. You'll need to focus intently on engaging your board and other stakeholders, urging them to invite guests personally and not rely on e-mail, texts, and social media.

A Philanthropic Approach to Audience Development

With this approach, you'll attract guests who have the means and motivation to drive bidding *over* the value of each item. At benefit auctions for schools, for example, very often parents bid far over value for auction items, especially those created by their children (e.g., a handmade cookie jar with children's thumbprints on it). Those parents are attending the auction to fundraise for the school. My motto is: It's not about what you get, it's about how much you give. At STAR, Inc., the board and gala committee work with a single focus to cultivate new guests to attend their fundraiser.

Keep your eye on what matters: fundraising and donor development. Ignore the rest. Strategic audience development is the top predictor of increased profits at benefit auctions. Engaging and retaining power bidders, donors, and sponsors is key to your long-term development.

Sonoma Creates Champions

As the consultant for the Sonoma Harvest Wine Auction, I advised the auction team to focus on a strong audience development strategy. This world-class wine auction always sold out at 600 guests, which provided an interesting challenge: how to increase income from the same number of guests. The best way to do this was to engage the local Sonoma vintners and growers to do what *they* do best—cultivate—except this time I was asking them to cultivate donors, not grapes. We focused the vintners and other key stakeholders on cultivating guests and strategically inviting *the right* new supporters. As a result, the Sonoma team more than doubled the money raised from the previous year. The second year, they shattered that record again, raising over $4 million, nearly triple the amount of money raised in the prior year.

Why Don't People Attend Fundraising Events and Auctions?

There are three reasons people commonly don't attend fundraising auctions. First, they aren't personally asked. Can you believe it? The top way to get someone to come to your benefit auction event is to ask them *personally*. Second, people don't think that they will know anyone at the event. Third, they think they're not going to have any fun.

Make a quick phone call or invite someone to lunch to easily address all three concerns. Role-play with your auction team, board, and table host members. Practice describing how each member is connected to your organization and what your group means to each of them.

Exercise: Inviting Guests

A simple way to help your auction committee put these findings into action is with role-playing. Try a 30-second mock telephone call to practice:

"Hi, Sally, it's Maura. How are you? Listen, I am so excited to invite you personally to our gala fundraiser event supporting California Labrador Retrievers & More.

"I've been a volunteer walking dogs and helping out with foster dogs and I just love what they do. I know how much you love Labs, especially since you've adopted that sweet senior yellow Lab, Maggie.

"I'm putting a table together. The tickets are $125 each. You're going to know so many people who will be there. A lot of our friends are coming. Would you consider joining us?"

When Sally says "yes," finish the phone call:

"This is going to be so much fun! It's a great night out for a great cause. Thank you, Sally!"

"I'll email you event and auction item details. Will you kindly send your check to Labs & More by the end of this week?"

Sally exclaims, "I'm writing my check right now. This is going to be great! Thank you!"

Attract More High Bidders

Price communicates. Consider raising your price. If your event registration prices are too low, you'll attract guests who will bid low or not at all. This is a negative consequence of a transaction mindset. The price of registration communicates the value that you put on your cause. Why does that matter? In the new philanthropy model, you want to make sure that every aspect of your event communicates the great value that you place on your mission and your impact.

Leveraging Spheres of Influence

Leveraging your stakeholders' multiple spheres of influence is one of the most overlooked aspects of developing and engaging audiences at fundraising events. Consider drawing on every single person you know, as well as their personal, business, and social media contacts. Create a huge and expansive list of prospective

Figure 5.1   Dedicated Donors Spheres of Influence

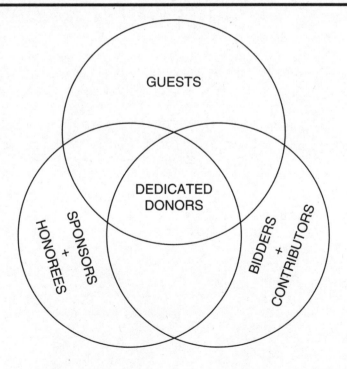

donors that reaches far beyond your direct constituency. How? When you're working with all your teams, ask the following questions:

- Who has the buying power now?
- Who cares about us?
- Who are the influential leaders and who are their colleagues?

This is when your board volunteers and major donors can be very helpful, because they have strong community connections. They might not know potential guests personally, but they probably know someone who can invite them.

Then look at the next sphere of influence. Brainstorm lists of potential supporters with your staff members, volunteers, neighbors, business colleagues, and everyone else you know, to push the boundaries of your sphere of influence. It's said that each of us has at least 200 people in our sphere of influence, and it's probably much more than that. Tap into those circles to make a difference.

Draw on Your Development Professionals Expertise

I'm always surprised when I hear that event organizers have not collaborated with the fundraising professionals at their organizations. Working closely and collaboratively with your development professionals throughout your planning process is a key strategy in the philanthropy model, because you're working to cultivate major donors for long-term giving. Remember, you're not just planning a fundraising event. You're creating your future. Include your fundraising professionals in all of your planning. They're a vital part of your team. Cultivation of major donors is a customized long-term philanthropic approach that's established over many years. You'll want to seek their advice as you integrate your guests into your advancement plan.

Empower Your Community of Champions

Honorary Chairs

Honorary chairs are individuals who lend their names, influence, and support to your event. Their gifts to you is their ability to leverage their spheres of influence to support you by inviting other influence leaders who will attend and/or contribute. They will then make introductions to *more* influence leaders.

Awardees

At many events, nonprofits present awards to individuals to honor their dedication and support. Awardees can make an exponential difference by inviting other guests who will contribute in order to honor their colleagues. They may also donate to the cause through bidding or give during the fund-a-need. Work closely with honorary chairs and ask them to fill a table or two, then invite your honorees to do the same. One year, the honoree for the Danbury Animal Welfare Society brought seven tables of supporters with guests who had the capacity to spend money at the benefit auction event. That not only translated to increased auction income, but also brought over 40 new potential animal lovers as donors.

Sponsors

Incorporate all of your corporate sponsors and media partners in to your audience development efforts. Sponsors have their own spheres of influence, and their collaboration will increase leadership, revenue, in-kind support, and visibility for your event.

A common question is, "What can we do to transform a potential 'no' into deeper sponsor support?" Fundraising is about relationships. You must cultivate long-term relationships over time. Sponsors really want to help you, but sometimes they can't do so at the same level as in the past. Be very kind to them. Ask, "You've been such a strong supporter—is there anything else you are able to do? Can you leverage your influence for new attendees at your table or for auction items or in-kind gifts? Can you help create an auction package equivalent to what you gave in the past? Are there other sponsors you know who care about our organization and our cause as much as you do?" This could include a monetary donation, in-kind support, premium items, a sponsor's participation on an auction committee, or much more.

Corporations may try to fill seats by sending representatives who don't have the capacity to spend money at your event. Here's a graceful way to help sponsors help you: "If you can't fill your table with the leaders of your organization, please return the tickets to us and we will be happy to resell them."

Vendors

Vendors are one of the most overlooked yet viable sources for new guest and sponsor engagement. This is one of my favorite benefit auction prospect areas. Did you know you already have a list with all the contact information you need, right at your fingertips? Just work with your finance office to review the list of business partners in your accounts payable file. This is a group of potential supporters you may not have considered, and they're right under your nose. Just tell the finance office, "I'd like to have a list of everyone to whom we write a check."

Your list might include a waste management company. There could be a printing company, a commercial management company, a lawyer, accountants, or a web designer. Invite them all. Then ask vendors about *their* second spheres of influence, the friends of friends, to maximize your fundraising efforts. Simply say, "I'd love to meet some of your vendors, friends, and business colleagues who care about our cause and our organization." This is a huge opportunity to leverage a vastly underutilized area for audience development.

The Super Connectors

As I was writing this chapter on audience development I realized there was a special group to feature. These wonderful supporters are already deeply connected to organizations and understand the impact of your mission. I call them "super connectors." Remember, people want to give to causes that they love. For super connectors, all you need to do is invite them in.

For school auctions, there are numerous super connector groups. When working with an educational institution or a school, the alumni, grandparents, aunts and uncles, and new families are great sources to develop your benefit auction audience. How can you engage them? Well, do you have a special outreach plan for new families? One school created a special alumni appreciation raffle, and the winning ticket won a donated upscale dinner for two at a popular new restaurant.

For wine charity auctions, your vintners, wine growers, wine industry vendors, specialty sponsors, and the media are knowledgeable and supportive of the profession. Golf charity auctions can focus on golf lovers, golf specialty stores, golf pros, and the golf media. Art charity auctions bring an exciting array of supporters including artists, dealers, brokers, collectors, art supply vendors, museum professionals and curators, and art lovers in general. Think about the possibilities for other arts and culture groups and for animal rescue and humane societies.

Neighborhood

Who are the geographic neighbors that abut your facilities and outreach services areas? It's time for a visit to share your impact in your community and invite their support. You'll be amazed. About 20 years ago, I directed a $1 million personalized brick campaign for Anchorage Town Square, selling personalized bricks to pave pathways. Armed with my three favorite fundraising tools—a brand new yellow pad, a mechanical pencil, and enthusiasm—I mapped out all of the businesses adjacent to the square. Then I personally visited each shop owner and talked about how this new park would bring more customers to his or her door. While sharing stories of how their gifts would positively impact their vibrant community, I made a lot of friends for the Downtown Anchorage Association and received an outpouring of sponsorships and brick sales. Today, Town Square stands as a stunning landmark built individual by individual with lasting pride. The lesson of Town Square is that people give to people for causes they care about, especially when the cause is local and they are asked personally.

Allied Professionals

Are you inviting other professionals with whom your organization shares a strategic alliance? Be sure to include anyone who's a professional allied with your profession. Consider those to whom you refer clients and those who refer clients to you. What about feeder schools or schools your students attend after graduation? Who hires the clients that you train, serve, or treat? Who attends the same professional conferences, hearings, and coalitions? Who is doing research, teaching, health care, or law in your area? In a philanthropic model, the goal is to connect people to your cause for long-term engagement and giving. Allied professionals are often overlooked. They're already there; just invite them in. This is a quick win!

Get Rid of Your Ticket Committee

Create an audience development team instead. Then put it on steroids. Recruit co-chairs who come from different backgrounds, and who are well connected. For example, you might have one co-chair who is in finance and another with a legal or health care background. The co-chairs can draw from their own spheres of influence, combing through their rolodexes, social media outlets, and business associates. Their job is to focus strategically on getting the right people in the room. The most effective audience development teams are composed of diverse leaders who have strong spheres of influence.

Ask Unabashedly: Perfect Your Pitch

The first rule of fundraising—we'll keep repeating it—is that people give to people, for things they care about. When you're looking for the best way to invite people to your benefit auction event, you might use save-the-date cards and invitations. However, the most powerful, potent, and effective way is to make a personal ask—not by e-mail or text! In person, over a cup of coffee, or at the very least, by phone.

The personal ask makes a huge difference. It's about cultivating a relationship early—before your benefit auction—and continuing that relationship during and after the event. Remember, you are now building relationships with your guests so that you'll continue to raise funds *after* your benefit auction. This is because you've designed the event as a cultivation event as much as a fundraising event. With nurturing, the relationship you started will continue for the long term. People give to people for things they care about.

What to Say? How to Ask? A Powerful Primer

As a young professional in my early twenties, I volunteered for a St. Louis YWCA event that provided excellent fundraising training. The presenter, a senior advancement officer at Saint Louis University Hospital who had just raised $60 million for a capital campaign, taught us the powerful words to use when making an "ask." He encouraged us to pass the wisdom forward.

Here's how I've adapted his invaluable words: "Would you be willing to consider donating (*fill in the specific dollar amount*) so that your gift will (*fill in the impact of the donor's gift*) for (*fill in the name of your organization*)?" Then, simply wait quietly. Don't interrupt. Hold the silence.

Use this model at your meeting and role-play with team members. Ask, "Would you be willing to consider purchasing two reservations for our fundraiser so that we can increase outreach at schools for the Colorado Symphony Orchestra?" Asking, "Would you be willing to consider" is not looking for a yes or no. You're just opening the door for the donor to consider the opportunity you've just graciously offered.

Kathy's Top Strategies for Audience Development

Here are four proven ways to easily and naturally engage your board and leadership to invite the right guests into the room, guests you already know will bid high.

- Use a table host or a table captain and half-table captains. This technique helps you engage guests in spending money during your benefit auction event. Table captains are responsible for communicating with the people at their tables. The table captain will likely make only three phone calls for a table of eight, because most people come to benefit auctions as couples. Other responsibilities are to invite friends and business colleagues and to fill the table with the right people. If someone says that they can't fill an entire table, suggest they serve as a half-table captain, which also reduces the number of phone calls.

- Create auction ambassadors. This is one of my hallmark audience development strategies. It's powerful and easy to do. Create a small group of 5 to 12 people who love you and will do anything for you. Tell them they don't have to go to any meetings. Simply call them up and say, "Would you be willing to help us focus on our number one strategy this year, getting the right people to our auction?" They're likely to respond, "I'd do anything for your group!" There are just a few jobs auction ambassadors need to do: Spend money. Bring a couple just like them who will spend money. Play along with the auctioneer (this is called the fun factor). When the auctioneer asks for more bidders, auction ambassadors bid again and again. They'll also ask the couple that they brought to do the same. Solicit premium live items you know they would buy. During the silent auction and dinner, connect guests to your organization's cause, ask them how they are connected, invite them to see the live auction items, and talk about the fund-a-need. Imagine having 5 to 12 new couples in the room that you know have the capacity to bid high. It changes the bidding dynamic instantly.

- Hold a kick-off event. Two to six months prior to your benefit auction event, host a kick-off event to talk about your mission. Hold this at a private home with cocktails and hors d'oeuvres. Invite your top donors, potential sponsors, and referrals. Ask your top donors to refer someone else who might be interested in supporting you. This will help spark a new group of participants for the next auction.

- Empower your stakeholders to go above and beyond. Being a table captain is more than just putting together tables. Table captains should introduce the individuals at their tables to the key people at your benefit auction, including the leaders, the VIPs, the honoree, top volunteers, and perhaps other guests who are developing close connections with your organization. They should bring guests over to silent and live auction items and say, "Wow! Isn't this great? Here's a great trip package. Let's take a look. Let's bid together."

Five Mistakes You'll Want to Avoid

Mistake #1: Not Inviting Everyone

Many people think that if they don't receive an invitation, they're not invited. Because you know that dynamic exists, make sure that people know they are invited by leveraging the power of personal follow-up. Think of the ramifications of forgetting to invite a strong bidder. Be sure to invite every single guest who has bid on an item or participated in the fund-a-need in the past. If someone gives once, they will most likely give again, especially if you thank them with a personal follow-up phone call.

Mistake #2 Not Choosing the Right Date Early

Another common mistake is missing the window to get on the social calendar of major donors or top bidders. It's important to know who schedules the calendars of major donors, sponsors, and top bidders. Also, cross-check community calendars. If you don't do this, your event could be half empty. Schedule your benefit auction event on a date when you can draw major supporters. Avoid dates when other organizations have events. Many communities hold scheduling meetings just for this purpose. Schedule as soon as possible, ideally 11 or 12 months or more prior to your benefit auction event.

Mistake #3 Believing Celebrities Are the Draw

Many people think having a VIP or a celebrity attend the event will increase overall event attendance. Yes, this might increase attendance, but it might also entice people to attend only to see the celebrity, rather than to connect to your cause and contribute. There was a famous VIP at one benefit auction who attracted people just to see him. Guests didn't attend for the cause, they attended to gawk at the celebrity. Bidding was dismal.

A celebrity can distinctly impact fundraising, however, by unabashedly serving as a spokesperson before, during, and after the event. Be sure to work with the celebrity's agent and give the celebrity inspiring talking points, in writing, in advance. Communicate your desire for him to use his celebrity to invite generosity from the audience. Keep the focus on fundraising. Help the celebrity understand that the most important role he can play is to invite others who can bid and give generously. How do you do that? Coach him. Write him a script. Get great photos of him with major donors. Hold a VIP party with key stakeholders and leverage the celebrity. Ask him for a unique specialty live item.

Best-selling novelist Dennis Lehane attended the Massachusetts SPCA—Angell Animal Medical Center auction and offered attendees the opportunity to be a character in his next novel. He was incredibly generous with his time at the event. He came up on stage, spoke from his heart about helping animals, talked about the dog he rescued, and spoke about how everyone can make a difference. He described his wonderful auction item, and then, as the auctioneer, I sold it for more than $11,000. The key is to keep the celebrity's focus on the mission of the organization, so he's engaging your guests to bid high.

Mistake #4 Believing Items Will Draw Big Bidders to Your Event

There's a myth that big items draw big donors. What draws big donors and strong supporters is a personal ask by someone they know, especially if they care about the particular cause. Your auction is not about the auction items. The number one reason someone will attend your fundraiser auction is because they have been personally invited (by phone or in person) by someone they know and trust.

Mistake #5 Not Including All Bidders — Even If They Can't Come

Some people mistakenly think that if they don't come to the benefit auction, they can't bid. When you're promoting the event, invite everyone to participate in bidding by asking if they'd be willing to consider an absentee bid. If there are no auction items that interest them, encourage them to participate in the fund-a-need by saying, "We have another opportunity called the fund-a-need, where you can offer a cash contribution at a level that is meaningful to you. The funds are going to support (*insert your program or activity*)."

We Sold Out! Create the Expectation to Give

Do you want your event to be a sell-out, crowded with people who are psychologically prepared to bid high on your items? Do you want an audience filled with guests who participate generously in your fund-a-need? Are you looking for long-term donors who are connected to you after your benefit auction event? Yes! Yes! Yes!

Fundraising at your event is paramount. However, cultivating and developing relationships with everyone who attends is vital to your long-term success as an organization. This begins with the very first communication you have with guests and continues long after your event is over. Everyone is a prospective donor.

How to Create and Sustain an Expectation of Giving
- Make pre-auction marketing phone calls.
- Follow up personally (call and visit) with prospects.
- When you follow up, share who else is attending, naming anyone they might know.
- Pre-sell auction items so that people come ready to be generous.
- Swipe credit cards for express checkout.
- Have well-organized logistics.
- Host a VIP party and a kick-off event with a preview of auction items to create more energy and momentum at your event.

Make Your Event a Signature Networking Opportunity

Many major gala events position their benefit auction events as major power-networking occasions. Why? It's THE place to be! When people come to a gala, they like to visit and they like to network. Have your auction ambassadors and your board members participate as hosts, so your guests are properly greeted and introduced to one another and can share impact stories about your cause. You can make your benefit auction a signature event for power networking and promoting your mission.

Engaging Community Leaders

The Koahnic Broadcasting Alaska Native Art Auction in Anchorage is a great model of how to create a signature fundraising event and giving networking opportunity, engage community leaders, and create an expectation of giving. As a consultant and auctioneer, I recommended that Alaska native leaders, together with KNBA Alaska media, make audience development their top priority. Their goal, in addition to raising money for the Native Youth Media Program, was to create a stunning signature event featuring native Alaskan traditional and contemporary artwork.

From 1993 to 1999, I had the pleasure of serving as the consultant and auctioneer for the Native Art Auction. The first year we raised $6,000, and the event was held in an upscale deli and market. Picture this. The only place to hold the silent auction was on trays in the front of the deli. Eight years later, this signature Native Art Auction raised $267,000 in the live auction *alone*.

How did Koahnic Broadcasting achieve that stunning level of success? We positioned the benefit auction event as a major signature event for native art in the state of Alaska. We also developed this event to be a major power-networking event, through focused and targeted outreach efforts and personal asks. That made all the difference in the world, because it meant the people with the capacity to give generously were at the event and primed to donate.

Audience Tip: Make It Easy for Parents to Attend

Here's a great idea from Trinity Catholic School in Maine. They extended the idea of after-school activities one step further. To raise more money on auction night, they offered free "evening activities" for children held right at the school. Aides supervised the children, providing games, movies, popcorn, and activities, while the parents enjoyed the annual auction. What a terrific benefit!

Conclusion

Build long-term connections that start at your auction fundraiser. Think of every guest as a long-term donor. Ask how you can align your guests with the work your organization is doing. Help your board members to discover the connections your guests have to the mission and to members. Understand each person's interests and core values and how they relate to the core values of your organization.

You want your guests to feel moved by your work, to feel deeply interested in the work you do as a nonprofit, and to be deeply touched by the difference you're making.

6

Procure Incredible Auction Items

STRATEGIC AUCTION ITEM SOLICITATION IS LIKE FISHING. Sound strange? Consider this: There's a huge difference between fly fishing and plain ol' fishing. Think Alaska. Think *Deadliest Catch*. Fishermen toss big crates out in the ocean. Not only do they catch crabs, they also haul a lot of by-catch (unwanted sea creatures). The same thing happens with item solicitation. When you throw out a big net for item procurement, you'll get heaps of extra low-performance items that no one wants.

Fly fishermen have a saying, "Match the hatch." This means match the lure to the specific insect upon which the fish you're targeting likes to feed. For example, an experienced angler knows that bottom-hugging crawfish lures won't entice trout if they are surface feeding on mayflies. A savvy auction chair knows better than to offer front-row Metropolitan Opera tickets at his or her high school ice hockey booster auction, because donated center-ice Stanley Cup seats, with dinner and a player meet-and-greet, is a real hat trick.

Steal this lesson for item procurement. Know who attends your fundraiser and what they want, then match unique auction items with the wants of your audience. With this highly strategic approach to item solicitation, you won't end up with auction by-catch and a room full of unwanted items that bore your guests to distraction.

In this chapter, I'll share how you can make your profits skyrocket by procuring top-selling auction items. By using my extensive insights and ideas on how to optimize "high-yield" auction items, you'll get those bid cards waving.

It's All about Relationships

From a strategic perspective, what drives a fundraising event is the opportunity to better know and build relationships with your guests, so they become more engaged, more passionate about your cause, and more willing to contribute. Before you begin procuring items, it's imperative to understand the buying behaviors of the guests and donors. The goal is to offer exciting auction items people actually want, so they can freely and eagerly support a cause they love.

Guest behaviors have changed. Auction guests are bidding much more intentionally. Let's face it: Not everyone really wants or needs another silent or live auction item. So it's vital for you and your benefit auction team to be quite strategic, and to make sure you exclusively procure and offer items that will keep the auction exciting.

Know your guests and curate your auction items. This is the most lucrative way to boost bidding and make more money. What's the very best way to know what your donors, past bidders, guests, and sponsors want? Ask them what they would love to bid on at your next auction. Then ask for their advice. Ask them what's missing at the auction. (See Chapter 9 on measurement for more ideas.) Study past auction data, list the top items, and note who bought them. Then focus on procuring those high-performing auction items.

Match your hand-selected auction items to your unique audience. If your audience loves and supports arts and culture, you just *have* to get sold-out Broadway or Vegas show tickets with a VIP back-stage meet and greet. Add airfare, a gourmet meal, and a luxury hotel, and that's a winning package. If you know your guests are baseball fanatics, make sure you have tickets behind home plate for one of the biggest sports rivalries in history: the Red Sox versus the Yankees. School auctions afford really unique bidding opportunities: Traditional best-sellers include chances to be head of the school for a day, have your very own parking spot, share a favorite teacher experience (like cupcake-making at Mrs. Smith's home), and, of course, own the class gift from each grade level, like that first grade cookie jar with each child's thumbprint and initials all over it.

Strategically procure your high-yield live auction items first. Don't waste your time and energy trying to get something for everyone. Design live auction items that will predictably fetch far more than their values. This is where you must focus your efforts.

Double your money. Always, always ask the donor if you can offer two packages on auction night. Be sure to let your auctioneer know when they can sell two!

What's *Hot?* Fulfill Fantasies, Hit Emotions

Solicit items that are experiences, personal and unique items, once-in-a-lifetime experiences, exclusive handmade gifts, one-of-a-kind travel trips, celebrity experiences, and sold-out or hard-to-get unique group experiences. Hot VIP tickets and experiences to sold-out sporting events, concerts, and shows are excellent. Dining and wine experiences are top sellers. Be sure to design items that are highly experiential and unique, and only available at your event. And always check state and local laws if you're considering offering wine or spirits.

What's *Not?* It's Personal

Avoid auction items that do not perform well, such as art, jewelry, business services, and medical services. Why? These categories typically sell far below value, because there's a high level of personal choice and individual preference. Someone on the team will select jewelry or art based on his or her tastes, which may not mesh with those of the audience. Unless you know you have several ready bidders prior to auction night, it's best to avoid these items. Look at your past auction performance results and bidding levels to help you analyze such items.

Have you ever been offered the opportunity to auction off a puppy? Don't do it. Buying any kind of pet at a charity auction tends to be an impulse decision, and you cannot guarantee that bidder will be an ideal pet owner. Your best advice is to heed the caution of humane and animal rescue groups, who almost universally do not support selling pets at fundraising auctions.

Only solicit auction items that generate a high rate of return. Hint: Think and act like a top marketer. Consider the performance of each auction item. In business, this is called the ROI, or return on investment. By knowing the performance ROI of each auction item, you'll start to realize which items are best, and will bring far more than their values.

Your ultimate goal is to acquire items that will fetch at least 100 percent of their values, ideally far more. My advice: If, historically, any of your auction items have received 50 percent or less of their values, dump them. It's not worth the time they take to sell in a live auction or the space they take up in a silent auction. Instead, offer these items as door prizes at volunteer appreciation events. Volunteers will be thrilled to receive gift certificates to local shops and restaurants.

How Many Items to Procure?

There's no magic number for how many items to have at an auction. It's more important to look at the strategy you'll use. Remember, your auction guests are increasingly strategic in their giving and bidding. Plus, I'm seeing a new trend of guests leaving events earlier than ever before. Leverage this trend and apply the proven adage of "less is more." Here are some guidelines to help.

Analyze Your Auction Data

What's the financial goal for your benefit auction? Break down that goal so you can look at revenue for each stream separately. This way, when you look specifically at your live auction goal, you can review your past performance and specifically the return on investment for your live-auction items.

How much money do you want to raise? Think first about your financial goals and the performance of each separate revenue stream—silent auction and live auction. Some simple auction revenue forecasting is invaluable here.

The most important step you can take is to calculate how well each of your auction items will sell, and how much they'll contribute to your financial goal. This will give you insight on how many items it will take to raise the money you need.

For benefit auctions, it's quite simple to calculate your ROI or item performance. It's the ratio between the value of the item and the final high bid. For example, a trip for four to the Caribbean that's valued at $4,000 and sells for $3,000 earns a 75 percent return. A VIP sold-out concert with a value of $2,500 that sells for $5,000 has a performance ROI of 200 percent.

Make a chart calculating the retail value, high bid, and percentage of value achieved. This will highlight how your items have performed historically, in past auctions. Look at items both individually and by category—trips, experiences, dinners, food, sports, entertainment, kids, and so on. By studying the last three to five years of ROI, you'll have a thorough under-standing of the kind of performance you can expect, and you'll be able to forecast how many items it will take to reach and exceed your financial goals. Go into your auction with your eyes wide open!

Use Time as a Guide

Is the auction the focus of your event? What else is going on—a dance? Entertainment? Is there a keynote speech? Are there awards? You have to think about where you'll position the key revenue streams of the live auction and the fund-a-need, as well as how much time you will allot. Remember, the "golden time" is the magic time that positions your live auction and fund-a-need for the most revenue potential. Never wait until the end of the evening for these two important activities!

What type of fundraiser event are you hosting? This often overlooked factor will help you determine how much time you actually have to budget for your live auction, because each type of event has specific characteristics that will affect your final number of items. There are five different types of fundraising auctions: gala auctions, classic dinner auctions, school auctions, youth/sports auctions, and specialty auctions such as wine, art, and golf auctions. Each type of auction can raise significant funds when you strategically factor in the proper number of items.

If you are hosting a gala auction, there are many other pro-gram elements that may occur during the event, such as awards and dancing. The auction is but one key fundraising activity. So you may conduct a live auction of only two to eight items of high value for the gala style auction.

In the classic dinner auction, the auction itself is the highlight of the event, with few activities other than a silent auction, the live auction, the fund-a-need, and some revenue activity games. For classic dinner auctions, the average live auction number is about eight to 15 live items.

School, youth, and sports auctions are unique, as they are typically *the* main annual fundraiser event for parents, supporters, members, teams, and alumni. The auction is the centerpiece and contains unique school specialty items such as class gifts and principal-for-the-day privileges. These auctions need 10 to 30 live items.

Each specialty fundraising auction (golf, art, or wine) has its own distinct culture. Golf benefit auctions typically have fewer items that are focused on golf; sporting events and trips top the charts. The highly specialized charity wine auction fundraisers are the culmination of multi-day exclusive food and wine events, typically offering two to three dozen extremely high-end travel packages, exclusive food and wine gourmet experiences with top chefs, and, of course, superb wines. Successful art auction fundraisers have both highly curated guests as well as art that matches the audience—typically, a smaller number of hand-selected pieces of art.

What else is happening at your event? Guests have shorter attention spans and leave events earlier than ever, meaning you'll need to curate fewer items of higher value and auction them as early as possible at your event. Consider what other program elements are scheduled during your fundraiser. Is there a silent auction, a live auction, dinner, a talk, awards and dancing, a performance, a stand-up comedian, or other entertainment? Write down exactly how much time you will allot to each element and create a minute-by-minute show flow timeline.

How many guests are attending your charity auction? In many cases, guests tend to attend and bid as a couple. This means that you'll need to calculate your bidding population by house-holds, not individuals. Consider a 1:4 overall ratio for auction items—that is, one item per every four households. If you flood your auction with too many items, you'll exhaust your guests and cause what I call "bidder fatigue." Remember, a confused mind never buys. With too many items, your guests' bidding behaviors are to stop bidding, talk to their friends, go to the bar, and, worst of all, leave your auction early. Don't risk losing money and donor engagement with too many auction items!

Who is your auctioneer? The pace of a professional benefit auctioneer is about two minutes per item. Volunteers or celebrities can take up to five minutes per live item because they're usually selling at a slower pace and not building as much momentum, so you'll need to factor in more time per item.

Here's your new benchmark: Balance the number of items with your financial goal. Fewer live items of higher value, sold earlier, is best. As you can see, each category of event has a different number of "right" auction items. Let the history of the event, past results, and the insights of the auction committees, staff, and board members guide you to the best number of auction items each year. Solicit items that have been successful in the past. Waste no time and space on items that don't bring high performance return. Study your results each year and only solicit items that are successful for you.

Making the Ask

When making an ask for auction item donations, remember that it's important to show how you are connected personally with the organization, so you can build rapport with the donor. Auction item donors are thinking, "If I donate an item, what good will it do for the organization? How does it connect to my values?" Begin an exchange and share a short impact vignette of success that is particularly meaningful to you. You are communicating the impact of the donor's gift, not just getting something to auction off.

Here's a tip from professional fundraisers when making any kind of ask: After you ask for the auction item, simply wait for the donor to respond. Many people avoid this important step, because it makes them nervous. Stop right after you have made the "ask" and be quiet, hold the silence. Listen. It may feel like you're waiting a long time, but skilled fundraisers know it's critical to have this time to let the potential donor think and respond. If the donor donates an item, be sure to say thank you and follow up.

No Is Not Always No

If you get a "no," don't give up. There are ways to follow up and turn an initial no into a yes. Ask people who say no if they would consider giving in a future year. Ask if there's anything else they might consider donating. When you get a no, investigate the opportunity to partner with the organization at a sponsorship level that would be meaningful to the potential donor. The more no's you get, the quicker you get to yes!

No to one request is not necessarily no across the board. Ask the donor if he would be willing to make a referral instead. Are there other organizations or businesses to which he could introduce you to? What about vendors? You can also ask him to underwrite part of your auction or a single expense, or perhaps provide a sponsorship or an advertisement for your catalogue.

Kick-Off Rally

As we've noted, the kick-off rally is a remarkably effective procurement strategy. This could be a wine and cheese event where you can incorporate a little bit about the organization's impact. Talk about the wonderful work you do. At the same time, include training on how to ask for sponsorships and auction items.

Each year, the Children's Trust Fund holds a kick-off party for their wonderful gala auction. This party includes a mini-workshop with training on how to ask for items, how to invite new donors, and how to more deeply engage the gala committee members. The party is held in the actual venue where the gala auction will be, and it's hosted at no cost to the organization. This event tends to bring many people, because it includes the opportunity to taste and select wines for the gala. The big benefit is donor cultivation in a unique setting.

Connections to Procure Auction Items

The Personal Ask

Item acquisition is all about who knows whom. Again, think about spheres of influence. These are the networks of connections of your committee members, board members, and sponsors, and they're as useful in procuring items as they are in finding guests, donors, and sponsors. For this committee, too, you'll want co-chairs who come from different backgrounds. For example, pair someone who works in the legal field with a co-chair in banking, health care, or a small business owner. Think strategically about potential committee co-chairs' spheres of influence. If they have all the same friends, they might enjoy the partnership, but they won't expand your influence.

Another powerful way to increase your auction committee's sphere of influence and develop relationships with donors is to have a liaison on your committee from a sponsor company. A sponsor's influence can bring items that a general auction solicitation committee or board does not have. If you can get a liaison from your sponsor, ask him or her to participate in item procurement. You'll be pleasantly surprised at the interest, especially when you start educating people about the items that sell best based on your analysis of past auctions.

Stakeholder Connection

Who is already involved in your organization? Your auction committee members, your chairs, your board, other key volunteers, and perhaps some awardees and honorees. Ask them to consider not only their friends, but their second spheres of influence, too. Who among their friends might take the opportunity to make a significant item donation? There's a high degree of correlation between board involvement in a fundraising auction event (e.g., attending, donating items, developing the audience, donor cultivation) and the event's level of success. Showcase your auction items and goal achievement with your board and stakeholders on a regular basis throughout the year-long auction preparation cycle.

Sponsors

Sponsors may provide cash contributions, but they can also bring their specialized influence, and this is a huge boost for item procurement. They have connections that you don't. Talk with sponsors about how they can leverage their relationships to help you procure best-selling items. Then consider a deeper step. Invite your sponsors to ask their vendors for auction item contributions and to tap their circles of influence to support you.

Vendors

We already talked about using vendors for audience development, but vendors are also my favorite new source for auction item donations. Review the list of businesses that are connected to your organization. Consider anyone to whom your organization or your sponsor organization writes a check. Remember to include all professional service providers, such as printing companies, waste management companies, accounting agencies, legal advisors, and so on, who are involved with the organization.

Celebrity Sphere of Influence

Ever wonder about how to leverage celebrities to find the right auction items? Like sponsors, celebrities have different spheres of influence and offer additional opportunities to procure auction items. If you're working with a celebrity and with the celebrity's agent, make sure they understand your cause and your specific practical needs. Be sure to receive written permission to use his or her name and image to promote the cause. If you are lucky enough to have the celebrity attend your fundraiser, ask him or her to help you promote an item and your cause at the event. Make sure you give the celebrity written talking points about your impact. Include an item that showcases that particular celebrity. For example, when I was the auctioneer for the Nantucket AIDS Network, Sara Jessica Parker was the honoree and offered the final *Sex in the City* script autographed by the entire cast. She spoke eloquently about the cause. Then I auctioned this wildly popular item for over $21,000, as Sara warmly encouraged high bids from the stage.

Regional Specialties and Themes

Consider regional specialties to create premium auction items. In New Orleans, creole is king. In Wisconsin, cheese. In Washington and California, wine. What types of items can you create from the region where you live? Tie in your theme, too. How about an exotic trip to India for your Asian Fusion theme? With a little creativity, you can come up with packages with extra allure for your guests.

Fresh Opportunities for Items

Invite new businesses. They want exposure and your benefit auction is a great marketing opportunity for them. Chambers of commerce are superb resources. Look in local papers and glossy city magazines. Tie into the hot "buy local" movement. After the auction, frequent your new shops, restaurants, and businesses and continue to engage their long-term support.

Favorite sources of premium auction items are the places where you and your volunteers, board, and parents spend money. Procure items everywhere and all the time! Keep auction item solicitation forms in your purse, briefcase, or gym bag, wherever you go. Solicit items throughout the year. For example, if you're at dinner or on vacation, meet the owner of the restaurant or resort, because he or she is the person who can make the difference in getting a "yes" response to your "ask," and it's great to develop a long-term relationship.

Auction Item Exchange

Remember the example of the high school hockey booster auction and the Metropolitan Opera front row tickets? Get creative. What if that local high school and regional arts organization exchanged items? Voila! Even though ski trips in winter climates are easy auction items to procure, anyone who lives in that particular region can easily ski there. Trade cool ski vacation packages with sister organizations across the country. Think how well ski buffs will bid for deep powder on their dream slopes, like Vail or Jackson Hole. Imagine animal rescue groups from San Diego and Boston exchanging a trip to the Channel Islands for a trip to Nantucket. Find sister organizations in your field, whether it's social services or animal rescue. Look for groups working with people who have similar disabilities; look for educational groups; look for regional or national organizations with similar missions. Be sure to exchange items that have approximately the same value. Put a written agreement in place with your sister organization to ensure that each group's commitment is clearly understood.

Getting Items from Your Neighborhood

Who are your actual neighbors, geographically? Try my yellow-pad map exercise. Map out every physical neighbor, starting next door and extending several miles in all directions. Take a few key people on your committee to visit those shops, restaurants, and businesses. Your neighbors are in your sphere of influence; meet them and invite their support.

Frazier Woods School is a small Montessori school in a semi-rural setting in Connecticut. As their auctioneer and consultant, I suggested a visit to a granite tombstone shop across the street from the school. A couple of committee members walked over and talked with the shop owner and came back with a great item. No, it wasn't a tombstone. The shop also made granite benches, and the owner of the tombstone company generously donated a granite bench, which I sold in the auction for $2,000. The high bidder won the bench for significantly more than the value of the item and, much to everyone's surprise, she donated the bench back to the school.

Seasonal Donations

Learn the budgeting cycles of local businesses, corporations, restaurants, and shops. You must make a request early in their donation cycles to be successful. Research each company's website for specific information about what causes they support and when they take requests for donations. Think about retail shops. At regular times during the year, they reduce inventory. If you'd like to get a nice barbecue grill for your auction, a store might not have availability in the summer, but you might score a great grill off-season, when they're trying to reduce their inventory.

The same thing is true for seasonal businesses. If you'd like to auction off a chance to "Win your weight in ice cream from Creole Creamery," approach the owner during their season. This is especially the case for special theme parks or ski areas, because when it's off-season, the owners often aren't even around.

A Few of My Favorite Things

Here are a few of my favorite innovative items that exceeded value.

- The Pope's skull cap. In 2014, a white skull cap worn by Pope Francis sold for $250,000 euros at an online auction. Proceeds benefited an Italian charity that was fighting child mortality in the Democratic Republic of Congo.
- An intimate six-course dinner. In Sonoma, 25 couples each paid $10,000 for dinner at Hamel Family Wines, raising $250,000 for the Sonoma Harvest Wine Auction in minutes.
- A 1950 GM Futurliner. A record shattering $4,650,000 ($4 million bid and $650,000 in additional pledges) was raised on January 17, 2015 at Barrett-Jackson, The World's Greatest Collector Car Auctions in Scottsdale, Arizona. The Futurliner was donated from the Ron Pratte Collection by Ron Pratte, a Vietnam veteran, to benefit the Armed Forces Foundation.
- Shoe frenzy. One of my March of Dimes clients auctioned off the opportunity for a family to have a one-minute shoe-shopping spree in a Famous Footwear store.
- The instant wine cellar. Each board or team member donates her favorite bottle of wine to create an instant wine cellar as one lot in the live auction. (Before doing this, check your state laws.)
- Once-in-a-lifetime sporting activities. Imagine a batting clinic with Derek Jeter, skating lessons with Kristi Yamaguchi, or a session with your favorite local coach.
- Sold out tickets. I once sold a set of *Oprah* tickets in a Chicago package for $8,000, right before the *Oprah* show was ending its run. The tickets triggered an intense bidding war between two women, who stood on their chairs amid wild cheering.

- A private cocktail party with the beluga whales at the Mystic Aquarium.
- Money made out of thin air. Handmade "sock-monkeys" lovingly crafted each year by the founder of a social services organization regularly sold for over $1,000 apiece.
- Immortality. How about the high bidder's name in the next book by a famous author? The purchaser of the item could be a hero or villain in the next story. The opportunity to put a dog's name in a famous author's next book fetched $9,000! I sold the head table at the Anchorage Boys and Girls Club for $45,000 for the *next* year's gala auction. Here's a booming success: I sold the opportunity to play the kettledrums with a symphony orchestra during the *1812 Overture,* performed immediately after the auction, for $3,000.
- A chance to wear the ring. The Boston Red Sox won the World Series several years ago after a very long hiatus. The president of a local medical center was closely connected to the team and wore his World Series ring to the benefit auction. On the spot, he offered to allow the winning bidder to wear his ring for the rest of the event. The opportunity to wear a World Series ring for roughly an hour sold for several thousand dollars.
- Naming rights. If you have a school campus, you could designate a hallway and auction off the right to name it. Name a small road in your town. Name your own deli sandwich or ice cream flavor, or create your own signature cocktail at a local bar.
- Items with no direct cost. School auctions tend to have classic items with no direct costs (front row seats at graduation, gifts made by each class, beloved teacher experiences...). At a Catholic school auction, front-row tickets to Christmas Mass always sell high. Don't forget to sell both sides of the aisle! Here's a creative auction package. A principal who was getting married shortly after a public school auction created a "reverse bridal shower" for 12 young girls. The winners came to the principal's home, each wearing white boas and big faux diamond rings. They ate cake, drank sparkling cider, got their hair and makeup done, and played traditional bridal shower games modified for children. They all got party gifts

from the principal. This item sold for \$1,200 to a group of first grade mothers and we doubled it for the fourth grade, too. It was a strategically brilliant item that engaged parents, students, and the school principal in a new creative endeavor.

Consignment items

Consignment auction items are offered by companies to be auctioned by organizations for fundraising. The organization makes money when it sells the item above cost.

The advantage of consignment items is that your organization has access to items it can't get through donations. This opens a vast choice of trips and experiences that are best sold when you base your selection on the makeup of your audience. There are consignment items that fit all sizes of auctions and may be sold multiple times. Consignment experiences are not a financial risk; if you don't sell them, you don't pay. However, it's vital to start the bidding at a price point above the cost of the consignment item.

According to Stuart Paskow, CEO of Mitch-Stuart, Inc., "The top auction fundraising success factor is selecting a variety of trips and experiences that match the demographics of the audience, so that your guests will be excited and open their wallets year after year. We have raised over \$1 billion using consignment items for 15,000 fundraising auction events in the last 21 years."

Review your donated auction items. Calculate how much you will raise with these items. If you need to raise more money and can't get more donations, or if you're seeking a special item, consider sprinkling in a consignment item or two.

As when contracting with any vendor, do your homework. Be aware that some guests and patrons wish to know if an auction item is donated 100% or if it is a consignment item, where a portion of their high bid will benefit the charity. This information can effect their desire to bid. In addition, ask the consignment company for references, not testimonials. Talk to other nonprofits and schools that have used the consignment company for a number of years. Be sure to read all the contracts and understand the financial arrangements.

Remember that fundraisers cannot rely completely on consignment items. However, in annual benefit auction events, many times the same people will donate the same items year after year, and the items can only be sold once, or airfare is not included, or the gift is date-specific. Consignment times can be utilized successfully to add a fresh component and new dollars. Unrestricted or choice travel dates will bring more dollars than a time-restricted item. Chosen strategically, consignment items can be used successfully in raffles, and silent and live auctions.[1]

The Dream Game

The Dream Game provides an inspiring interactive experience that engages volunteers and donors while teaching auction procurement. Perfect for an item solicitation rally, a kick-off party, or a board meeting, it offers an opportunity for every person to share the dream item they would buy. "Buy" is the operative word. Start by sharing a mission moment story, something that had a powerful impact on the people you serve. Have everyone close their eyes and imagine that they have the opportunity to select any item they, personally, would love to see auctioned. Then ask each person, "What would you like to buy?" Someone might say, "I'd love to go on a cruise to Greece." Another person might say, "I'd love to have tuition to this school paid for my child." Capture everyone's dream item in writing.

Then discover connections within the group to procure those dreams on the spot. Ask, "Does anybody here have any connection whatsoever, direct or indirect (perhaps a second cousin or neighbor) to any of these items?" It's almost like magic! There's always a good number of listed dream items for which someone says, "Yes, I know my uncle's brother's friend works for a Greek cruise line, I can get that."

While playing the Dream Game at a choral organization, I had someone say, "It's been my dream to play violin at a symphony." Someone called out, "My cousin plays first chair at the Cleveland Symphony." Boom! Instant connection. Another time, a donor quietly revealed, "I'd love to take my husband to Tuscany for our 40th anniversary." Across the room a new volunteer shouted with excitement, "We own a travel agency that specializes in Italy tours—ciao bella!" You'll make powerful connections to terrific items that your guests already intend to buy.

About 10 years ago, I was conducting the Dream Game at the kick-off meeting for my international adoption agency client. As volunteers and board members shared dream items, a volunteer actually started crying. "I can't offer anything," she sobbed. "We just adopted a baby from Russia. We used all our funds and have no money to buy any auction items and I certainly don't know anybody."

Her friend, who was sitting next to her, tapped her on the elbow and said, "Doesn't your son know somebody?"

The mom said, "Well, yes, but my son's dyslexic, you know."

Everyone was quiet. The rest of us were thinking, where is this story going?

The woman went on, "My 12-year-old son has a dyslexic pen pal." Who was the pen pal?

"He writes back and forth with Jay Leno once a week," she added. Until that moment, she didn't realize her powerful connection. Through her son, the group was offered tickets to the show and a meet-and-greet with Jay Leno. Isn't it amazing who may be within our spheres of influence?

Conclusion

The number one question asked about benefit auctions is, "How do you get auction items that sell the best?" Remember, the most important thing to "sell" is the donor's connection to you. It's not about auction items. Today, guests and donors are very strategic about their giving and with their bidding. Not everyone wants a silent or live auction item. Not everyone wants to be involved in competitive bidding. Through the new lens of the Philanthropy Model of Fundraising Auctions, focus on the spirit of giving. When you remind your supporters that it's not what they get that counts, it's what they give to make a difference, your donors will be sold on you.

Note

1. Stuart Paskow, personal communication, October 9, 2014.

7

Make Your Show Flow

IN THE WEEKS BEFORE YOUR AUCTION, it's easy to forget how much fun you're about to have. This is theater! You're about to put on a show! The magic of that can get lost, because benefit auctions are intense work. Inevitably, you will spend countless hours planning, organizing, and preparing for your event: attracting the right guests, determining the right mix of revenue streams, choosing just the right auctioneer, selecting meals, and recruiting and training volunteers (just to name a few myriad tasks on your benefit auction list). These ingredients are necessary for a successful event, but they are not sufficient.

When you shift your mind-set to the Philanthropy Model of Fundraising Auctions, you realize that what's even more important is the strategic orchestration of your benefit auction and the surrounding event. Like a combination of a Broadway director and a small business owner, you have to take charge of the flow: choosing the most advantageous opening and closing times; using marketing techniques to display your items for high return on investment, precision timing fundraising opportunities and emotional impact. You must intentionally design the event and direct its pacing, letting excitement and momentum build for maximum revenue flow. Think timing, pacing, spacing, and gracing (gracious guest engagement).

This is what I call *show flow*. The term is borrowed from the entertainment business and performing arts and refers to the sequencing of an entire show. Your guests are audience members, and they have an unspoken expectation that they're going to be entertained in some way, shape, or fashion. Why not leverage that expectation by positioning the fundraising elements of your event in the right place in the show. In this chapter, we'll walk through an event from A to Z so you can see how a successful benefit auction is choreographed.

Planning Your Show Flow

First, make sure that you plan the show flow for your benefit auction event on paper. It will probably take several drafts to finesse the actual show flow or written timeline. There are layers to show flow, so make one column for the elements of the event and a separate column for the production of the event. Each will have a different schedule or timeline.

Insist on seamlessness. When it's time to start, the event runs with no lag time. The biggest enemies of fundraising are boredom and distraction. Strategic show flow can help you position your mission in the best way possible.

Intentionally design and build a high level of excitement, letting the momentum crescendo with the fund-a-need in the live auction.

Less Is More

Less is more in several ways, starting with the number of items you auction. Less is also more in terms of the timing of the event. As I've noted, guests are tending to leave 30 to 40 minutes earlier than they used to. Take advantage of this with a less-is-more approach. Condense your event elements so that you have the most exciting, compelling, and on-target fundraising auction event possible.

Avoid Bidder Fatigue

Guests expect to attend a fun, upbeat, lively event. Attention spans are short, so keep things moving. Your organization cannot make money if the guests are gone. If guests are bored or there's been too much lag time, their attention will go somewhere else. We want to keep them focused on your mission and why they should support you generously at the auction.

My number one rule for show flow is "No BS!" By that I mean, "No Boring Speeches!" Why? In benefit auction events, time is money, and boring speeches will cost you—not make you—money. I've developed formulas you can use to calculate how many dollars per minute and per square foot you want to make.

To calculate the dollars per minute you need to make in your benefit auction event, simply divide your target fundraising goal amount by the number of minutes that will elapse from the second your doors open until the event's triumphant ending.

If your event drags out and is not well-orchestrated, it can cost you revenue for your cause, and you run the very high risk of losing the interest of your audience in the short and long term.

Make Every Minute a Revenue Minute

To calculate the dollars per minute you need to make in each segment of your benefit auction event (i.e., silent auction, live auction, fund-a-need), multiply the dollars per minute you need to raise for your benefit auction event by the total time allocated for each segment.

You can also assign a value to other revenue-generating activities. Share this information with your auction committee and board members to help them understand that time is money.

Brief, Inspiring Remarks

Here's my rule: *Anyone who holds the microphone for more than one or two minutes is eating into prime fundraising time.* This is important to understand from a financial standpoint, but it's also important from a momentum standpoint. To illustrate how crucial this rule is, please take out a piece of paper and write the word "SPEECHES" on it in large letters. Then, take your pen and scratch it out as hard as you can. Replace it with the word "REMARKS." Ask the chairperson of the board who will tee up the live auction to make brief inspiring remarks instead of a speech or keynote address. Ask your client who will tell her first-person story for your Fund a Need to make first-person inspiring remarks. That phrasing alone will make a huge difference in the expectation of everyone participating in your event.

> **Kathy's Five-Step Formula for Starting an Event Fundraiser**
> 1. Welcome
> 2. Thank You
> 3. Why We're Here
> 4. Introduce Your Auctioneer
> 5. Raise MONEY

Anatomy of a Benefit Auction

Specific activities will happen at the beginning, middle, and end of your auction. Let's go through the entire event so you can see how this will flow.

Before the Doors Open

After months of strategic design decisions and careful research, networking, and preparation, it's time for the big event. On the day of your benefit auction, you'll start by setting up the venue, training volunteers, and having final run-through rehearsals, sound and light checks, and final auction meetings with your team and auctioneer.

The Event Begins

The doors open and guests register. You may have a VIP or special patron event prior to the auction. After that or during the silent auction, volunteers sell opportunities for extra fundraising for the Heads and Tails game, a raffle or any special activities like mystery grab bag, a wine pull, or interactive games. (See Chapter 14 for more ideas for strategic income streams.) Many organizations hold their silent auctions during the cocktail hour. (See Chapter 11 for an in-depth look at silent auctions.)

Make Transitions Smooth and Efficient

Moving guests from your silent auction to your inspiring program is a critical transition. Whether the two will be held in the same room or in separate areas, there will always be transition time. For the smoothest and most efficient segue possible, assign volunteers to invite guests into the live auction venue from the silent auction. Your benefit auctioneer should also graciously invite everyone to come into the venue. Make sure to have a great sound system for the silent auction, the live auction, and the transition between the two. (See Chapter 11 for my innovative technique, the Clam Shell Offense, for quickly moving guests from standing at your cocktail hour to seating themselves for your inspiring program, live auction, and fund-a-need.)

Before starting the program, make sure everyone is seated. That job goes to your emcee or benefit auctioneer: Get everyone seated and ready for the program. For an event using food stations, the meal service and silent auction must be completed by this time. For seated dinners, preset salads should all be dropped at the exact moment that you close your final silent auction section. Placing salads on tables in advance saves you time. Everyone is hungry at this point, so when guests see the salads being served, they will naturally move toward the tables, making a natural transition from the silent to the live auction.

Design an Inspiring Program

Show flow is really about designing an inspiring program. Key components of a benefit auction that affect show flow are the welcome and thank you, food, and meal style. Make it memorable!

Welcome and Thank-You Remarks

Where you position the welcome and thank-you remarks is critical. Ideally, this should occur within five minutes or so of guests being seated, because it alerts the audience that you're beginning your program. This is a good time to offer a perfunctory thank you to the sponsors, the committee, and the board. Recognize board members and committee members at their seats. Ask them to stand for a warm round of applause. You'll save time and build momentum.

You may want to give the auction chairperson flowers or a small gift. Take care of these tasks now, so they don't interfere with the show flow crescendo to the big emotional moments that open hearts and wallets.

It's Go Time

Your guests are seated, eating or chatting. There's a magic moment to begin the fundraising piece. I call this "go time." It's a serious moment when program elements start ratcheting up. Everyone's attention is riveted on the speaker, and there is absolute quiet in the room.

This is when you'll have an inspiring and compelling speaker make wonderful and momentous remarks for *less than two minutes*. This is different than the first-person story that leads into the fund-a-need. These remarks are about transformations, results, and the benefits of your organization.

WWH: Why We Are Here

Next is the communication about the *impact* of the contributions your guests will make.

There are several ways to offer brief inspiring remarks about your organization, which help your audience understand why they are at your event. One option is to have an individual make those remarks. Another is to have a montage, where three or four people each say one or two sentences about how your organization has transformed their lives.

Whichever you choose, you want your speakers to make their remarks about the compelling impact of your organization *immediately* before the live auction. The timing makes this powerful. The speakers will have more of an impact by making their remarks first, and then introducing themselves. Look to the performing arts for expertise on how to perform this segment well.

An Inspiring Live Auction

Next, we turn to the live auction. Introduce your auctioneer personally from the stage saying, "We're here to raise as much money as we can for (*your cause*). Here to help us do just that is our auctioneer, (*name the auctioneer*)." From a strategic standpoint, it's very important for the leader of the organization to introduce the auctioneer and to shake hands, which bestows credibility on the auctioneer.

Your benefit auctioneer should then talk briefly, highlighting the compelling and exciting points about your cause, and kicking off the live auction. Expect the auctioneer to intersperse bullet points about your organization throughout the live auction. Many benefit auctioneers are trained to do this, but some are not. Help your auctioneer transition from the "why we are here" remarks to the live auction by giving her compelling bullet points to use during the live auction.

Time Allotments

The time allocation for each live auction item depends on the skill level of the auctioneer but should be close to two minutes per item for a professional benefit auctioneer. An auction game, like heads-and-tails, takes about seven minutes. The fund-a-need takes about 10 to 15 minutes. The key point is to budget every single minute in a written timeline.

Make Every Minute a Revenue Minute

There's a hidden contest happening inside your fundraiser event. The contestants are time, money, and the attention spans of your guests. We want money to win every time—but you must be strategic!

When you design a benefit auction event, one of the most commonly overlooked mistakes by auction planners is working from the *wrong* auction timeline. Instead, make every minute a revenue minute by strategically sequencing and pacing the silent auction, the live auction, and the fund-a-need activities. Benefit auctions have myriad event details, and getting this "show flow" right is critical to maximizing every single dollar and creating an environment that will build audience engagement for future events.

Transitions: From the Live Auction to the Fund-a-Need

The best time to conduct the fund-a-need depends on what else is going on at your event. It can be in the middle of the live auction or at the end. Either way, the transition from the live auction to the fund-a-need is critical in terms of your show flow. There should be no gaps at all.

One way to make sure you don't lose momentum is to ask the auctioneer to have audience members clink their glasses to get everyone focused immediately following the sale of the last item. Always ask your guests to be quiet in a very gracious way. Have the person telling the first-person story for the fund-a-need at the side of the stage ready to go so there are no gaps in the show flow. She'll make her inspiring remarks, tell her story, and then go into the appeal portion by asking guests to raise their bid cards at a level that is meaningful for them.

Transitions: From the Fund-a-Need

If the fund-a-need is in the middle of the live auction, the benefit auctioneer should start right up with the next live auction item, so that no momentum is lost. If the fund-a-need is at the end of the live auction, the auction chairperson or board president should immediately come up and thank everyone. Then go to the next part of the program seamlessly.

Positioning the Fund-a-Need

If you have fewer than a dozen live auction items, position the fund-a-need immediately following the live auction. If you have more than 12 live auction items, place the fund-a-need right in the middle of the live auction. During the middle of the live auction, guests are paying attention and they're typically physically in the room, so the fund-a-need will have the most impact. If guests are tired or bored or they've left the room, it's highly unlikely that they will give you money.

Starting the Inspiring Program

Within five minutes of having all of the guests seated, have your benefit auctioneer quiet everyone and introduce whomever is making inspiring remarks. It's very difficult for someone who is not professionally trained to quiet and focus an audience, but if you get everyone quiet before the first person speaks, you'll set the right tone for the entire event. If you have a plated meal service, at this point, guests are eating their salads. Spiritual or religious groups might offer a blessing. It's important to invite guests to "please enjoy your meal now." If they wait to eat, it will throw off your entire evening, so be sure to include that in the script for your emcee or auctioneer.

Run on Honorees

What do you do when an honoree talks too long—actually one hour too long? Yes, it's true, we have actually had this happen twice. Even though as an auctioneer I sounded the alarm to the executive director and the auction chairperson, they did not feel there was anything they could do. That's not true. Of course there was. You need a plan to get the hook, graciously. In both cases, because of the lengthy speeches, the live auction and fund-a-need were pushed to the very end of the event, so late that over half of the audience was gone, gone, gone. Each organization lost over $50,000 and did not come close to what they had raised the previous year.

But that's not the crime. Think of all of those guests who were so bored and tired that they left or felt stuck in their seats just wishing they could be home. They were deprived of hearing the inspiring fund-a-need story and giving to a cause they care about. When I think back on this, it still makes me sad because they lost so much money and did not even realize it!

Entertainment, Dancing, Awards

At the conclusion of the live auction you may have awards, entertainment, or dancing (if the fund-a-need is in the middle). A fun way to focus guests on bidding is to say, "Bid now. Dance later." Once guests get involved in the entertainment, like dancing, it's nearly impossible to refocus them on bidding. If you have music during the dinner hour, make sure that you don't play dance music right before or during the live auction, because that will reduce your ability to raise money. Play upbeat dinner music that's not danceable because it will create momentum and start building energy up to the live auction. Get all your fundraising done before you move to awards, dancing, or entertainment.

After the Live Auction

Don't open the auction checkout until after *all* fundraising is complete. This includes the live auction and the fund-a-need special appeal. Strategically speaking, you'll want your audience focused on how they can make a difference, not worrying about a checkout line. Sometimes, especially in nonprofits for performing arts, there may be a post-event party or a VIP party.

After the event is a great time to raise money, as you follow up with all your guests, donors, and sponsors. Go to each table and thank guests for bidding and attending, and make sure you invite them for next year too.

Food Choices Have Consequences

You can choose from several different food styles during the silent auction. Whether it's hors d'oeuvres or food stations, what's critical is that food service is completed *prior* to your inspiring program. If you want to raise money, every guest must be seated when that program begins.

Stand-up cocktail parties with heavy hors d'oeuvres don't work well to raise money. (Think Manolo Blahnik stiletto heels for the entire night—ouch!) Some groups inadvertently sabotage their events by having a cocktail party and an inspiring program going on at the same time, which detracts from the focus of the benefit auction event: fundraising. When your guests are seated, you have the opportunity to get them riveted and excited about your cause. That's when you can really see transformation and you have the opportunity to build loyalty to your nonprofit organization.

Choose the Right Foods

Integrate food stations into silent auction tables. Make food choices that will promote bidding in the silent auction. For example, if you choose food that requires a fork and knife, like carving a turkey or pasta, guests will need to sit down. Sitting down during a silent auction is the enemy of fundraising! Instead, choose finger foods that guests can pick up with a toothpick and put on a napkin. There are some fabulous hors d'oeuvres choices that can fit any budget. Also, be aware that though turkey and pasta, chocolate fountains, and carving stations are showy and reasonably priced items for food stations, they take up a lot of room, create boring lines, and make guests sleepy (think Thanksgiving), which is the antithesis of momentum and energy.

Seated Meals

For seated meals, the silent auction typically is scheduled for about 60 to 90 minutes from when guests arrive until they are invited to be seated to start the inspiring program, live auction, fund-a-need appeal, awards, and entertainment. If guests arrive at 6:00 P.M., close the last silent auction section by 7:30 P.M. Have a 10-minute transition time to the venue where you have your inspiring program. Make sure that you have plated salads served at every table before guests enter the room. Tell your caterer that the last guests will come in and be seated at 7:40 P.M. and that you want the salads plated and on tables by 7:30 P.M. so that they are not serving them as guests are coming into the room. You want guests to sit down and immediately begin eating their salads.

Food/Dinner Stations

With food stations, guests walk around and sample different food choices at stations during the silent auction and cocktail hour. Food stations require approximately a one and one-half hour to a two-hour period from when guests arrive. Remember, this is your guest's meal. If they are hungry, they will leave before your fundraising and you will loose substantial funds. If the invitation says the event begins at 6:00 P.M., schedule 6:00 to 8:00 P.M. for gourmet dinner stations, the silent auction, mingling, and any VIP reception you might have. The time period will vary based on the market where you live, the time of year, and the distance guests drive to the benefit auction event. Be sensitive to the time needed for your guests to drive to your venue. In many larger cities, the starting time for a fundraising event may be later that in a small community where there is less traffic and commuting concerns.

BBQ Ribs Make Sticky Stuck Bidders

Barbeque ribs make sticky stuck bidders. Even if you have a theme (e.g., Western, jewels and jeans, etc.) and even if you have country attire and Western-style food, try very hard not to have sticky foods (e.g., chicken wings or ribs) to eat during the silent auction. Why? It's physically impossible to eat chicken wings and ribs standing up when you are bidding. When people are eating they're not bidding! Choose finger foods that are not greasy, that are easy to eat, and that don't leave people's hands feeling too dirty to pick up a pen. This holds true no matter which way you choose to serve your guests: passed hors d'oeuvres, small hors d'oeuvres stations in pods, or bigger food stations. No sticky or messy food choices! Food choices have significant consequences. Work with the caterer to come up with ideas that help you achieve your number one objective: bidding. Make it easy to bid.

Consider the amount of space you need for the types of food you choose. For example, food stations that include pasta and carving stations are a good choice because they are economical, very showy, and guests like them. However, you better have a lot of room, because they take up more space than another food station service. In any kind of food station, you want to avoid lines.

At an event in Colorado, there were 100 people standing in line for only one carving station. There was a beautiful round of beef being hand-carved for each guest, like at a wedding reception. If your guests are standing in line, guess what they are not doing? Bidding! Make sure that your guests can get their food easily and move on. Some very astute event planners and auction consultants say that they don't have any plates or forks whatsoever. Think about it. If you have finger food that you can have on a napkin, it means that your guests are not going to sit down and they don't need to use a knife and fork to cut. If you have something messy that could soil a dress or shirt, your guest is going to want to sit down. The minute your guests sit down, getting them up to continue bidding is nearly impossible. Be sure to plan your silent auction thoughtfully and strategically so that you are not inadvertently making choices (e.g., food selections, stations with lines) that are actually counterproductive to your primary objective for the silent auction: bidding. Think about anything that could inadvertently cause lines and then remove them ahead of time.

My well-known disdain for buffets is based on the fact that you make zero dollars when your guests are standing in a boring buffet line. Take the same buffet items and create separate food stations interspersed with silent auction items instead.

Shrimp Cocktail—Your Secret to Big Silent Auction Bidding

Claim the best areas where your guests can drool over and bid on silent items. Place the most desirable food stations around the space to draw guests all over the venue to view your item. Place your best silent auction tables in this prime space. This is why supermarkets put the milk in the back of the store.

Don't Let Dessert Make You Lose Money

Time the dessert when you have finished your fundraising. If you choose to bring out dessert before the end of your fundraising, be sure to finish the first half of the live auction and get the fund-a-need done. When you have two auction items left to go, bring out the dessert. If dessert is served in the middle of the fundraising, you will lose $10,000 or more because you will have lost the attention of your audience. Even if you have a lovely and charming benefit auctioneer, exciting auction items, and your fund-a-need speaker makes compelling remarks, you can lose a lot of money if dessert isn't timed properly.

Chocolate fountains attract guests, but they're detrimental. Believe me, I believe that chocolate is the forgotten mineral. However, everyone clusters around a chocolate fountain, and it's almost impossible to raise any money. Instead, have a plated dessert. Dessert buffets don't work because the timing conflicts with the live auction and the fund-a-need.

It's best to bring desserts to guests when they are seated at tables. These can be served family style or on individual plates. In different regions, dessert has different connotations. For example, in New England, as soon as guests have dessert, they are ready to go home. Have a special volunteer called the dessert controller who stands at the catering door and makes sure that the dessert is served at the right time—when it will have the least impact on your ability to raise money for your organization.

Timing

Back up the closing of the final silent auction section to the conclusion of the two-hour time period. If you end at 8:00 P.M., close the last silent auction section at 7:50 P.M., leaving a needed 10-minute transition time to the live auction. If the venue for the live auction is far away from the silent auction, use a stopwatch to determine how much time it will really take to move all of your guests from the silent to the live auction. Based on that information, you can create an accurate transition time. For the sake of understanding an ideal sequencing, assume that it takes 10 minutes. This means that you close the last silent auction section at 7:50 P.M. Assuming you have two silent auction sections, you close the first section at 7:40 P.M. and the second section at 7:50 P.M. This timing exercise is good to do with your auction committee and pencil and paper.

The Most Profitable Time for Fundraising

Remember, less is more, and your guests are tending to leave earlier than ever. Position your fundraising activities early. During a seated meal service, position the live auction and the fund-a-need when you have the opportunity to raise the most money. Imagine a bell-shaped curve. The golden time for fundraising is before or at the top of the curve when guests are at the height of food and alcohol consumption. You can actually feel the golden time for fundraising. Position your live auction and the fund-a-need when guests are on that upswing. If you wait until guests are going down the backside of the curve when they are settling in and relaxing, it's really challenging to get them motivated to bid. Don't wait! Conduct your fundraising early in the event.

Get Into the Fundraising Right Away

If you have a great sound system, which I know you will, think about a couple of times when you can have your "go time," when you begin the why-we-are-here remarks, the live auction, and the fund-a-need. Did you know that when the last plate goes down, about 45 percent of guests have already completed eating their meals and are starting to get bored? This is the perfect time to start the why-we-are-here remarks. These typically take two minutes. Then, introduce the auctioneer and start the fundraising. It works fine for servers to clear plates during the live auction. However, during the fund-a-need, servers need to take their seats. Make sure that you communicate this to the banquet captain beforehand so that he is crystal clear that everyone, including servers, needs to be absolutely quiet during the fund-a-need.

Booze Is Better for Bidding … Right?

There's a myth that the more alcohol an event guest consumes, the higher he'll bid. Don't believe it. Remember, alcohol is a depressant. Research shows that there's a biphasic (two-phase) effect of drinking alcohol. During phase one, the body experiences a positive, euphoric response. But during the second phase, the negative effects of alcohol become apparent (losing a buzz, becoming tired, acting drunk, etc.).[1]

Imagine a bell-shaped curve. You'll want to schedule the live auction and fund-a-need while your guests are still in the first phase of the biphasic response. On a bell-shaped curve that's on the upswing, that's when all of your guests are energized and ready to support you generously.

Bust that old myth. Do not wait until the end of dinner or worse yet, at the end of the event. That's why it's imperative to hold your vital fundraising of the live auction and fund-a-need early in your event.

Regional and Cultural Norms

There are regional differences across the country regarding the meal service and the live auction. For example, in the South, many groups consider it rude to conduct a live auction when guests are eating. However, in New York or California, guests are eager to move the event along—think dinner theater. (Note: be sure to have an outstanding audio system.) It is accepted and appreciated to conduct the live auction and fund-a-need during dinner—or even during your first course! Work within the cultures and norms of the area where your benefit auction is located, and also consider the impact of how you sequence your fundraising activities. Find ways to maximize fundraising while observing cultural norms.

When to Close the Silent Auction

You will make more money if you close a traditional paper bid sheet silent auction (as opposed to mobile bidding) before you start your inspiring program. Close it as close as possible to when guests move into the venue for your live auction. This creates momentum and excitement. Your benefit auctioneer can make announcements to close the silent auction and get guests thinking about bidding. If guests did not buy something in the first section, there might be something in the second section. If they did not get something in the first two sections, the auctioneer can encourage them to bid in the third section.

Close the Final Section

Sometimes, the final silent auction section is open at the end of the event during dancing. This is most common in school auctions. It's better to close the final section as soon as the last auction item is sold or the fund-a-need concludes, whichever happens last. Why? Experience has shown that there is no best time to close the silent auction. In other words, the timing of the closing of the silent auction (i.e., before, during, or after the live auction) does not affect your silent auction revenue. But closing the silent auction late will hurt other aspects of your event. When you close the silent auction, there are a lot of details, including paperwork and moving items. Focus on getting the logistics right so guests can get through the checkout line efficiently.

Create an Unforgettable Inspirational Moment

There are a few moments when you can create that compelling emotional mission moment during a benefit auction. The first moment is during the "why we are here" remarks. When you have an individual or a montage of three or four people sharing how your nonprofit organization has impacted them personally, it's really compelling.

The other time is during the compelling first-person story for the fund-a-need about how your organization changed the speaker's life. For example, this could be a compelling true story about how one of your rescue animals found his or her forever home or how one of your alumni benefitted from your outstanding education. (See Chapter 13 for more ideas on fund a need stories.) Guests remember love, and they remember transformational stories. The audience will fall in love with your nonprofit organization and your cause because of the way you have designed your event. When you follow up with guests after the benefit auction event, draw on these stories. Make sure that you start with your schedule and show flow, and time your event to optimize fundraising.

Run Your Auction Like a Track Meet

My experience as an athletic director and coach for volleyball and track for blind runners has helped me tremendously as a consultant and benefit auctioneer. Think about organizing and running your benefit auction like a track meet. The first thing a track coach needs is a stopwatch, and you need one too! It's very important to time out every single element of the event.

In a track competition, the next runner is "on deck" and the one behind her is "in the hole." The same lineup works for benefit auctions. At the beginning of your event, the chairperson, board president, or executive director makes the welcome and thank you remarks. Immediately following those remarks, go right into the montage about the transformational aspects of your nonprofit organization. Set this up so that you have speakers "on deck" and "in the hole." Put six or seven chairs on the side of the stage and insist that everyone who is making any kind of remarks is seated in chairs 10 minutes in advance of when they are speaking and line up in order of stage appearance.

Add a Stage Manager and Speaker Handlers

One of the best ways to maintain control of your strategically designed show flow is to engage a dedicated stage manager. In a track meet, that person is called the clerk of the course. She oversees the timeline, queues up the competitors, and ensures that everything happens on time.

At your event, have volunteers to bring speakers right to their tables and escort them to the stage before it's time to make remarks. These people are beloved to your organization, and your guests want to visit with them. But that slows down your timeline. You may want to have one handler for each speaker to escort the speaker to the side of the stage, wait with him until it's time to speak, and then escort the speaker from the stage back to his table following the remarks. It's also a good idea to have backup people who stay with the speakers in the queue so that they don't scoot away. Sometimes speakers request to stay at their tables until it's their turns to speak. Unless there is a really compelling reason why they cannot sit with the rest of the speakers in the queue (for example, they have a disability) it's critical that *all* of the speakers are on the side of the stage ready to go. It helps the momentum and the physical flow of the event to have everyone who is making remarks lined up and ready to go with your stage manager right there.

Kathy's Super-Secret Show Flow Tips

Here are my super-secret tips for show flow:

Plan Show Flow

You can have the best auction items and the most compelling, exciting, and riveting speaker who shares a transformational first-person experience, but if you position the elements of your event at the wrong times, you will lose money. Plan your show flow on paper and in advance.

Co-Create Show Flow

Invite your board members and key members of your committee to understand how powerful show flow is. Co-create your show flow with them.

Enter the Room Early

Moving guests from the silent auction to the live auction can be challenging. One way to help make this transition more efficient is to have some of your key auction committee members move to the live auction venue five to seven minutes early so that other guests will follow the unspoken leaders. This creates momentum toward the live auction because guests start saying, "Where is Tom? Where is Mary? Oh, they are already in the room!"

Use an Experienced Enthusiastic Voice

Have your benefit auctioneer or your emcee use his or her voice to get everyone into the live auction venue. The total time for this transition needs to be less than 10 minutes so that you don't cut into critical fundraising time.

Design Brief Inspiring Remarks

The speaker who welcomes and thanks the audience to kick-off the live auction needs to have very rich, distilled, and compelling remarks. Long speeches are the enemy.

Note

1. D. J. Hanson, "How Alcohol Affects Us: The Biphasic Curve," *Alcohol Problems & Solutions* (2014). Retrieved from www2 .potsdam.edu/alcohol/HealthIssues/1100827422.html# .VFBVEPnF91Z.

8

Communicate Donor Impact

YOU ARRIVE AT THE GALA, ACCEPT a glass of wine, and begin to meander through the silent auction. A prominently placed poster on an easel grabs your attention. The resolute expression of the woman in the photo captures you. Her compelling words: "I've worked with a number of children who've been severely shaken. No child deserves that. The Children's Trust training helps to make sure it never happens again. Even if it's only one family, that's one child that will not suffer."

This is communicating impact.

In the Philanthropic Model of Fundraising Auctions, organizations are called to optimize opportunities for guests to become engaged in different and deeper ways to raise more funds. Donors are looking for ways to support something they love and believe in—you. It's vital to emotionally connect with guests about the difference their bidding and contributions will make in *every* aspect of your strategic marketing plan.

My most successful clients are the ones who take this approach. They repeatedly share success stories about "hitting it out of the park" and exceeding their fundraising goals because their guests and donors understood and felt how their support makes a difference. In this chapter, I'll share some of my most effective—and often overlooked—communication and promotion tips for benefit auctions.

It's Not the Plane—It's the Destination

Imagine that you've just come back from a great vacation. Did you think about the details of the plane on which you flew? Probably not, because you were remembering relaxing on that warm sunny beach in the Bahamas or experiencing the exhilaration of thigh-deep powder swishing down the slopes in Park City.

The lesson here is that people don't buy the plane, they buy the destination. It's the same in fundraiser auction events. Your guests want to know the impact of their high bids and contributions at your event (the destination). Don't bore them with statistics and program details (the plane). Instead, tell actual stories that show the results and benefits of their gifts to your cause.

As you continue this exercise, invite your auction committee to talk about how they feel when they give to your organization. Identify the feeling that you want to create at your benefit auction event, which is your destination. Then, craft the content and messaging that reflects that feeling. Integrate those remarks into your show flow. This is a great approach that you can use immediately at your next auction committee or board meeting.

Riveting Remarks Raise More Money

Create the expectation that all remarks to be made your benefit option event must be approved by you. A month or more before the event, start working with the people who are going to say something on stage and help them understand that their remarks need to be about the transformation, results, and impact of your nonprofit organization. Creating purposeful remarks will make a huge difference in your momentum.

Avoid having speakers make statistical remarks, such as, "We serve 100 at-risk youth," or "We taught 2,347 kids to read." Having speakers who share transformational results about your organization, however, *will* inspire your audience to give generously. Try this: "In our organization, our youth musicians have improved their grades at school. They've all been accepted to college.

They've had the benefit of high-quality music instruction, which has transformed their lives." This will rivet the audience in a way that numbers and statistics cannot.

Know What Your Audience Loves About You

It's critical to know your audience—the guests at your benefit auction—as well as your supporters, donors, volunteers, and board members. Your target audience is *everyone* involved in your benefit auction. And marketing is all about your target audience. This means that in order to understand how to communicate effectively with them, it's important to learn about them. What other important things can you learn about your supporters? Do you know why your donors give to you? Do you know why they care about your mission? There are a number of reasons why people support causes, some of which you can likely name off the top of your head. However, it's really important to know specifically why *your* benefit auction guests and donors support *your* cause. The more you know about your supporters, donors, and their bidding behaviors, giving behaviors, and reasons for giving, the faster you'll develop a laser-focused approach to marketing.

Getting to the Heart of Your Message

Let's talk about branding your message. The point is to inspire the spirit of giving for your cause. What is your message? What do you want your guests to remember long after your benefit auction is over?

These are important questions for the entire auction committee. The message needs to be simple and powerful—especially because many of your guests will be sipping champagne and thinking of a million other things until you capture their attention. Ask yourselves, "What does the money do?" In other words, from a donor's perspective, what is the power of my gift? Whether it is a sponsorship, silent auction item, live auction item, or a fund-a-need gift, be able to describe how the funds you are raising will be used.

Next, ask, "Why should my guests care?" If you really want to get to the heart of your message quickly, ask my famous question, "So what?" If you can get beyond the "So what?" question and clearly articulate the impact that someone's gift will have, your message is on target.

Extreme Focus on Fundraising

Carefully crafting your mission message is essential, and it must be done early in the planning process. Typically, the majority of benefit auction planning happens in committees, and it's not uncommon for committees to have difficulty staying on task. Inspiring the spirit of giving for your cause may be a new concept for your auction committee. Focusing members on this concept can make or break your benefit auction.

What's your approach to marketing? What's your philosophy? Here's one of my pet peeves about marketing: Imagine that you go to your mailbox and find an envelope. On the outside of the envelope, there's a photo of the Eiffel Tower. You tear open the flap. Inside is a beautiful invitation. It's obvious the auction committee spent a lot of money on this. On the front is another image of the Eiffel Tower with the words, "April in Paris." Nothing else. When you open the invitation, it describes a big party to celebrate a social service agency. There's no branding of the nonprofit mission. The name of the organization doesn't appear. It's all about the party.

This is an example of the old transaction model. There's no communication about how your guests' attendance and contributions will make a difference. Even though everyone will be excited when they open their invitations, there's no branding mission message and no call to action. There's no information saying that the invitation is to a benefit auction event. Please don't *ever* do this!

Kathy's FAB Formula

I've developed a simple formula to help focus your marketing: the Kathy Kingston FAB Four Formula. F is for fundraising. A is for auction. B is for benefit. You *want* your guests to know this is a fundraising event. You want them to expect to bid at an auction. And you've got to remind them who their money will benefit, and how.

The fourth factor is psychological. When your guests read that invitation or save-the-date card, poster, newspaper ad, or video, do they feel there is an expectation to give? The fourth factor creates inspiration and the expectation for giving because this is a fundraising event. Be happy and unabashed about that. Use the words, "fundraising auction benefit," and create the inspiration and an expectation for bidding. This is not a Spring Fling, April in Paris, or the Festival of the Trees. Those words tell you nothing! Create ways to graphically and psychologically help your guests understand the power of their gifts.

Leverage Your Sponsors' Marketing Power

I learned the value of sponsors when I worked as the statewide marketing director for Ogden entertainment company, a Fortune 500 company when I lived in Anchorage, Alaska. My job was all about promoting entertainment. Specifically, I had to fill two sports arenas and a convention center with entertainment—everything from Sesame Street to Snoop Dog to ice skating shows.

This taught me how to work with VIPs and sponsors. They were our lifeblood, and they're also the lifeblood of benefit auctions. There are many ways you can work with VIPs and sponsors to maximize your fundraising impact.

For example, it's easy for sponsors to put a link on their homepages to your benefit auction webpage. Studies show that donors use the Internet to find information about nonprofits and for charitable giving. For example, a Google study showed that 75 percent of donors engaged in Internet research to find out about charities, and 47 percent visited charities' websites prior to giving. Strategic use of your website to promote your cause and your benefit auction events will get you a lot of eyeballs, good impressions, and support.

Ask sponsors if they would be willing to lend their marketing or public relations services to help promote your benefit auction as a form of sponsorship. Many companies have internal marketing departments or they work with outside marketing vendors and agencies.

Sponsors can also provide a well-placed staff member or two to serve as a liaison to the sponsorship committee. These staff members have great ideas and resources, which we are often unaware of until they start volunteering for a benefit auction event.

Media Sponsorships

Media sponsorships can be powerful. Whether it's print or broadcast (e.g., television, radio, or streaming), the most important thing is to get a one-on-one meeting with potential media sponsors to request a sponsorship. Print, broadcast, and electronic media can cover your benefit auctions with advertisements or banner ads, which you can customize with each media partner.

Choose your potential sponsors deliberately. If you're going to promote a country music star, go to the country music stations and ask them to become a sponsor. What could a radio station do for you? Free ads are one option. Another is "call liners," when a DJ says, "We have Blake Shelton country music star coming to our city, and we are a sponsor. We hope you can come." The radio station can help create the radio spots. Sometimes they will do this pro bono, and other times they'll split the costs with you. This is a highly effective way to promote your benefit auction event.

Sponsors Can Provide VIPs and Celebrities

You can also ask a media personality to come to your event and be a spokesperson or emcee. This is *not* to suggest that the media personality is the auctioneer. You'll want a professional benefit auctioneer to conduct your fundraising activities and live auction.

Sometimes, when you partner with media, you can request that they provide live coverage. For example, when I worked with Kate Snow, an anchor and correspondent at NBC News, she was very close to Friends of Karen, the organization that serves families of kids with cancer. Kate was an eloquent and passionate spokesperson for the organization and really understood their mission. She was the perfect match, and her engagement in the benefit auction event helped donors to Friends of Karen feel glad they'd made generous gifts and happy about the way their contributions would help families.

Sponsors Have Powerful Relationships

Third party co-promotion can also increase your event's reach. Permit your sponsor to invite other businesses to join with them to sponsor your event. For example, let's say you have a bank as your auction sponsor. Invite them to involve some of their key business colleagues or partners, or even their media contacts, to put together a promotion and advertising package that leverages their individual strengths. Using this technique, you bring in additional advertising and an additional vendor to create a marketing package. You can ask them for "in-kind" contributions to print your promotional materials (e.g., invitations, posters, catalogue). You can also ask them to create and underwrite your advertising—a bank could cover credit card fees; a wine store could donate wine for the meal.

The Gift of Influence

In 1986, I was honored to serve as the director of an international competition for blind athletes, organized by the United States Association for Blind Athletes (USABA) in St. Louis, Missouri. Because St. Louis is the international headquarters of Anheuser-Busch, we invited the company to be a sponsor and asked them to consider inviting their other business partners. At our first meeting, the Anheuser-Busch representative said, "We want to bring in our good partner Chrysler, plus their advertising agency, FleishmanHillard." The support of these three immense sponsors working in tandem lifted awareness for blind and visually impaired athletes and support for USABA to unprecedented heights. Co-promotion is a powerful tool. Go further and invite your sponsors to consider offering you their gift of influence. Sponsors care about your cause and want to be connected to you. They are happy to introduce their other colleagues and businesses to your organization.

Public Relations

Public relations is an important way to get news about your event to the media and your target audiences. Consider recruiting a volunteer who likes to write to handle this. You can create a short overview of your event in the form of a press release and send it to all of the media outlets in your area. There are services that will do this for you, including releasing your information online and posting your event on the Internet.

It's important to get your press release out at least a month in advance and follow up with key media outlets. Just because you send a release doesn't mean anything is going to happen. Follow-up is critical. A personal phone call is the best. For local media outlets, you might even consider hand-delivering the press release.

Why is a public relations strategy so important? People give to people for things they care about. It's the same with the media. Make sure you have a hook—a story angle that will get their attention—and make it personal. How? Create a list of your local media outlets and send each a custom press kit, addressing it to a particular reporter who's likely to be interested, and including the release and background information about your organization.

Specialty Newsletters and Publications

Media outlets also include specialty groups with newsletters and magazines for various interests—parenting, theater, music, donkey rescue, you name it. Because you are raising funds for a specific cause, these groups can make great marketing partners. Often, they have monthly newsletters that are printed or online. For example, for a school auction, you might consider the Montessori School Newsletter, which has a national audience. For a horse rescue group, look for horse clubs that are connected to people who really care about and support horse rescue.

Social Media Marketing for Benefit Auctions

There are many ways you can use social media to market your benefit auction for maximum impact fundraising. Social media includes blogs, LinkedIn, Facebook, Twitter, YouTube, and many

other venues. Enlist board members, volunteers, auction committee members, and others to reach out to their personal spheres
of influence with social media. The goal is to keep everyone
informed, energized, and up to speed. Social media includes powerful tools that you can use to reach that goal. Use social media
to update everyone about the event. This might be about a new
sponsor, the honoree, or the menu. However, research shows that
while social media are excellent for soliciting and communicating
with volunteers, very few funds are raised with social media.[1]

Item Solicitation and Procurement

Use social media to supplement your auction item procurement
and promotion. At the same time, use this vehicle to communicate
the impact of your donor's giving. Let's say your auction item is a
stay in a superb hotel in a great location with tickets to an exclusive
show, but you don't have dinner included. Send out information
about the item with a request for dinner to complete the auction
package: "We need a dinner to complement this amazing live auction package." Or you might say, "We have a lot of people who
really want to go to Tuscany. Does anyone have any connections to
a Tuscan resort?"

Once you've procured an item, use social media to tell everyone about it with a description, a photo, and a link to the item.
This is a form of pre-promotion that will help keep up energy and
excitement about your benefit auction.

Get the Word Out Immediately: *Tweet*

Create Twitter posts that are preformatted and ready for posting.
Ask your volunteers to tweet and retweet. When you tweet information about your benefit auction, leave space for people to add their
own personal comments when they send out a tweet. Use Twitter
to share success stories, such as, "We just got a trip to the Bahamas
for our benefit auction!" Get information out there so it can work
for you.

Linking to Sponsors

Use social media to create links to your sponsors through all of your social media venues: Facebook, LinkedIn, Twitter....Include information about the sponsors and links to their websites. That is powerful! Ask sponsors to include links back to your benefit auction event in any of their social media venues.

Videos, Photos

As you are preparing for your benefit auction, take pictures or video and use social media to share the images through Instagram and YouTube. For example, you might have pictures of the auction committee preparing for the event. This keeps everyone engaged. Cardigan Mountain School students created two fun creative videos: one was an invitation for fellow students and parents, and the second promoted hot auction items. With humor and fun props, this innovative marketing piece helped sell out the annual auction.

Marketing *before* Your Fundraiser

Okay, who really wants or needs a silent auction or live auction item?

Nobody...

Unless you *intensely market your event and auction items* before *your benefit auction*, you may be leaving thousands of dollars in the room. Why? In the not so distant past, nonprofit and school auctions could always count on their guests bidding on everything and anything without much pre-auction promotion.

However, auction guests are far more strategic and discriminating about bidding at charity auctions than ever before. Why? In my own experience, I have seen auction buying patterns changing, even though benefit auctions are booming! Savvy donors are showing a preference to donate directly to the mission at the inspiring Fund-a-Need Appeal rather than fight crowds in the silent auction or bid on lackluster live items.

More than ever, nonprofits and school auction committees must intensely market auction items *before* their auction events to vastly increase their fundraiser auctions bottom line.

Fundraising Auction Website. Websites play a key role in communicating. Is your website prominently showcasing one of your biggest fundraising opportunities? While most organizations have a website, many do not maximize visibility and excitement about their auction fundraiser. Do you have a page dedicated to your benefit auction? If you do, does it include all of the information (who, what, when, why, where, and how) about your benefit auction event? Does it tell people how to buy tickets? Does it include the names of sponsors? Your benefit auction webpage should also include auction items, calls for volunteers, or anything else you need. Add an icon to your homepage, making it effortless to get to your benefit auction webpage.

Leverage your auction webpage. Make sure that your auction webpage includes full descriptions, links, donor links, photos, and special notes about the items. Place a button graphic on your homepage that says: "Check out our awesome auction items now." Get creative! Drive bidders to your website to inspire greater giving to your cause.

Save-the-Date Cards. Before your benefit auction, send out save-the-date cards. In different parts of the country and the world, save-the-date cards should go out at different times, generally from two months to eleven months ahead of your event. For example, in Alaska, we sent them out about 11 months in advance of a benefit auction event, because Alaskans travel often and have very busy schedules. Savvy auction committees know that. Be sure to send a save-the-date card out early and then send follow-up emails. Save-the-date cards are more than reminders. They are important communications to remind your guests that you are fundraising. They serve as a call to action to your guests to include your date on their calendars. Use the save-the-date card to immediately capture the attention of existing and potential sponsors and donors.

Make sure that the save-the-date card clearly communicates the purpose of your benefit action event. What does it say? Does it say *Fall Follies* or *Spring into Spring* or *Kid's Cabaret?* What does that *mean?* Do you know from reading the card that this is the main fundraising event for the organization? Do you even know who will benefit from generous bidding? Whatever you do, do *not* just write the name of your auction with the words "Save the date!" Add mission messaging. In too many cases, sadly, the save-the-date card emphasizes the party, not the philanthropy.

A group called buildOn sent save-the-date cards with a photograph of a 16-year-old girl. The wording? "I'm 16. I changed a life today. Who am I? Find out at the November 18th buildOn Benefit Auction and Dinner. It is your night. It is their future." Think about the power of, "Who am I? Find out..." That's the hook. The card provided key messaging about buildOn's cause, and it created intrigue. How can you be creative and integrate your message into your save-the-date card?

Invitations. What do your invitations really say to your supporters? Just "gala and dinner"? Do you let people know that this is an auction event and there will be an opportunity for guests to give? Do you say the word "fundraising"? Do you say "benefit"?

In some parts of the country, there are people who prefer not to go to an event that has an auction. In some areas there are people who would rather donate in other ways than a benefit auction. There are some people who dislike events and auctions, but they're generous donors to causes that are close to their hearts and values. I always suggest that organizations include, "Fundraising auction to benefit..." Then, add a transformational sentence.

An invitation from Friend's Program, which provides social services in New Hampshire, featured a photo of a volunteer and a woman sitting on her couch at home with the quote, "When I gave up my car, I lost my independence. Because of the volunteers who drove me to my medical appointments, I have it back." This invitation also included the first names of the volunteers and the woman whom they drove to medical appointments. The picture was worth a thousand words. With the quote, there was no doubt how the funds raised in the Friend's Program benefit auction would be used.

Auction Information Volunteer Packets

Consider this to be "internal marketing" to your volunteers. Create an auction information packet for board members, auction committee members, parents, and volunteers. This detailed packet should include an event and auction fact sheet—powerful talking points that they can use in conversation with donors or potential guests. The messages should focus on success stories. Also include item solicitation forms and brochures about your organization. Arm your volunteers with outstanding information and build their confidence. You can also have a role-play session to make sure that they understand and can explain how your great cause transforms the lives of your clients. Board meetings, procurement rallies for auction items, parent meetings, and volunteer gatherings are all great places to train volunteers to promote your mission messaging.

E-Mail Signatures

Create an e-mail signature that everyone in your organization (from board members and key sponsors to staff and volunteers) can use. Here's an example: "Join us at the Food Bank Gala." Include the date and a link to purchase tickets. This is a powerful way to promote and market a benefit auction event. Think about how many e-mails you send out each day. Imagine the communication power you will have if everyone includes an e-mail signature to promote your event!

Your Tagline Message—Everywhere

Think about your tagline. Where do your guests, prospects, volunteers, and board members see the tagline of your logo? Is it on every single letter? Is it on your website? Is it on your auction forms? Make sure there is a constant, powerful message. Are you just singing, or are you changing the world through song? How do you take your specific message and relate it to every single audience member in the room?

Auction Catalogues

Are auction catalogues even worth it? *Yes*. From a strategic marketing standpoint catalogues are an important written piece to showcase your cause, provide messages from your leaders, display photos, thank board members and volunteers, honor your guests, describe your auction items, list the auction rules, and recognize your sponsors and donors. The most successful clients send auction catalogues to every registered guest. What a powerful way to connect to your donors! *Think about the oomph of a catalogue with a message or an inspirational quote at the bottom of every page.*

Marketing during Your Fundraiser

Every place your donors look while they're at your event, they should be reminded of the impact of giving to your cause. Remind your supporters why they're here with you. Unfortunately, many organizations unintentionally overlook this crucial marketing strategy. Make sure your guests visibly and emotionally know what nonprofit or school they'll be supporting. Visibly marketing the *impact* of your mission at your event builds a crescendo of emotion and inspiration, propelling your guests toward your biggest revenue opportunities—the live auction and fund-a-need special appeal.

How can you maximize the time you have with your guests and donors to build an intimate relationship while they're right there at your fundraiser event? There are many ways to get those bid cards waving. First, let's look at what you can do to spotlight your work and your message. Before, during, and after your event, your mission message should communicate how guests can make a difference. Showcase your mission messaging in every nook and cranny of your fundraising auction venue. It's about transforming your event through maximum impact fundraising auction marketing. Here are some of my favorite techniques.

Table Tents with Mission Messages

Brand your message everywhere. Place colorful images, quotes, and logos between every single silent auction item as well as on high-top tables and dinner tables. Remember, a big font is better. My favorite table tent comes from The Children's Trust: There's a photo of a small child smiling, and the card simply reads: "Be Generous."

Big Banners

A banner is a bold way to communicate. One of my favorite examples of effective use of a banner is Saint Mary's Hospital. Their stunning banner had a wonderful image of a mother with an infant and the tagline, "Where hope changes lives." Saint Mary's was raising funds for their neonatal unit, and they used a photo that captured a loving look between a mother and her infant. Placed on stage, it created vibrant emotion, and its message was lost on no one.

Impact Posters (One of My Favorites!)

We live in a visual world. Communicate vividly by displaying an inspirational photo with a stirring quote on easels or tables, strategically located in different sections of your silent auction and around your venue. Here's a powerful example of how STAR, Inc., captures attention during silent and live auctions. Giant impact posters are elevated on silent auction tables. The beautiful images portray STAR, Inc., clients active in the community—working in a bakery, library, or other job environment. Each poster displays one huge word, such as "employment" or "reliability."

Girls' LEAP, a self-defense organization for at-risk girls, has a poster featuring a photograph of a young girl with this quote, "When I acted courageously, I found that I felt empowered, strong, and assertive. To be courageous, I had to stand up for something I believe in." Underneath the photo next to the Girls' LEAP logo, it said, "Jana—Age 13." That's impactful! Cool tip: Move your impact posters to the stage or up front so your guests can be inspired during the rest of your fundraiser for generous giving all night long. (You can use these in your office and for other events too.)

Auction Forms

Do your silent and live auction forms include your logo and tagline? Are they on your auction receipts? If you're using mobile bidding, be sure to include your logo in the design of the bidding application.

Mission-Focused Centerpieces

How can you use centerpieces for marketing your cause? Here's a great example. At the auction for El Hogar, a school for children in Honduras run by the Episcopalian Church of America, the committee created meaningful centerpieces out of backpacks, books in Spanish, dolls, and school supplies, and arranged them artfully in the middle of the tables. As part of the live auction, I conducted a special auction of these centerpieces that raised much needed funds for El Hogar, and the backpacks, full of supplies, were then sent to each student at El Hogar. What a win, win, win.

Special Thank You Gifts

Would it surprise you to know that recognition gifts have no bearing on donors wanting to contribute more funds to your organization?[2] Some groups will give a thank you gift at an event. When a zoo raised funds for an elephant exhibit, all of the guests received a small stuffed elephant at their tables. Other organizations present gift bags filled with goodies to guests as they leave. Thank you gifts and goodie bags are costly and take a good deal of volunteer time to prepare. If you are thinking that those guests will write a bigger check because of that token, think again.

On the Back of BIG Bid Cards

Print your tagline on the back of your bid card. For example: American Cancer Society, The Official Sponsor of Birthdays. That placement is superbly beneficial to your presenting sponsor. (Strategically, this is valuable with only *one* logo; you don't want it to look like the back of a 5K race T-shirt.)

Auction PowerPoint Slide Shows

Focus your guests' attention on your cause during the silent and live auctions. With so many distractions at your event, intentionally position your organization front and center in the minds and hearts of your supporters. Use inspiring images and quotes that highlight impact. Sprinkle in sponsor logos and live auction item highlights. Pump up momentum as your guests enter the ballroom. When it's time for the live auction, create one PowerPoint slide per live auction item. Sell the sizzle and excite your audience.

Climb the Golden Ramp

Each year I have a compelling theme for my clients. Recently I advised my clients to intentionally envision a profound paradigm shift in marketing. Climbing "up the golden ramp" means strategically showcasing the impact of your donors' contributions from on a continuum, from the moment your event ends to the next year's invitation, to the cultivation of guests during the cocktail hour, and to the inspiring climax—your fund-a-need special appeal. What's imperative is to build an ascending ramp of supporter engagement year-round, as opposed to limiting yourself to promotion of a single event.

Design your golden communications ramp to include every moment you touch your supporters. Start now and map out a detailed communications plan so that each time they receive any written, electronic, phone, or personal communication, you are developing a deeper relationship.

When I'm consulting with clients, I help them choreograph their show flow and speaking program so that energy and donor impact build throughout the event. Every single time you have the opportunity to address your beloved donors and valuable guests, make it count. Craft your program to be short, surprising, and of great interest to your audience. Build more excitement as each person makes brief, inspiring remarks. (One minute—really!) This includes your auctioneer, board president, parent, and the person telling a mission moment story. No one should be making remarks off the cuff. Keep it tight and compelling.

Try this: Insist that everyone who holds a microphone also say why they love supporting your cause and what it means to them—in 59 seconds. Your audience is bored stiff with the same old talking heads and long boring speeches. Change it now. Make your program short and unforgettable. Show gratitude for the generosity of your donors and connect the dots. Get everyone excited!

Most importantly, thank donors immediately and meaningfully showcase how their contributions are making a difference. Invite your supporters to become more deeply engaged with your cause after your fundraiser event. This approach stands in sharp contrast to the old, single-event advertising campaign with the goal of getting a person to attend one event.

Conclusion

The most potent and powerful way to interact with guests and donors is personally. High-tech/high-touch has never been more relevant. The more we dive into social media, the Internet, e-mail, and texting, the more important it is to develop a personal relationship with donors and sponsors. In the world of development professionals, this is called *cultivation and stewardship*, which simply means understanding an individual supporter's motivation and building a relationship based on that. Use marketing strategically and intentionally to build excitement, emotion, and impact throughout the year.

Notes

1. P. Burk, *The Burk Donor Survey: Where Philanthropy is Headed in 2013* (Chicago, IL: Cygnus Applied Research, 2013).
2. Giving USA Foundation, *The Annual Report on Philanthropy for the Year 2013* (Indianapolis: Indiana University Lilly Family School of Philanthropy, 2014).

9

Measure Impact

IN THIS ERA OF HEIGHTENED AWARENESS about measurement and big data, it's easy to get wrapped up in—even obsessed with—statistics and accountability. Often, we compile and analyze without even knowing exactly why we are tracking this data.

Consultant John H. Lingle invites us to ask the right questions: "You get what you measure. Measure the wrong thing and you get the wrong behaviors."[1] Rather than viewing your fundraiser as a stand-alone event, concentrate instead on positioning it to create a culture of philanthropy for long-term donor support. Strategically engaging supporters after your fundraiser event has the greatest impact. (See Figure 9.1). Only then will the right questions and measurements emerge. Begin by focusing on outcomes and asking *why*. What difference are you making? What is your real need? What is important to your donors? How do you measure the impact

Exhibit 9.1 Doorways to Greatest Impact

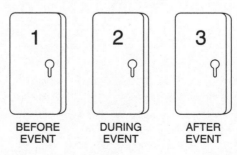

Choose the door that Leads to the greatest IMPACT.

1 — BEFORE EVENT

2 — DURING EVENT

3 — AFTER EVENT

of donor gifts? How can you quantify results? How do you communicate those results back to donors?

While not within the purview of this book, there are specialized models, created by experts in this field, that measure overall organizational and donor impact. An excellent model is the GuideStar Exchange Charting Impact Report. Nonprofits self-report impact information based on these five questions:

1. What are we aiming to accomplish?
2. What are our strategies for making this happen?
3. What are our organizational capabilities for doing this?
4. How will we know if we are making progress?
5. What have and what haven't we accomplished so far?[2]

There are key metrics to analyze how your auction and fundraiser is performing, but without a clear understanding of the difference you make and why you do what you do, collecting data is a wasted exercise. This chapter showcases the essential (and simple) measurements necessary for organizations to analyze their success.

Legendary thought leader in marketing Peter Drucker understood the nuances of measurement: "Your first role...is the personal one.... It is the relationship with people, the development of mutual confidence, the creation of a community.... It cannot be measured or easily defined. It is one only you can perform."[3] As such, fundraising and donor engagement centers on cultivating relationships—not on statistics alone. Here lies the core of strategic auction philanthropy.

Your Auction Data Is a Goldmine

For many, the idea of working with databases is daunting. However, mining your auction data is a lot easier than it looks. Once you adjust your mind-set to think strategically about leveraging your information, working with databases can actually be fun and inspiring. What it all comes down to is you'll learn much more about your supporters, how they participate, and what they love about your cause. And in the new Philanthropy Model, that connection is the core purpose of your auction.

Know Thy Audience

Use your auction event data to examine both the demographics and psychographics of your past audiences. Demographics include data such as gender, age, where people live, their professions, and their income levels. Psychographics are data that tell you about who a person is—his or her likes, interests, and leisure pursuits. When you look at your data, you'll likely see patterns you've never noticed before. Analyze those patterns, and you'll begin to understand how to invite your guests, what they care about, and why they fund your cause.

Make it easy. When you invest in benefit auction software that easily imports and exports data with your existing donor management systems, you can help your auction team and development staffers think more strategically. There are several outstanding benefit auction software packages that produce over 100 kinds of reports, putting all that excellent, readily usable data at your fingertips.

Performance Snapshot

"Uh, okay, I think we raised…"

How much money did you *really* raise? It never fails to surprise me how many auction organizers don't know. It is vital to understand your real event net profit and the origin of each revenue source. You can compare these results from year to year, getting a big picture you've never been able to see before, and observing trends that help you plan for success.

Create a simple fundraising event performance snapshot.

Here are some easy measures that every event planner, board development chair, and auction committee chair must understand to maximize revenue and increase donor engagement.

Funds Raised

- Overall event revenue
- Overall event expenses
- Net event profit, (expenses minus revenue—aka, a dose of reality)
- Profit from each individual revenue stream

    Before: reservations, sponsorships, donations, program ads

    During: live auction, silent auction, fund-a-need, revenue games

Guests

- Number of guests who attended
- Number of guests who gave
- Percentage of guests who gave
- Percentage of guests who gave to fund-a-need
- .Top 20 silent auction bidders
- Top 20 live auction bidders
- Top 20 overall donors

Auction Item Performance ROI

- Silent auction return on item value, ($ value of silent item high bid)
- Live auction return on item value ($ value of live item high bid)
- Top 10 performing silent auction items, based on ROI
- Top 10 performing live auction items, based on ROI

Fund a Need Performance

- List of cach giving level with number of donors per level
- Lead gift, matching gifts, incentive match gifts
- Fund-a-need giving level with highest participation

(Note: If you already use fundraising auction software, make sure you're benefiting from the dozens of valuable reports it can generate. Learn more about specialized benefit auction software and technology in Chapter 10.)

Here are some suggestions for data collection that will put specific results and donor information at your fingertips. Start by going back three to five years and reviewing your benefit auction data. Who came to your auctions each year, and who were the top 20 bidders? Make a list of what they purchased, their levels of giving in the fund-a-need, the number of years they attended, and their donation records over the years. Determine who's missing from your benefit auction guest lists. Is there a top bidder who fell out of the loop and has not been invited back? Identify those guests, because they can create incredible bidding intensity. What percentage of board members attend your events? What percentage of staff members? What percentage of your volunteers contributed?

If You Don't Do It, You Blew It!

Be sure to collect every single guest's contact information—name, street mailing address, e-mail, and phone numbers. Even if they're registering at the door on the evening of the event, insist on receiving contact information at that time. You will also need to link guests with their bid numbers to keep track of their winning bids and contributions throughout the fundraising event. Many times organizers do not understand that this essential data is the golden key to building a long-term relationship with donors. Let's face it, you and your board have worked tirelessly on planning and conducting your fundraising auction and event. But if you do not collect contact information on each guest, you will not know who is attending your event. Worse yet, you will have no way to follow up personally and meaningfully after your event. Change your mind-set. It's simple to require each guest's contact information at registration. Period. We'll talk about how to follow up with your supporters after your auction event in this book's last chapter.

Priorities for Measuring Impact

As you develop your strategy of what to measure and how much data to collect and analyze, keep this simple priority in mind: Donors first, then revenue, then things.

1. Donors: Audience, donors, volunteers, sponsors, auctioneer
2. Revenue: Revenue streams and expenses
3. Things: Event logistics, meals, beverages, check-in and check-out, chocolate lava cake consumption, entertainment, and so forth

Avoid Fundraising Event Budgeting Myopia

Do you truly know how much net income you produced from your auction fundraiser? Many organizations only report the gross overall revenue. I'd like to invite you to go deeper. It's vital to know your bottom line of net profit. However, be sure to factor in this often overlooked cost factor for auction and event fundraising: volunteer time and energy.

Hidden Cost Factor: Your Volunteers' Time and Energy

Did you leverage your volunteers' time and energy in a way that could maximize fundraising and deepen donor engagement? In other words, did you empower your dedicated volunteers with responsibilities for raising funds and developing deeper relationships with your supporters before, during, and after your event?

You can find this out by analyzing the number of hours your volunteers spent on each specific area of your auction and event. Also, measure the total volunteer hours spent in fundraising and donor activity. Analyze the number of volunteer hours invested. Then try to determine the extent to which the volunteer hours invested actually raised funds and engaged more donors. Make sure that your most valuable resource, your volunteers, are inspired, not tired out by time-consuming tasks such as decorating, moving tables, selecting meal choices, picking out the band, soliciting silent auction items that have a 40 percent return, or putting together baskets for raffles that do not yield a high level of funds. You get the picture.

From a strategic perspective, you'll want to focus your volunteers' efforts on activities that deepen the relationship of your guests to your mission. Volunteers should be involved in strategic audience development, cultivation of new sponsors, serving as table ambassadors, procuring high-profit live auction items, and soliciting matching or lead gifts for your fund-a-need special appeal.

Beyond the Numbers

Even after all the donations are collected, the bidding is tallied, and the statistics have been analyzed, how can you tell if your event was a success? The information we've been discussing is quantitative—statistics, financial results, and numbers. There is another way to measure impact at your benefit auction: a qualitative method that measures behavior and the reasons for that behavior.

I use qualitative methods all the time as a professional fundraising auctioneer; I'm analyzing audience behaviors as I go, reading the body language of guests and the energy level of the event from start to finish.

- Are the guests smiling? Are they nodding their heads yes?
- Are their eyes bright with energy?
- Are they talking to other guests, and if so, what are they talking about?
- Are they walking around, bending over to bid at the silent auction?
- Are they writing bids furiously on silent auction bid sheets?
- At last call, is the response furious mobile bidding on smart phones?
- How fast are they raising their bid cards during the live auction?
- Is there laughter?
- Are guests seated, attentive, and energized, or walking out the door?
- Do guests wipe away a tear of emotion during a well-told fund-a-need story?

The point is very simple. Are your guests happy at your event? Here are other questions you can ask to determine if you are creating impact at your fundraising auction. Do your supporters feel connected to your cause? Are guests excited to bid over value in the live auction? Do they entice all the friends at their table to support you during your fund-a-need special appeal? Do they smile? When do they smile? Are they walking around during your live auction and not paying attention? Do they quiet down when you share an inspiring success story? Do bid cards fly up fast? Do guests get emotional or even shed a tear during your inspiring mission moment testimonial story? Do they happily bring their friends the following year? Do they encourage others at your event to contribute more funds? Do they get involved in other ways, such as joining the board and volunteering for other programs? This list of questions is a small sampling of what I'm qualitatively measuring on a moment-by-moment basis.

As a consultant and fundraising auctioneer, I intentionally walk through the entire venue before, during, and after the event, listening to what's being said and studying the behavior of guests. From the jittery hour before people arrive until the weary cashier heads home, I'm listening and talking with guests about the impact of their contributions and how it makes a difference to the cause. This is a special sixth sense that I've developed as a professional fundraising auctioneer. I provide an extra set of expert eyes and ears to help clients identify and correct any problems in the moment, and to more deeply engage guests in active bidding and in conversations about your mission. I continually gauge the audience and immediately adjust techniques to generate momentum and bidding excitement, and to communicate the impact of the donors' bidding and giving at the fund-a-need through mission moments and adding fun. All of this happens in nanoseconds.

I have to admit that I love to hear what guests are saying. Most of the time, event guests are not engaged in talking about your mission or why they care about your cause. They're chatting about whatever is on their mind—vacations, sports, new shoes. Wouldn't you rather hear them talking about how they've been moved by your organization's work and how impressed they are with what's been done with last year's donations? You can.

In this chapter, I'm introducing two of my simple qualitative methods that you can use to better understand your donors' behavior and the underlying causes that shape it. With this kind of information, it's possible to strategically plan to more meaningfully and personally engage your supporters.

Kathy's PILI Method: Purposeful Informal Listening In

I've developed an easy assessment and feedback strategy I call Purposeful Informal Listening In, or PILI, that you can use at your auctions and fundraising events. While walking around, I'll often hear something that may indicate a problem is ready to develop. I tell the auction chair, and the situation is resolved immediately. I enjoy talking with guests, volunteers, and sponsors about their interests in the cause and hearing their stories about why they care. You can adopt this same strategy to generate meaningful connections with your guests during all phases of your fundraising event.

Here's a very simple yet powerful example of the benefits of leveraging my PILI method. During the silent auction at a recent gala fundraiser for a humane society, I heard two couples wondering aloud about the Tuscany live auction package. "Should we bid on this? Did the package include airfare? How close is Rome? Was there a special Tuscan dinner and wine included? How many does it include? What do we do with this bid card? How will we know if we are the winners? How do we pay? When is the expiration date?" And many more questions. As their auctioneer, I smiled and introduced myself, then personally escorted them to the live auction display. I showed them the beautiful color display with photos and a detailed trip information sheet as well as the item description in their auction catalog. As first-time guests at this auction, I explained all the details of this enticing vacation as well as how their generous bidding would help animals through the emergency pet medical fund. Further, I shared best ways to bid at a live auction and assured them that I would attentively watch for their bidding. All four were so excited that they were the high bidders. Bellissimo!

> Kathy's Purposeful Informal Listening In (PILI) Method
> 1. Walk around your event
> 2. Listen in
> 3. Take action if needed
> 4. Report problems immediately to event chair for action
> 5. Continue throughout all phases of your event
> 6. Memorize what you are hearing
> 7. Debrief and adjust for next year

Here's a perfect example of how Joe Viesta[4], a dedicated board member at STAR, Inc., embraces the PILI method. At each STAR gala auction, he intentionally walks around the cocktail and silent auction area with two goals in mind. First, he wants to engage guests and strategically direct their conversations about STAR. He intentionally and informally listens to what guests are talking about, then joins the group, introduces himself, and talks about STAR's impact. Sometimes Joe will share a brief impact story about a particular program or result; at other times he asks about their children, many of whom are clients at STAR.

The second important action Viesta takes is to make sure guests are focused on fundraising and actively bidding on the silent auction items. If he sees a gathering of people talking, he goes up to them, introduces himself, asks about the items they've been bidding on, and points out some great silent auction items. Viesta says this usually spurs his guests to bid more on the silent items. During the live auction, Joe drives fundraising energy with his own generous bidding and gifts at fund-a-need, but also with good-natured competition and encouragement with his friends and colleagues throughout the evening. "When it all comes down to it," he says, "on the Monday morning after the fundraising auction event, I need to know that we have made a difference."

Here's another example of the power of the PILI method. When I was consulting at a very large gala auction and I was walking around the audience during the live auction, actively practicing my "PILI" method of listening in and wandering throughout the audience, a spotter stopped me and said that bidder #427 was very upset. Bidder #427 thought he was the final bidder for the item that just sold—the gourmet dinner and wine experience. Immediately, I told the executive director. She was very happy to know of this potential crisis in donor relations. She explained that her board had been cultivating this influential business leader for two years, and this was the first time he had shown interest in their cause. I suggested immediate action: Create an exact duplicate of that live auction item and immediately go over to him to let him know that we were able to double it on the spot. (This final high bid fetched over three times the value, so financially, it was very easy to instantly double that gourmet dinner/wine experience.) The bidder was thrilled and received a personal and immediate solution to what could have been an irreparable donor disaster. That's the power of PILI.

Here are some tips for you to incorporate purposeful intentional listening in as you do your strategic planning. Hand-select several key leaders that you trust to walk throughout all aspects of your fundraising event from start to finish. Ask them to listen to what guests are talking about, graciously engage them, solve any problems immediately, and smile and thank them for their support. They should never carry a clipboard, so that their hands are free to shake hands, and always a smile, showing gratitude. After the event, they should have a deep debrief on what they heard and saw.

Kathy Kingston Fundraising Auction Impact Scale

How can you get a quantitative reading on such seemingly intangible impacts as guest enjoyment and such challenging issues as checkout lines, guest engagement in various parts of the event, and even the level of fun? Strategically, I'm suggesting that you use my simple measurement instrument to focus on more qualitative aspects, such as the quality of your guests' experience, the level of involvement for your board and key volunteers, guests' engagement in bidding in the silent and live auctions, and the giving during fund-a-need.

Select areas on which your organization specifically wishes to focus. It could be an area where you have experienced challenges and wish to understand more or you could focus on new areas for fundraising. Simply, this is a Likert scale from 0 to 5, with 0 being lowest and 5 highest. You can measure different aspects of your auction and event and take immediate action if necessary, then review your results at your post-auction evaluation meeting. To utilize this simple Fundraising Auction Impact Scale, you'll need to create a team of top volunteers who will each measure a specific aspect of your event, as directed by you. Be sure to create training and support for your volunteers and to have a post-event debrief meeting.

You Get What You Measure

Be very strategic and select exactly what aspects of your event you wish to measure and understand in more depth. Each year you may choose to measure different aspects, depending on your goals. To get you started, here are four of my favorite impact areas. For full reading of impact, select predetermined time intervals. You will find that there's great value in measuring each live auction item and each fund-a-need giving level.

1. Standing in Lines Impact (wasting your guests' valuable time in lines such as registration, coat check, bar, food station, checkout). Scale: 0 = lots of guests stuck in a line, 3 = a few people in line, 5 = no waiting.
2. Silent Auction Fundraising Impact. Scale: 0 = no bidding, drinking and talking, facing away from items, 3 = half of

crowd moving through the silent auction space and actively writing bids, 5 = most of crowd furiously bidding, stealing pens, standing guard over items, or bidding on their mobile devices.

3. Live Auction Fundraising Impact. Scale: 0 = guests out of room or driving home, 3 = a few brave souls raising bid cards, 5 = wild bidding, cheering, clapping, final bids exceeding value.

4. Fund-a-Need Impact. Scale: 0 = out of room, talking, yawning, 3 = listening, minority of guests giving at some level, 5 = applause, tears, bid cards in air, majority of guests giving at some level.

These are just a few examples of ways to implement my Fundraising Auction Impact Scale. You can easily adapt this method to measure your impact at your own event.

Conclusion

Use the Philanthropy Model approach to measure the impact of your fundraising auction and events. Keep your core purpose of fundraising and donor engagement at the forefront of all your strategic planning, so you can measure your impact in meaningful ways. Remember, you get what you measure. Create your own Performance Snapshot for simple statistical analysis of your financial performance. Utilize Kathy's PILI method to measure event impact factors but also as an on-the-spot donor communications opportunity. The Fundraising Auction Impact Scale gives you a fresh approach to understanding and measuring key sectors of your auction and event to provide a new level of strategic insight. Organizations can leverage both quantitative and qualitative information to take their fundraising and donor development to the next level.

Notes

1. J. H. Lingle. In Bullseys! Hitting Your Strategic Targets through High Impact describe the unintended consequences of measuring the wrong things, which can lead to the wrong behaviors.

2. GuideStar, "One Web Site Enables Nonprofits to Tell Their Stories, Commit to Transparency, and Define Their Impact," press release, 2013. Retrieved from www.guidestar.org/rxa/news/news-releases/2013/2013-08-14-charting-impact-integrated-into-guidestar-exchange.aspx.

3. R. Klitgaard, "On the Drucker Legacy," letter, Claremont Graduate University, 2006. Retrieved from www.cgu.edu/PDFFiles/Presidents%20Office/Drucker_Legacy_May%2006.pdf.

4. Joe Viesta, personal communication, September 24, 2014.

10

Leverage New Technology

WHY WASTE VALUABLE STAFF AND VOLUNTEER time and energy in redundant, time-consuming, mundane activities and problems that have been elegantly solved with new technologies? From a strategic fundraising and donor development perspective, it makes more sense to empower your volunteers and staff to focus on what really counts.

One of the greatest new impacts on benefit and charity auctions is the rapid growth of specialized fundraising and auction technology for the nonprofit, school, and charity marketplaces. Benefits of new technologies include increased efficiency, decreased labor intensity, and reduced stress and burnout of development professionals and auction volunteers. Benefit auction software has systematized and streamlined myriad details for fundraising auction logistics and donor communication.

Technology is enabling efficiency and effectiveness for auctions, making life easier for the people who are organizing and staffing them. This chapter examines the various types of technological advancements and suggests specific pros and cons to consider before choosing what to implement.

Fundraising Auction Software

Consider investing in fundraising auction software. These products keep track of all the details you could possibly think of related to benefit auctions. They will help you decrease staff and volunteer burnout, lower stress, and significantly increase efficiency and effectiveness. Instead of entering data on a computer multiple times, you can spend that time cultivating relationships with potential new sponsors and donors. To find top fundraising software companies, you can conduct a search on the Internet for "benefit auction software."

Two Hidden Bonuses

Benefit auction technology can boost your fundraising efforts and make them far easier to manage. There are many advantages to leveraging benefit auction technology. Here are two key examples where charity auction software can help you take your event to the next level: donor management and auction item procurement.

As you move beyond the single-event mentality and look at your constituents over the long-term, donor cultivation and long-term relationships with your auction guests, donors, and sponsors become paramount. Benefit auction software will give you the ability to analyze your guest's contributions event over event. The bonus, when you're an auction organizer, is that you will have complete information on what each donor has given or won in each revenue stream, year after year. (Note: most auction software will allow organizations to import and export auction event data into their donor management software.) Save time, stress, and burnout with the ability to see at a glance what a donor has given and what that contribution delivers to the bottom line of the auction event.

The use of benefit auction software to manage auction item procurement is immensely important. To truly understand what auction items sell best, organizations must look hard at the numbers and leverage the return on investment (ROI) of each auction item, using a category analysis. Software shows you what items sell well, what items don't sell well, what is actually being bought, and for how much. Knowing the actual metrics behind each gift is invaluable when you're trying to raise more revenue every year.

How New Technology Can Support Donor Development

Leveraging event and fundraising auction technology helps you develop and retain your audience. If guests need to wait in a long line to check out, they'll leave with a negative feeling about your benefit auction event. That lowers the chance that they'll return next year or invite new donors. Technology makes the registration and checkout processes efficient and effective.

With the advancements in technology, there's no reason to have *any* check-in or checkout wait lines at a fundraising event. People go to benefit auction events to have fun, be engaged, and contribute. The last thing they want is to have to stand in a big, long line to support you. Make it easy. Accept credit cards securely at fundraising events. Avoid the old-fashioned paper forms (known as "knuckle buster" machines) that have a high potential for security breaches. Networked credit card swipe machines are far more secure, and they can be used in a stand-alone environment.

The other alternative is a USB credit card reader that securely plugs into a computer at your check-in or checkout. Many companies offer credit card swipe terminals and smart tablets with mobile card readers.

Debby Roth-Bush, relationship manager at Greater Giving, told me that about half of their clients run events using mobile smart tablets with cloud-based software. Tablets allow credit card payment at the door, log raffle sales, a wall of wine, party board sales, payment at the bar, and priced items such as event T-shirts, headbands, and water bottles. Instead of using cumbersome paper forms, volunteers and staff can roam the event with tablet in hand, helping guests buy and contribute. There are no more stacks of paper or crowded tables—everything is captured directly by the benefit event software, reducing the line at checkout and at item pickup. What's most important is that this software also allows you to import and export donor data easily into your existing donor fundraising management software. And that's an essential strategy to track and cultivate donors.

Caveat emptor. Not all mobile card readers are the same. Be sure to select a mobile card reader with a high level of safety and security when capturing credit card payments.

The reach and impact of benefit auction technology companies is immense. According to Debby, "Since 2002, Greater Giving has helped nonprofits raise over 3.5 billion dollars and supported 40,000 fundraising events for 10,000 nonprofits nationwide."

Technology Supports Key Marketing Efforts

Benefit auction software helps you manage your event much more effectively. You can track who attends, what they buy, and how much they spend. You can generate reports and create databases for sponsors and volunteers. You can even integrate all of your correspondence into the software. Auction software can provide you with the ability to build databases over time, which will make it very easy to create a benefit auction marketing plan specific to your organization and audience. Additionally, with a stronger web presence and online auction and mobile bidding, you can give greater recognition to your donors by featuring them in your promotions and providing links to their websites.

Perry Allison, vice president of sales and marketing at Bidding-ForGood, makes an important recommendation: "If your goal is fundraising, then make sure you organize your event so that your guests don't have to do too many things at once, such as hosting a big party that competes with a fundraising auction or having a casino during the same time as closing your auction. It's great having impact and helping great organizations raise money. Help your guests show that they care, driven by their passion for your organization and great cause."[1]

Online Auctions Offer New Possibilities

The right software also allows you to offer online auctions, which can build awareness of your mission, heighten interest in your cause, and leverage additional fundraising opportunities for your organization. Online fundraising offers customizability, affordability, and incredible security. Many people consider putting some of their auction items online. Then they invite all of their constituents—supporters, members, alumni, or whomever—to visit a webpage that lists all the auction items for sale.

Online auctions are increasingly popular because they expand your organization's reach. By offering an online auction, you open up your event so that you can invite people who love you but aren't able to attend the live event. You can invite the whole world to participate if you choose! It's an extraordinary asset. Online auctions promote fundraising events and auction awareness, stimulate competitive bidding, and bring in supplemental revenue. If your nonprofit is national in scope—an educational institution, for example—far-flung alumni will be able to support you without flying in for your event. An online auction offers them an opportunity to participate and feel connected, as well as providing a new revenue source.

When to Do an Online Auction

An online auction can be a stand-alone event, or it can be scheduled a couple of weeks before your regular benefit auction, closing a few days beforehand. You can even do one *after* your event. However, it's complicated to try to do an online auction *at the same time* as your main event.

To integrate online and in-person auctions, have a "preview only" online auction that features all of your silent auction items (or a few preselected items) upon which people can bid. Then, start your benefit auction bidding with the top bid from the online auction. Be careful with bringing online auction bids to your benefit auction event, because you may have a backlash from guests. Those guests who spend money and time at your benefit auction may take exception to this practice. Be sure to talk to your board of directors and auction committee members about this before moving forward.

Who Are Those Online Bidders?

BiddingForGood has developed a demographic profile of those who bid in online auctions. Twenty-seven percent of Americans participate in online auctions; of these, 71 percent are women. Why? Typically, many women don't like the pressure of live auctions, but are more willing to bid online. Online auctions also attract an increasing number of younger adults.

Get a demonstration of online auction capabilities by conducting a Google search for "charity online auctions." BiddingFor Good is the best online auction site I'm aware of (biddingfor-good.com).

The Cost of Online Auctions

Pricing for online auctions is based on the level and type of service purchased. Factor in the cost of features such as credit card processing, as well as fees that are applied on top of the online auction service. It's great to have this in one software package so that when the online auction is over, it's neatly tied up and you receive your funds. Request a customized quote in writing. Do your research. There are some online auction costs that you need to consider carefully, including annual licensing fees, long-term contracts, cancellation fees, updates, technical support, and customer support.

Marketing an Online Auction

Let's compare and contrast the cost of marketing an online auction. Say you're a collector of Hummel pieces, and you only have one Hummel left to collect to complete your collection. You find this piece on eBay and then check on the bid 24 hours a day, seven days a week, until the bidding is over, because you have to have that Hummel.

Contrast that with a wonderful nonprofit school charity auction with various interesting goods and services, but no urgent demand. The trick is to build excitement by creating an exciting marketing campaign when you launch the online auction. Sprinkle in new items regularly to keep up the momentum. Technology companies have data indicating the best time of day to start and stop online auctions, as well as what items sell best. The key is to keep people excited through your whole online campaign.

Mobile Bidding

New mobile bidding technologies work with smartphones and similar handheld devices. For silent auctions, mobile bidding moves the experience from sheets of paper on a tabletop the night of the auction into your guests' hands 24/7. No one can sit on the silent auction bid sheet; no one can cheat and add a late bid. Benefits for guests include the ability to bid from anywhere easily and securely. They can set a maximum bid at any time and have the guaranteed purchase option, paying a premium on a silent item (150 to 200 percent of value) to win the item on the spot.

These devices can help you reinvent the boring, tired, old silent auction model. Silent auctions can be crowded and poorly lit. People don't want to fight and push for items. If you have a huge audience, people may be unable to get close to the items. They don't know when they are outbid, and often there's a lackluster closing, or, worse yet, no closing at all. Mobile bidding devices can really enhance a silent auction, which is where they are most effective. They are most powerful when connected to software and payment systems integrated with your credit card processing.

With mobile electronic handheld bidding devices, anyone can bid from anywhere in the room. These devices use web-based software, similar to an app on an iPad. This frees bidders to go anywhere in the venue and maintain constant vigilance over their items without returning repeatedly to the silent auction tables. They can relax, engage with other guests, and have a good time while they're bidding.

Mobile bidding devices work for silent auctions, and they can also be used for special appeals and fund-a-needs. However, they are *not* effective for live auctions, because they don't create excitement and interactivity. In fact, mobile bidding significantly reduces the excitement, energy, and bidding in a live auction room. Electronic bidding won't capture the heart and passion of the bidder. Mobile bidding won't replace the energy, excitement, fun, audience engagement, and high revenue of a live auction.

With mobile bidding devices, there are no bid sheets; there's no paper at all. You can still create silent auction displays if you like, or you can omit the displays in the room because the items are already featured online. When guests register, they use their smartphone or a special mobile device that's preloaded with all silent auction items. In either case, guests will receive regular updates on the bidding for silent auction items. For example, if a guest bids on a big chocolate basket and she's outbid, her mobile bidding device will buzz with a message. She can then decide whether she'd like to place another bid. When the item closes, the device sends a confirmation message to the highest bidder.

Does It Pay to Use Mobile Bidding Devices?

Do your research. There are technology companies that have dozens of years of dedicated experience serving nonprofit and school auction communities nationwide. There are also new companies emerging in all these technology markets. Ask for data and costs. Mobile bidding technologies are not inexpensive. Read your contracts and understand what services will be provided. When comparing companies, remember that they may need to create an enhanced wireless environment in your venue.

Do a tight cost analysis. You must forecast if you will net more revenue using the mobile device. Be thorough. When analyzing your event, figure out how much more money you'll need to make to cover the costs of online bidding, and how much you expect the mobile bidding devices to enhance your fundraising. Be sure there is enough financial gain to make this technology cost-effective for your silent auction.

Mobile bidding devices *can* be used for fund-a-need events as well, but with several important caveats. First and foremost, include an inspiring first-person story—the mission moment testimonial that rivets and inspires generosity. Second, retain an excellent auctioneer with strong experience in benefit auctions, fundraising, and mobile bidding who can successfully focus and engage your audience throughout the entire process. Third, do your homework. Select a mobile bidding technology company that has an excellent technology and customer service track record in the nonprofit and school auction communities.

When you introduce mobile bidding technology, you're also offering your guests an opportunity to disengage from your mission and not be as fully present. It's easy for your guests to get lost in checking e-mails, Facebook, and texting when they're placing their gifts on their smartphones.

Top Strategy for Fund-a-Need Mobile Bidding

The best way to combine fund-a-need and mobile giving is to use a hybrid model that preserves the best of a live fund-a-need, using both bid cards and mobile bidding devices. Your auctioneer plays a huge role in keeping up the excitement and energy of donating during the fund-a-need. She must focus the entire audience and prepare them to listen to your inspiring "mission moment story." Then she'll invite guests to raise their bid cards at levels meaningful to them, starting high and going lower with each level, while a volunteer records each number. This way, your organization won't lose funds.

One challenge has been that some guests raise their bid cards or pledge at higher levels, and then, when it's time to enter their payments into their mobile devices, they change their minds and give at lower levels or not at all. Writing down bid card numbers at each level will eliminate this problem.

Only introduce the mobile giving opportunity at the lower levels. It's very important that your auction continue to promote your cause and maintain the spirit of the event. Direct your guests to use their phones for giving by being both inspiring and all-inclusive: "Now it's time where everyone can make a difference. Will you kindly pick up your phone or mobile bidding device?"

Here's the rub: When you invite guests to pick up their phones, you never know if they are actually pledging the amounts they said they would, or checking their e-mails. Keep the energy high, be clear about intent, create excitement at the moment of giving, and encourage everyone to give. A leader board can then be activated at the lower levels to show who is bidding.

What does *not* work is for the emcee or auctioneer to simply say, "Now get out your phone and give." A successful fund-a-need is a completely designed and rehearsed experience in which you're counting (literally) on your auctioneer to be the ringmaster and cheerleader for your cause for the entire duration of giving. In many instances where no bid cards were used and there was no inspiring story, results were less than satisfactory.

I know from experience that a "soft ask" fors fund-a-need does not work. Driving guests to pull out their cell phones without instructions and an enthusiastic ask for donations never yields the best results.

Be sure to work as a team with your auctioneer, staff, and mobile bidding company as you plan the exact execution. Make sure the mobile bidding company is customizing their technology to achieve what is best for you, not what is best for them.

Guidance for Mobile Devices

To make sure your online effort is effective, have someone with experience in engaging and directing audiences guide the entire mobile bidding process. The best choice is your benefit auctioneer, because fundraising auctioneers know how to use their voices and they understand momentum, timing, and tone. Make sure you announce the close of your silent auction sections, calling guests' attention to your mission and engaging them, or you will have disappointing results. It's still important to have your auctioneer make the announcements, get people involved and excited, and explain how the silent auction works.

Wireless Connectivity

From a technical standpoint, mobile bidding devices require strong and consistent wireless connectivity. Be sure to confirm the wireless service before your event. Some companies will bring in a wireless infrastructure, which is very expensive, but fail-safe. If the venue does not provide wireless for you, you'll have to set up the network, devices, and cords yourself.

Mark Wehrmeister, vice president of technology and operations for Greater Giving, emailed me this comment:

> Now that Internet access has become ubiquitous, the use of online technology for auctions has accelerated and will continue to grow.
>
> This is evident in the rapid growth of Greater Giving Mobile Bidding and in the decrease of offline software at events, which must be installed, upgraded, and synchronized. The Internet has also introduced user experience (UX) design principles that make auction tools vastly easier to learn and use when embraced. We've utilized UX design in our online event interface, Greater Giving Go Time, and our users have been delighted with the ease-of-use.

Questions to Ask about Benefit Auction Technology

Here's a summary of questions that you can ask technology providers to determine their level of experience and ability to customize capabilities for your unique fundraising situation.

- What is the wireless connectivity in the venue? Is it sufficiently robust? How do we test it?
- What do you do if there is not enough wireless connectivity?
- Can the wireless connectivity handle a large volume of many hundreds at once and over a period of several hours?
- What is the level of customer service? What is the training program? Do you send a team to work at the event?
- What is your proven backup plan if something goes wrong?
- How much money has been raised at events with your technology? How much of a change have you seen in similar fundraisers for the first year, second year, and beyond?
- What is your experience in silent auctions?
- What is your experience for fund-a-need special appeals?
- How do you register guests?
- How do you handle payment?
- How do you integrate mobile bidding with existing registration and cashiering systems?
- Does the system display names? Do you have the capability to show names and contributions? Can you show names only?
- Does the mobile bidding system include an image of a thermometer to show increasing levels of giving that displays on a screen? How many ways can you customize the image and timing of the thermometer giving levels? Can you turn it off?
- What is your level of commitment to work as a team with our organization, our auctioneer, and other key staff?
- Please provide references and case studies.

Conclusion

Today's technology offers the tools that can enhance fundraising, donor engagement, and guest experience. Avoid the temptation to obsess on emerging technologies at the expense of what matters most. Focus instead on technology you're sure will heighten board and volunteer energy and help you raise money and develop donors. A key benefit of mobile bidding, online auctions, and online giving is that these new technologies allow you to expand your community to the world. But remember that it never makes sense to use technology for technology's sake. Get demonstrations of online auction capabilities by conducting a Google search for charity or benefit online auctions including a demo from Bidding for Good.

Note

1. Perry Allison, personal communication, October 10, 2014.

Section III

Conducting Strategic Benefit Auctions for Donors and Dollars

11

Optimize Silent Auctions
for Loud Results

CITY LIGHTS GLISTENED ON THE WATER BELOW. A stunning backdrop, replete with fragrant night-blooming bougainvillea, enthralled the auction guests. The parent-teacher public school auction committee was thrilled at the chance to serve cocktails and heavy hors d'oeuvres on this gorgeous balcony. Imagine the allure! Silent auction, dinner, live auction, and dancing were set inside a gorgeous indoor ballroom.

Can you guess the result? Out went all the guests to the balcony to enjoy the view, bar, and food. The committee mistakenly believed that guests would come inside to bid on silent auction items. Not the case. Predictably, everyone stayed outside on the balcony, and virtually no one came inside to bid. This silent auction disaster raised far less than one-third of its value and left many items unsold.

This chapter focuses on intentional and proven strategies to maximize bidding and more deeply engage donors. Silent auctions have been a mainstay of benefit fundraising events for many years. Regardless of how much you raise through silent auctions, never lose track of the reason you're holding your event in the first place: to raise *more* funds and to engage *more* donors. Even though a silent auction may be an income producer, the precious time during the silent auction is often overlooked as a wonderful cultivation time. Be strategic and strengthen your relationships with guests during the silent auction/cocktail hour and visit with your supporters about the impact of your great mission. Let's talk about how you can leverage silent auctions to showcase the mission and impact of your organization.

Too Little Money for Too Much Work?

Silent auctions are arguably the most labor-intensive, detail-ridden, volunteer-time-sucking activity of any special event fundraising. Many silent auction items fail to raise even 50 percent of their value. You're wasting valuable volunteer energy and time, and it can seem to take forever to procure, collect, and track items, write up descriptions, set up displays, close them out, and pack them up. I'm exhausted just thinking about it!

Are Silent Auctions Worth It Anymore?

Ask these qualifying questions before planning your next silent auction:

1. If our volunteers spent half the time inviting the right guests that they typically spend on silent auction tasks, would it be more effective?
2. What is our Silent Auction ROI? If our items bring less than 70 percent of their value, should we even proceed?
3. How are we creating awareness about our mission at the silent auction?
4. How are we cultivating guests?
5. How are we engaging our leadership during cocktails and the silent auction?

Strategically Cultivate Guests during Silent Auctions

Not engaging your guests and stakeholders more deeply in your cause is one of the most overlooked opportunities of special event and auction fundraising. Nowhere is this more evident than during your cocktail reception and silent auction. This is the exact time to exhort your board, stakeholders, and leaders to get to work building relationships with donors. Silent auctions, VIP receptions, and cocktail hours are the most strategic times to cultivate guests at auctions and fundraising events.

Empower Your Leadership Team Now

In Chapter 3, I showcased my "Magic Question" for donor cultivation at any event. Try this: During your silent auction, empower your board and leaders to go up to three guests they do not know and say, "Hi, I'm _____. How are you connected to (*the name of your organization*)?"

Ask them to share any of the ways your cause has touched them. Immediately, the power of this engaging activity is apparent. The energy in the room shifts. Now your attendees and stakeholders are talking about your mission and your impact. It's palpable and powerful to focus your guests on how their generous bidding and contributions will make a difference.

Erica Donnelly is the annual campaign manager at The Providence Center. She and her leadership team are incredibly thoughtful and strategic in their cultivation approach. Donnelly assigns 38 key volunteers and staff to talk with specific attendees and donors during the VIP reception and the silent auction. She matches up staff members with donors who have an interest in that staff member's program and encourages them to visit. For example, the director of a veterans program will talk with guests he knows really care about veterans in their communities. The goal is to make their guests feel special and heighten their awareness of the organization's impact.

Your Auctioneer Is Your Ambassador Too

Leverage the expertise, energy, and voice of the fundraising auctioneer at your silent auction. Starting with initial pre-event planning, many auctioneers bring insider-proven best practices to you and your team. During the event, benefit auctioneers can play a critical role in cultivating guests and talking with them about your cause. Remember, your auctioneer is an ambassador for your mission, not just a voice on a mic.

Learn from the Retailers

In retail, businesses use strategic profit-making design concepts to promote sales. You should, too. Did you ever wonder why milk is always in the back of the grocery store? Because on your way to the dairy counter, you'll see a wide array of additional items and fill your cart with them. How does that apply to silent auctions? Deliberately place the bar as far away from the entrance of the silent auction areas as possible. Quite intentionally, place some of your best silent items on tables along the pathway to the bar. Now your guests have to walk past your inviting silent auction displays if they want a drink.

Great retailers use eye-catching "end cap" displays at the end of each row to attractively promote high-profit items. Bookstores place best-sellers right up front to draw in shoppers and promote sales. Purposefully display your exciting silent auction best-sellers, such as trips and dinners, right where your guests mingle most.

Claim the Prime Space

Remember, your silent auction is a fundraiser, not a wedding or a private party. When you evaluate a possible venue, look at the floor plan and do a careful walkthrough with the caterer or the banquet manager. Identify the prime "real estate" in the space where you will hold your silent auction. Where is the highest traffic? Claim this space. Many times it's the center of the room. Don't allow crudités, giant cheese stations, or ice sculptures to dominate your event. Instead, focus on displaying photos that show the impact of your mission on the community alongside your best silent auction items.

Amazing Grazing

Remember the story about the auction that failed because of the night-blooming bougainvilleas? Don't lose money. Place high-end food item stations close to expensive silent auction items. Avoid putting all of the same food items together or having one giant food station. Divide the food stations into several smaller areas and place them around the room. When someone asks another guest, "Where did you get the scallop wrapped in bacon?" the guest will respond, "See that sign that says 'Super Silent' with those gold balloons? Go over there."

Don't line up silent auction items around the edge of the room or put all of the food in the middle of the room. Don't plunk the bar right where guests enter the room. Why not? This ineffective, dated layout highlights food and drinks rather than your core goals: raising money with silent items and focusing guests on your mission.

How Many Silent Auction Items?

This is one of the questions I'm often asked. There's no simple answer. What's the financial goal for your silent auction? How many guests are coming to your event? More importantly, how many *households* are coming to your event? Most people come as couples. You want to keep an item-to-household ratio that is no greater than one. Less is more. Some of the mobile bidding technology companies report that the highest yielding silent auctions have a 4:1 ratio (e.g., for every four people, there is one item). In other words, if you expect 100 people at your benefit auction event, have 25 silent auction items. This is a good rule of thumb. However, school auctions will likely have many more silent auction items than gala auctions, which tend to have only a handful of items.

Packaging items is another great option. Arranging items in baskets is popular, but please, please, please don't put cellophane plastic around baskets! Cellophane does *not* sell! "Mmm, look, over 100 Godiva chocolates!" Guests need to experience and see silent items close up. "Ooh! Look at our sixth grader's work on these mosaic garden tiles!"

How Do You Spell Silent Auction Success?

S: Spread Out Items
I : Interval Closings
L: Light 'em Up
E: Elevate Your Items
N: Announcements
T: Tactical Design

Apply the 2 × 4 Butt Rule

Have you noticed that guests seldom walk around a silent auction setup alone? Instead, they're talking while strolling through the display. Here's a simple way to place the right amount of space between your silent auction items. Use my "2 × 4 Butt Rule." Remember, when guests bid, they bend over to write. Intentionally design for two guests bending over to bid at opposite tables while two more guests stroll through the aisle—all without risking the dreaded "butt brush."

This is especially important when you close your silent auction sections, because you strategically want to create an open space for a competitive bidding frenzy that will carry the price as high as possible for each item.

How do you determine exactly how much spacing for traditional paper bidding? With my 2 × 4 Rule, you'll avoid bidder fatigue and butt brush. Strategically design your silent auction to make it easy for your guests to bid and buy items. To raise more money at your silent auction, intentionally design more space for bidders to see, graze, touch, and bid comfortably and competitively. For mobile bidding at a silent auction, you can display items more tightly or not at all, because your silent items will be displayed on everyone's mobile device.

Interval Closings

Stagger the closing times for your silent auctions by setting up separate sections that close in timed intervals. From a physics standpoint, you increase the surface volume of bidding so that your guests have more bidding opportunities more often.

If you close all silent auction items at once, your guests only have one chance to buy their favorite items. In contrast, closing a silent auction in staggered sections creates more opportunities for competitive bidding, which greatly increases fundraising potential. It's exciting, because if bidders don't win any items in the first section, they can go to the next section and bid again. I recommend closing sections 10 minutes apart, creating energy and movement right before you enter the ballroom for your program, live auction, and meal.

Capitalize on the Three Musketeers of Silent Auctions: *Urgency, Demand, and Closure*

Urgency

As you announce the closing of a silent auction section, create a sense of urgency so people think, "Oh! Gosh! Is it really closing? I've got to keep bidding!"

Demand

When sections close, there are fewer and fewer items left to bid on, which creates demand that translates to higher revenue.

Closure

When it's gone, it's gone. Be "happily intrusive." Start packing up your closed silent auction section right away, giving your guests a gentle and timely nod toward the next section and into the ballroom for your program.

Generate Crowd Momentum

Strategically move your guests to the next phase of your event and energize them about what's to come. First, think about where you want your audience to go after the silent auction is completed. Let's say the silent auction is in an atrium adjacent to the ballroom where you will hold your program, live auction, and meal. Close the section farthest away from the ballroom first and close the section closest to the ballroom last. This systematically creates a natural movement of your guests to the ballroom, allowing a smoother and quicker transition.

Close the sections in a logical order to keep the crowd moving in the direction of their ultimate destination: your live auction and fund-a-need. You never want to have your crowd swimming upstream like salmon. Your auctioneer can promote closings with clear announcements about the specific tables that are closing.

Here's a sample: The auctioneer announces, "Ladies and gentlemen. We have three silent sections closing. The red silent section closes at 7:30 P.M., the white silent section closes at 7:40 P.M., and the blue silent section closes at 7:50 P.M. Our program and meal begins at 8:00 P.M."

How Many Sections?

How many sections should you have in your silent auction?

- Plan on between 20 and 40 items in a section.
- Factor both the activities and space into this decision.
- What else is going on in the space?
- How is the room laid out?
- Make your priorities fundraising and guest engagement.

Elevate Your items

Strategically display your silent items and point of sale sign at the eye level of your guests. Why? Because your guests first "shop" from about 10 feet away. If they cannot be enticed to come closer, no bidding will occur. It helps to think and act like a high-end retail display designer. Let's face it, no one can see items if they're flat on the table. Creatively elevate all your silent auction items so they are visually accessible to all of your guests. Try two-tiered tables.

Superb Sound

Be sure to have a superb sound system tailored for the silent auction area. Remember, the noise is *loudest* in the *silent* auction section, so you'll need to strategically add more audio speakers there. This often gets overlooked, which is a big mistake. As you close silent auction sections, promote auction items that need attention and create a bidding frenzy. My favorite announcement: "Bidder number 472, you were just outbid on the deluxe Disney family vacation. Come back to our gold silent auction section!" The transition after silent auction closing is critical. Make clear, well-timed announcements to ensure smooth and efficient transitions. For example: "The silent auction is now closed. We invite you to kindly take your seats in the ballroom for our program, live auction, and dinner."

At school auctions, where there are more silent auction items, there are usually more announcements than at a luxurious gala auction where announcements don't fit the profile of the event. It's a good idea for the auctioneer and organizers to stay in close contact during the entire silent auction, so they can react to any situations that might arise. This is a perfect example of why my PILI ("Purposeful Intentional Listening In") assessment is priceless.

Avoid the Top Three Problems in Silent Auctions

1. **Item Overload:** One of the biggest problems with silent auctions is too many items crammed on too few tables. Unfortunately, when items are jammed together, no one can get near them to place their next bids. Many times these items are not curated to your audience and will net dismal results.
2. **Bidder Fatigue:** Don't exhaust your guests by requiring them to push into a crowd just to see items they don't want or need. They will be fatigued for the rest of your event. What a huge deterrent to generosity and spirited bidding! Limit items and time for silent bidding. Get to the core—your inspiring program, live auction, and fund-a-need appeal—sooner.
3. **The "Butt-Brush Factor":** Retail anthropologist Paco Underhill found that women shoppers are far less likely to make a purchase if they are "brushed" from behind—by a person, a display table, or a piece of merchandise—while examining retail goods. Underhill's finding, backed up by extensive video research, carries a corollary: Retailers should avoid jamming narrow aisles full of merchandise.[1] It's not different at your silent auction. When your guests are viewing and bidding on silent items and the space is too jammed, naturally people will "brush" against each other. Auction guests will stop bidding and leave the uncomfortable area.

Silent Auction Quad Pods

Whales thrive in pods, and your silent auction can benefit from this strategic grouping too. Create pods that contain the four key elements listed below. Then strategically place numerous pods around your silent auction room for maximum giving.

Four Key Elements for Silent Auction Success

1. Silent Auction Items
2. Food Station
3. Bar or Soft Drink/Water Station
4. Mission-Based Messaging

A silent auction pod includes a few silent auction item tables, an inspiring branding poster about your mission (e.g., a lovely photograph with a quote on an easel), food, and drinks. I believe the best layouts for silent auctions are large round tables and serpentine tables with plenty of space around each table. Both encourage flowing bidder movement where bidders can actually watch others outbidding them. It's easier to flow around a serpentine or round table to bid again, which means higher prices for your items. If you're concerned that you just don't have the room, big hint: You need a bigger venue. A small, cramped, silent auction and venue will hold back your fundraising and guest experience. Start looking for next year now.

Kathy's Clamshell Offense

Figure 11.1   C.L.A.M. Four Steps to Seat Your Guests Fast

Want to make a lot more "clams" at your fundraiser? Use my Clamshell Offense!

Use four simultaneous actions at the exact moment your final silent auction closes.

1. *Clamshell* Closer: Position numerous volunteers around the outside perimeter of your silent auction and cocktail reception rooms. At the exact minute your silent auction closes, instruct "clamshell volunteers" to smile, walk up to each group of guests, and politely invite them to take their seats at this time. Why a clamshell? Just imagine a wide-open clamshell closing as your volunteers walk deeper into the room, inviting guests to take their seats. See how quickly you can close your "clamshell" and enjoy the energetic movement of your guests into the next phase of fundraising.

2. Follow the *Leaders*: Instruct and expect board members, sponsors, volunteers, chairs, and committee members to sit down first. Many times, these leaders are the last to be seated, and guests are watching and following their behavior. Change the momentum and other guests will notice and follow.

3. Auctioneer *Announcements*: Leverage the energy and voice of your auctioneer. Ask her to make gracious announcements inviting everyone into the next room and asking them to please be seated now. Your auctioneer can facilitate guest movement by being visibly present in the cocktail and silent auction area on the microphone. Create hospitable one-liners such as, "Dinner is now served, kindly step into the ballroom," or, "Our exciting program and fundraising auction are just about to start, so please find your seats. The bar is now open in the ballroom."

4. *Momentum*: Close the other bars, the silent auction, and the food stations. Do it now. Waiting costs you more than you know in energy and revenue. Instruct the bartenders and banquet staff to stop serving in the pre-party cocktail and silent auction areas. Hint: Immediately open the bars in the main room and open your ballroom early to a preset first course. The faster you get your guests seated, the more funds you will raise. If seating your guests cuts into your program, your fundraising will drag, too.

Timing: When to Close Silent Auctions

Do you make the most money by closing the silent auction before, during, or after the live auction? A few years ago, Northwest Software Technologies, Inc., did a study that asked that exact question and found it doesn't matter.[2]

When you factor in all of the details related to a silent auction (e.g., paperwork, cashiering, data entry, and packing up), it makes sense to close before your live auction. You can tie up loose ends from the silent auction during the live auction. Also, this way, guests aren't distracted by going back to look at silent auction items during the live auction. At the end of the evening, you're all set.

In nearly three decades of work specializing in fundraising auctions, I have not seen any appreciable increase in silent auction proceeds when the silent auction tables stay open later. The exception would be with use of mobile bidding devices that are strategically predetermined by the auction committee. Remember, the major revenue at your event is the live auction and fund-a-need appeal. If you hold the silent auction open too long, you can lose significant dollars later.

However, suppose you are using mobile bidding, you have a big dance after the live auction, and you want to keep the silent auction open during the early part of the dancing? That's fine—just don't confuse your guests. Make sure that you have a very clear announcement to that effect, so that your guests aren't worried that they'll lose a silent auction item during the live auction. Be crystal clear about this on your signage.

Volunteers Are the Key to Success

Volunteers are the heart, soul, and backbone of benefit auctions. A high-functioning, enthusiastic team is vital for auction success. Try these new ideas for a higher quality guest experience.

Captains and Concierges

Even with the greatest plan in the world, if your volunteers are not well-trained and prepared, a silent auction can fall apart. Appoint a silent auction captain who is responsible for training all of your volunteers to make sure they check in, get their assignments, know what sections will be assigned to them, and review final information at a run-through rehearsal.

Add a concierge or personal shopper volunteer team who give special attention to your guests while they are bidding. This is critical if you use mobile bidding. These individuals can help explain and promote items while they connect with guests: "You like to travel—I see you've been bidding on this exciting Cancun travel package. Did you know we have a trip to Bermuda on the next table?" In this case, you'll want to showcase your silent auction concierge volunteers. Here's another excellent silent auction table layout tip. Consider designing tables in a triangle or square so that two or three silent auction concierge volunteers can personally and easily engage your guests by standing in the middle of this table arrangement, for higher bidding and greater discussion of your great cause.

What's New in Silent Auctions? Mobile Bidding

One of the most exciting developments in auction technology is the use of handheld bidding devices (see Chapter 10). There are numerous mobile bidding companies that utilize guests' smartphones or provide handheld bidding devices such as an iTouch. You can preload items on them, so that guests can walk around and bid on items no matter where they are. But if you use these devices, you'll still need an auctioneer with a great announcing voice who can focus the audience when the silent auction is closing. Remember, the majority of bidding happens 10 to 15 minutes before a section closes, so your auctioneer must create an even greater frenzy to energize the bidders right before the close.

As we've said, mobile bidding devices work best in silent auctions. They solve the problems of crowded bidding, a large audience, or complex venues. There are significant costs to having a handheld bidding device, but guests have fun with them, so do the math. Figure out the cost-to-value ratio to determine if it makes sense for you financially.

Conclusion

There is nothing more important to your organization than fulfilling its mission. Silent auctions have great potential to raise funds for your organization's cause. Use these proven silent auction strategies and techniques to ensure record-breaking fundraising. How do you spell success? S-I-L-E-N-T!

Notes

1. Underhill. P. n.d. "Why People Buy: The Science of Shopping." Strategic Marketing. Retrieved from HYPERLINK "http://www.etstrategicmarketing.com/smjan-feb3/art10.html" www.etstrategicmarketing.com/SmJan-Feb3/art10.html.
2. Jack Wilson, personal communication, October 8, 2014.

12

Maximize the True Worth
of Your Live Auction

"THE RIGHT TO NAME A NEWBORN DAIRY CALF?" "Are you kidding me...?"

I began the auction: "And now, Live Auction Number 6. Ladies and gentlemen, everyone—one of the most unique items that I have ever auctioned. One lucky winning bidder will have the exclusive right to name and visit a newborn dairy calf at the farm that supplies our fresh milk and cheese to our community food pantry. Your generous bidding will help hungry families in our community to receive nutritious lunches every day from the Saratoga County Economic Opportunity Council. Thank you to our wonderful donor and board member, Jane, who owns this farm. Your generosity helps your neighbors who are struggling daily with hunger. For many, this is their only meal of the day. Your gift will touch someone you may never know in a life-giving way.

"Here we go, the auction's on! This happy heifer is due any moment now. Who'll bid $100? Now $200? $300?" In a flash, surprising even me, bidding burst open. Up, up in just a few breaths—700! Amid the entire crowd's cheering and clapping, driving them forward, two bidders emerged from the crazed frenzy, $800, $900, how about $1,000? A bidder shot up, "Yes!" she cried, her bid card high. "Sold for $1,000!" I seriously couldn't believe it myself. Then, just as I said "sold," barreling toward me with her cell phone on her ear (and I could not make this up) dairy farmer Jane yelled, "Kathy, sell two! Bessie just had twins!" Instantly, we raised $2,000 for the community food outreach program.

I ran right up to the first bidder and said, "Wow, thank you so much. We all want to know, what will you name the baby dairy calf?" She smiled warmly. "Olivia. That's my granddaughter's name, and I want us to visit the farm together so I can show her how this food helps people who need it the most. I know how my money will be used and I want my granddaughter to learn firsthand." The audience went wild.

Twin Morals of the Story

First moral—you can recite it with me by now—It's not about what bidders get, it's what they give. *Always* tie your mission into the item description to showcase the impact of your guests' generous bidding. Second moral: Double your money. Always ask your donors for a second package. On this occasion, even Mother Nature conspired—we had no idea twin calves would be born at the exact time of the auction!

Twin Strategies for Ultimate Live Auctions

Illustrated in this fun and insightful true story are two indispensable strategies for live auction success: maximizing profit and energizing guest engagement. At a glance, live auctions seem simple: Just get somebody to call out numbers and sell items out loud during your event. Then cross your fingers and hope to raise money. That's the old way, a Transaction Model relic that will predictably lose thousands of dollars and leave donors wondering how fast they can bolt away from you and your event.

To achieve record-breaking live auction success, you need a highly strategic perspective and months of careful pre-event design that includes a whole choreography of strategies. What you and your audience see on the live stage is just the tip of the iceberg. In this chapter I pull back the curtain and reveal top-level thinking to take your live auction to the next level.

Why Live?

An entertaining, highly profitable focal point of the entire event, the live auction adds sparkle and fun while inspiring the audience to bid ever-higher, raising more money for your cause. In the old Transaction Model approach, a live auction could be simply defined as a sale in which the auctioneer offered selected items for bid with an oral outcry method, selling each item to the highest bidder.

But looking through the lens of the Philanthropy Model, a live auction is a top revenue stream in a strategically designed fundraising auction. High-profit, curated auction items raise more money offered in the live auction than in the silent auction. During the live auction, in fact, many items sell for more than their value, a happy phenomenon I have named "philanthropic bidding." In the old Transaction Model, bidders had a one-time shopping mentality and wanted a bargain. In the new Philanthropy Model, they're inspired to pay more than the value for live auction items in order to support your cause.

Stop Selling Items—Start Selling Your Cause

It is essential for an auctioneer working at a benefit auction to inspire guests and show them how high bids will positively impact the cause. The auctioneer should make strategic comments about the mission throughout the live auction. During the bidding process, he can intersperse key talking points about the mission of the organization.

Here's a snapshot of the live auction through the lens of the Philanthropy Model. The auctioneer briefly describes the item, building excitement and desire. Rather than reading the boring description that guests have already seen, "Spend six days in Cancun," he entices bidders: "Imagine your feet sinking into warm, wet sand this winter, ahhh." Next, the auctioneer begins selling this trip and taking bids from the audience. A skilled fundraising auctioneer knows how to start bidding with zest and keep up energy for both bidders and nonbidders.

Why Risk It?

You and your dedicated auction committee work for months on end, then on auction night you turn your entire event over to your auctioneer. Why? Because you don't want to leave money in the room. With a professional benefit auctioneer who has wide experience, proven fundraising ideas, and a dedication to good causes, you will raise more money. I typically see an average increase of 20 to 200 percent in live auction revenue when I am the professional auctioneer following a year that an organization uses a volunteer, celebrity, or VIP personality. That's because I know how to engage the audience, move bids along to reach the highest possible amount, keep the focus on the nonprofit mission, and create a lively and entertaining event that maximizes your fundraising and leaves your guests eager to return the following year. Remember, investing in a professional auctioneer does not cost you money in the long run, because you will generate more profit.

Feel free to contact me kathy@kingstonauction.com for information on finding experienced benefit auctioneers in your area. (Note, there is an in-depth discussion of auctioneers in Chapter 4.)

> As a nonprofit executive director at STAR, Inc., watching every penny and wanting every dollar raised to go into programs, it was hard thinking about paying for an auctioneer. But as our fundraiser grew we knew we needed professional help to take it to the next level. We were concerned that a professional auctioneer would not be sensitive to our families and clients and we feared we would lose our intimate family centered approach at our fundraising gala. We learned that there is a specialized group of professional auctioneers who specialize in fundraising and consulting for auctions. They understood our values and helped us weave those values and our mission into every task associated with the gala event, making it even stronger.
>
> The first year alone with a fundraising specialist auctioneer our revenue catapulted over 33 percent. The value of the auctioneer's professional consultation impacted our donor cultivation and longer-term fundraising plans. The professional fundraising auctioneer not only gave us technical advice but became our cheerleader, reminding us of all we could accomplish.
>
> **—Katie Banzhaf, Executive Director, STAR, Inc.**[1]

Stand Up Front and Gain a New Perspective

Auction organizers, try this enlightening tip. During the live auction, face your audience and see what the auctioneer sees. Many organizers sit in the audience or stand in the back of the room and watch the auctioneer. From a donor relationship standpoint, it is much more powerful—and revealing—to watch your guests. Stand up front, near the auctioneer, and you'll experience a different dynamic. You'll be able to focus on all the action. You'll see exactly who is bidding, who is not bidding, which guests are focusing at which moments, who is more engaged during which live items, and who is not even in the room. This rich information will be invaluable to you as you create your donor follow-up and cultivation plans. Knowing on a firsthand basis exactly what your guests are actually doing during the live auction and how they are participating will give you strategic insights on the best way to make personal connections after your event.

Combo Auctioneer and Emcee

In some instances, you may have the benefit of both an emcee and an auctioneer; at other times, you have one person filling both roles. Here are some strategies to optimize your live auction. If you have both a VIP or celebrity emcee and an auctioneer, be sure to communicate in writing each person's roles when you provide the timeline. Require both individuals to come early for a run-through and sound check before your event doors open. This will ensure that you have a professional, fast-paced event, and your emcee and auctioneer know how to smoothly work with each other.

A Hidden Benefit of Live Auctions

From a strategic perspective, the live auction builds a crescendo of energy and emotion right up to the exact moment of your fund-a-need special appeal. At this peak time, the auctioneer must simultaneously quiet and excite the audience as he transitions to the inspiring story for the fund-a-need. Here's one of my secrets for a live auction: Ensure that your auctioneer keeps this transition *tight*. Without the auctioneer expertly choreographing this moment, many organizations lose thousands of dollars and donors' gifts. Construct your timeline to build to a climax and then gracefully shift the momentum. Retain an auctioneer who can deftly manage that transition, and has expertise in both live auctions and fund-a-need special appeal fundraising. (Note, the fund-a-need special appeal is discussed in Chapter 13.)

Increase Generosity: Prepare Your Guests to Bid

Bidder behavior has changed. No longer do guests come to charity auctions with the express purpose of bidding no matter what. Now, your supporters are much more strategic—so you have to be strategic, too. Leverage this trend and design a comprehensive, personalized approach to market your live auction items heavily before your event. The best-selling live items are trips and experiences. Many live items are group experiences or are date specific, such as a Tuscan villa for 12 people, a Ladies Latin Night for 12, a lobster Bake for 20 people, a gourmet dinner for six with flights of wine at a board member's home, or a full luxury box at a major sporting event. Each of these live auction packages requires the buyer to plan and prepare far in advance of the auction. So pre-promote the items.

Create a specialized marketing campaign before the event to showcase and build excitement about your live auction. An often overlooked yet powerfully effective strategy is to mail an auction catalogue in advance to all your guests. Prepare them to give generously. Your stakeholders should "talk up" your live auction items by personally speaking to your previous top 20 to 30 bidders and letting them know about hot live auction items that they, especially, will love! To get more bid cards in the air, you must prepare your guests in advance to bid generously.

New Stakeholder Leadership for Higher Bids

Invite your table captains, board members, VIPs, and sponsors to bring their guests to the live auction display and talk up these live items. Ask the same people to be responsible for thanking the guests after the event. Here's my favorite strategy for board members and other leaders to engage bidders at their tables during the live auction. Ask them to simply nod their heads and smile and say, "Yes, bid again. You are making a big difference for our cause." They can encourage their entire tables to cheer and keep up the energy and excitement. It will make an enormous difference in your bottom line and in donor fun and engagement.

Curate Your Live Auction Items

Waste no time or space on live auction items that do not bring a return of at least 85 percent of value—and shoot for items that sail over the value! Remember, less is more. Fewer items with higher values will fetch more profit. Hand-select premium items. Act and think like a top marketer: Match your auction items to your guests. Study your live auction results each year and only procure items that are incredibly successful for you. Make a chart calculating retail value, high bid, and percentage of value achieved. Study what your group loves to bid on. Go get more of these top revenue producers! Solicit live auction items that are personal and unique: once-in-a-lifetime experiences, exclusive handmade gifts, one-of-a-kind travel, and sold-out and unique group experiences. (For more in-depth discussion of auction items, see Chapter 6.)

Here's an outstanding example of a live auction procurement strategy that proved itself four million times over (yes, that was the net revenue, $4 million) at the Sonoma Harvest Wine Auction. Each of the key vintners and growers created their own superb specialty live auction item well in advance of the auction. They then personally marketed their live auction lot to the guests and donors they knew would be seated at their auction table, as well as to everyone in their circle of influence, including their wine club members. For example, the honorary co-chairs of the Sonoma Harvest Wine Auction designed and promoted a superb live auction lot. The Gloria Ferrer Caves and Vineyard donated a luxury trip for two couples to Barcelona, curated by the Ferrer family and brimming with VIP experiences customized to the winning bidder's preferences. It sold for $80,000.

The Fun and Profit Factor at Your Live Auction

Live benefit auctions are fun! How do you plan fun and make money, too? See Chapter 14 for fresh ideas on ways to diversify your revenue streams by adding fun auction icebreakers and revenue games. Engage your audience's hearts, minds, and pocketbooks with such games as heads-and-tails, a centerpiece auction, or auction chicken. It's also fun to add one or two items upon which virtually everyone can bid. This could be a year's worth of your favorite ice cream, a specialty live item that ties into your theme, or something unique to your organization, such as the opportunity for a walk-on role at a local theater or dance troupe. Remember, when your audience is having fun, they bid higher and are excited to return and bring friends who love your cause, too.

"Auction-tainment": Lights, Camera, Auction!

Make your live auction entertaining. Set your live auction apart from the rest of the evening and engage more of your guests. Strategically incorporate music, theater, dance, and higher production values, using live video and professional sound and lights. Pump up excitement by playing a short snippet of exciting upbeat music when the auctioneer says "SOLD." At that moment, your winning bidder and your entire audience are thrilled, and when you add music, the excitement rises even higher. If you have a live band or DJ, they can play a lively snippet of music, different in mood, to lead into an item's sale. Musical fanfare keeps everyone engaged and adds that all important ingredient, fun.

To more deeply engage and thank your donors and winning bidders, have exuberant volunteers deliver small gifts to their tables, or bring a mischievous surprise, like a top hat and boa. Be creative. To further provide on-the-spot recognition, use new benefit auction software that allows the auctioneer to see the name of the winning bidder and instantly personalize her thanks.

Generate even more momentum by highlighting your mission. For example, several years ago, I was the auctioneer for a small regional theater that was raising funds for the youth acting troupe. In their upcoming season, they were producing the legendary *Annie*. As their consultant, I suggested that it was vital to showcase the entire youth cast at the auction. Here's what brought the house down. Right before the live auction, I quieted the audience and focused their attention. Intentionally waiting several seconds, building the suspense, the local teen who was playing the lead role as Annie entered from the back of the ballroom. Belting out "The Sun Will Come Out Tomorrow," she wove her way through the audience to the stage. When she climbed the stage steps, the youth acting troupe came out to join her and sang along with the entire audience, "Tomorrow, tomorrow, I love ya, tomorrow. . . ."

To lift off the live auction, I simply said, "Let's show how much you love our youth acting troupe tonight. THAT is why we are here." The live auction was an energetic, fun, and profitable success. And their production of *Annie* sold out quickly to appreciative fans!

Double Double—Dollars and Donors

Doubling a live auction is an oftentimes overlooked fundraising opportunity that has the potential to raise a lot more money. To be strategic, always ask your live auction donors, before the event, if they would consider offering two packages. With a doubled item, you will engage more bidders *and* their supportive friends.

Benefit auctioneers are skilled at doubling your money on live auction items. At one of our charity auctions, the featured live item was a barbecue for 40 people to be served by the board. It sold for $22,000. On the spot, the professional benefit auctioneer went over to the board president, who was standing right up front during the auction, and asked, "Could you find it in your heart to offer a second package?" Of course he said yes. Now, that's making money out of thin air.

When Bigger Is Better—Bid Cards

Bid cards are not the right place to get creative. At a charity auction in California, dedicated volunteers spent untold hours making bid cards out of folding flowered fans for an outdoor event in the evening. They hand-wrote bid numbers on the folding fans using magic markers, which were impossible to read at an outdoor event in the evening in a tent. No doubt, the idea of creating bid cards to double as fans was creative, but it got in the way of the core purpose of the event: raising funds for the organization's mission. Imagine the impact if these same volunteers focused on audience development instead!

Keep bid cards simple. Use white card stock with a black number. If the volunteers who created the fans for bid cards had spent that energy getting a few more qualified people in the room, think about how much more money they could have raised!

The Value of a Live Auctioneer Team

Given your live auction's high revenue goals and guest engagement expectations you may want to consider using professional auctioneer bid assistants. With large audiences or unique venues, your lead auctioneer needs an assistant responsible for engaging the audience and spotting and relaying their bids.

For example, I was lead auctioneer for the Nantucket AIDS Network Gala several years ago. Because there was a crowd of 600 guests, I brought two additional professional auctioneers to assist me. During the live auction, they were both working inside the audience, smiling, creating energy, engaging guests, relaying bids, and paying close personal attention to bidders and non-bidders.

Sara Jessica Parker was the honoree that night, and as I mentioned earlier, she offered a wonderful gift of a script from *Sex and the City* autographed by the entire cast, including Mr. Big. While Sara was on stage with me, we bantered about her show and her commitment to the Nantucket AIDS Network and the cause worldwide.

Bidding for her script quickly reached $8,000, then abruptly stalled. Were we done? Sara wondered aloud. The two top bidders stopped bidding and started talking to friends at their tables. However, by reading the energy in the room and understanding the body language of both guests and my professional auctioneer team members, Steve Schofield and D Byers, I knew we were not anywhere near being done fundraising. (In fact, the bidders were conferring with their friends about the auction item.) Then the top bidder turned to our auctioneer in the audience. Do you know what he whispered? "I can't possibly go more than $21,000." My assistant encouraged him to bid again to support the cause, which set off another round of bidding that ended with a flourish. Sold at

$21,000! That's the power of having professional auctioneer bid assistants. Not only was an additional $13,000 raised, but the guests were entertained and engaged during the spirited bidding contest and inspired by the philanthropy of a beloved celebrity.

Engage Donors in New Ways

Anyone can throw party. Only you can develop relationships with your guests that will help them realize the impact of their gift on your cause. How do you engage auction guests, whip up your live auction, focus on your mission, keep it fresh, get those bid cards waving, and make sure your guests return year after year? After almost 30 years of consulting and auctioneering for all sizes and types of nonprofits, charities, schools, and associations, I've experienced every imaginable live auction situation. Here are six of my favorite strategies so you can turbo-charge your live auction:

1. First and foremost, focus on fundraising! If your event has been planned like someone's dance party and your live auction is an afterthought, you are leaving untold thousands of dollars in the room. However, if you strategically design your benefit auction as a fundraiser and purposefully create a dynamic culture for giving, more funds and goodwill for your nonprofit will be raised. Kingston Tip: Intentionally script brief compelling mission-related remarks for *every* speaker. These remarks should illustrate how you transform the lives of your clients. Inspire your guests to bid high and make a difference. Every one of your guests needs to understand what the funds raised will support, who the funds will benefit, and how your nonprofit makes a difference.

2. Communicate impact before you start the live auction. Insist on making emotionally inspiring remarks (limit to two minutes, maximum) about how your guests' high bids will change lives. Kingston Tip: Immediately before your live auction, remind supporters "Why We're Here!" If you can effectively communicate this, you'll rivet your guests' attention and wrap people's hearts and minds around your mission and seriously increase your guests' generous support. Prepare your auction guests to bid generously!

3. Sell the sizzle. Show an exciting PowerPoint slide for each live auction item. Make sure your guests know exactly what

is being sold. Remember, a confused mind never buys. Your audience won't look at boring or crowded slides. Kingston Tip: Use high-quality photos of what you're selling. Each slide needs the name of the item (its title) and item number. Bidders will memorize the item numbers they're going to bid on, and they often don't pay attention until that item comes up. For trip number 3 to Greece, create a PowerPoint slide with a couple of great pictures (the whitewashed buildings of Mykonos, perhaps) and a few key bullet points. Be sure to include the name of the donor as well. That's all you need on the PowerPoint slide. Use one slide for each item. Locate these visuals strategically, so the audience is facing both the benefit auctioneer and the presentation.

4. Insist on a professional, fundraising-quality sound system. You must also be strategic about placement of the audio speakers. Kingston Tip: Make sure that you place individually powered audio speakers on stands to surround your room, not just at the front of the room. This ensures that everyone in the room can hear your live auction clearly. Plus, your auctioneer needs a dedicated handheld wireless microphone set to his or her voice. Remember to add a good sound system for your silent auction, too—there's a lot of noise in silent auction areas and it's critical that your bidders hear your announcements and understand when the silent auction sections are closing. Not investing in a great sound system is a surefire way to lose money and your guests' attention.

5. Conduct your live auction far earlier than you used to. Don't put the live auction at the end of the evening, or interest will fizzle. To keep the momentum of the auction and narrow the focus, put the live auction earlier. Kingston Tip: Conduct the live auction before dinner or start your live auction during dinner. A lively and energetic live auction makes for inspired bidders who spend their money happily for your cause. However, beware of the dreaded "auction fatigue" that can cause your fundraising auction to be dull and boring and, worst of all, fail to bring in money for your cause. You will recognize auction fatigue. It often occurs when the live auction is scheduled at the end of the event, when your guests are done in. No one can raise money when guests are tired or already heading for their cars!

6. Pre-promote your live auction items. Gone are the days where your guests will automatically come to your auction and bid high. Help your supporters learn about and get excited about your amazing live auction items. Remember, hot items are trips and experiences and that means your guests need to check their calendars and prepare *in advance* of your live auction. Kingston Tip: Create a compelling mini-promotional campaign with personal contacts, e-mails, letters, and social media to stimulate buzz and create competition far before your fundraising event. And remember that *less is more!* Hand-select fewer live auction items with greater value and make sure they match your guests' interests and tastes.

Instant Live Auction Makeover

Here are the six most important things to do immediately to make your live auction successful:

1. Insist that every single person is seated for the live auction and for your inspiring program.
2. Turn up the lights so the auctioneer can see the guests and the guests can see each other.
3. Engage a sound professional who will install speakers on stands that surround your audience.
4. Showcase your live auction items with PowerPoint slides that focus the attention and energy of your audience.
5. Start with compelling and brief (ideally, less than two minutes) remarks to share a "Why We Are Here" and communicate the impact of your auction guests' generous bids.
6. Retain an experienced professional auctioneer who provides consulting and specializes in fundraising and benefit auctions.

Note

1. Katie Banzhaf, personal communication, October 29, 2014.

13

Ignite Generosity with Fund-a-Need Special Appeals

I'd like to tell you a true story—my story. My name is Taylor Robinson. We are here right now to raise as much money as we can for Boston Gay Men's Chorus. I grew up in rural South Carolina, in a very conservative county—a hard place to grow up gay.

So coming out as gay when I started college meant that I lost everything. My college roommate, who I had known since I was four years old, moved out without saying goodbye. I had already lost my childhood home to foreclosure. When I came out, I lost my parents too.

After college, I moved to Boston for a full-time job. I was alone. I looked for a way to get involved and to make friends. Finally, a friend told me about the Boston Gay Men's Chorus. I nervously auditioned and was accepted. For the first time, I had unconditional love and support. There were 175 people who cared about me. It was the first time that I felt like I had a family that accepted me for who I am. The chorus taught me how to express myself and be *myself*.

And now, by supporting the chorus, *you*—every single person here tonight—are giving a home to celebrate each other, and without BGMC, that space will not exist.

And that is the power of the Boston Gay Men's Chorus. The magical power of music to heal hearts and minds and to promote respect and understanding.

And as you can imagine, there are so many others who are just like me, who need your generous support—right now. That's why we are here, to raise as much money so we can to do this transformational work together! I cannot ever do enough to repay the Boston Gay Men's Chorus for all they have given me, and I hope that by sharing my story, you will consider doing the same. Thank you in advance for your generosity.[1]

Taylor's heartfelt true story inspired a standing ovation and record fundraising for the Boston Gay Men's Chorus during their fund-a-need special appeal that night. In the moment after his story, as their auctioneer, I invited the entire audience to consider making a contribution at any level that was meaningful to them. The result was a generous outpouring of record-breaking donations and the high point of the entire event! What a superb way to communicate impact; Boston Gay Men's Chorus creates musical experiences to inspire change, build community and celebrate difference.

Double Your Income in 10 Minutes

This chapter dives deeply into one of the most lucrative and exciting strategies to raise funds at *any* event, even if you are not holding an auction.

Consider Fund-a-Need Special Appeals

Did you know that there's a way to equal or more than double your live auction revenue in just minutes? The fund-a-need special appeal often exceeds the revenue generated in live auctions. It's a hugely rewarding and powerful technique to raise exponential funds in a manner of minutes.

The fund-a-need is one of the newest and most exciting parts of a live auction. Also called a special appeal, fund-a-cause, or paddle raise, this is a powerful technique you can use at any fundraising event. Conducted as part of the live auction, it's the number one way to raise money today. This new and profitable auction revenue stream gives your guests an opportunity to raise their bid cards for a special project, a service, or a facility that your charity really needs. It also gives your guests a chance to make a tax-deductible cash contribution.

What types of special projects might be appropriate for a fund-a-need? It could be a playground for children at a homeless shelter or scholarships for low-income kids to go to college. It could be a program to teach entrepreneurial skills to at-risk youth. It could be to support hospice volunteers or create a new technology center for an elementary school.

You name it.

Inspire Generosity and Goodwill

Unlike the silent and live auctions, which involve competitive bidding, the fund-a-need promotes collaborative giving, which is very powerful. Bidding starts at a higher level and decreases in increments to a lower level, giving everyone an opportunity to give, make a difference, and feel great about doing it. This is a wonderful way to inspire giving and get the message out in a very interactive and compelling way.

Research conducted by the National Auctioneers Foundation shows that the fund-a-need can yield more revenue than a live auction.[2] Today more than ever, it's critical to have guests at your benefit auction event who have the capacity to give generously in the fund-a-need. Because not everyone wants or needs a silent or live auction item, the fund-a-need offers all guests a superb way to support your cause.

The most important thing you can do in fund-a-need is to have a compelling and inspiring first-person story told in 59 seconds. I call this the "Kathy Kingston 59-Second Pitch." You want your guests to be riveted so they get behind your cause. A compelling first-person story is a true story told from the heart. Immediately following the story, the benefit auctioneer invites guests to participate at a level that is meaningful to them.

What the Fund-a-Need Looks Like

Usually, the fund-a-need is introduced during the live auction. But you can successfully use a fund-a-need at any event to maximize inspired giving. It begins with brief, inspiring remarks, typically a first-person testimonial underscoring a specific appeal. The auctioneer uses the testimonial to encourage guests to bid at a level that is meaningful to them. Unlike a regular auction, the fund-a-need starts high and, level by level, goes lower. The auctioneer calls out each bid number at the amount on which it was bid, and this is recorded by the auction recorder or the clerk. In a matter of minutes, many thousands of dollars are raised, and everyone feels great.

Nonprofits that don't include this very effective fundraising technique in their events can lose tens of thousands of dollars. They're literally letting money walk out the door. Across the country, benefit auctioneers and nonprofit leaders are seeing a trend. Bidding in silent and live auctions is all over the map. Sometimes bidding is up, sometimes it's down, sometimes it's flat, and sometimes there are great increases in the silent and live auctions. The fund-a-need is the one benefit auction revenue stream that is consistently financially strong.

How to Raise as Much Money as Possible

Let's look at auction night. Envision your benefit auction event. You have several hundred guests in the room, a handful of live items, and a multitude of silent items. Here's the big question: How can you ensure that you raise as much money in as little time as possible? Engage your guests to contribute and demonstrate right then and there, with the force of a laser beam, exactly how these funds are going to benefit your cause.

The fund-a-need does just that.

What's in a Name?

The fund-a-need has many other names. It's also called fund-an-item, fund-a-mission, fund-a-cause, fund-a-dream, fund-the-hope, and fund-the-scholar. Generically, it's called a special appeal or a paddle raise. You might even hear it called an emotional appeal. As you design your event, you may create your own name. Make sure the name makes sense to you and your guests. "Fund" is an important part of the name because it's an active verb and it's incredibly self-explanatory. "Fund" is also important because at events, guests are enjoying adult beverages and they are in a social climate, not a business meeting. "Fund" is specific and will hold their attention. What follows "fund" is really up to you. For example, if your appeal is for scholarships, you might name it fund-the-future.

Great Fund-a-Need Ideas

Here's a list of proven fund-a-need ideas:

- Scholarships of all kinds
- A new stove for the soup kitchen
- A new technology center with computers for a school
- An outreach program for theater that includes performances and classes for at-risk youth
- An expansion of a music program for people living with autism
- A new entry kennel for dogs at an animal rescue league
- Camper-ships for a kids' space camp
- Funding for mammograms and breast health care for low-income women
- Professional development for teachers at a school serving students living with disabilities
- Dance and movement expression classes, including performances to local area schools
- Matching funds for Big Brothers and Big Sisters to offset a long waiting list
- Expansion funding for a fatherhood training program for fathers just released from prison
- Cutting-edge augmented communication devices for people living with disabilities
- Expanded after-school activities at a Boys and Girls Club
- A premiere of a new choral work
- Counseling programs for homeless veterans

One of the most unique, poignant, and successful fund-a-need appeals I've ever conducted was for a wildlife rehabilitation program for youth at a residential school for children with emotional disabilities. The children would learn by caring for the animals and bringing *them* back to health. As their compelling fund-a-need video ended with a rehabilitated juvenile eagle taking flight, hearts and donations soared.

What all fund-a-needs have in common is that they are achievable, exciting, and emotional. The most critical quality of a fund-a-need is that the money raised goes to a specific program.

The Secret Ingredient

Penelope Burk's work on donor-centered fundraising teaches us that it's important to communicate the impact of the donor's gift at a fundraising auction.[3] An inspiring story that captures your audience and motivates generous giving is the key ingredient for fund-a-need success.

Communicate Emotionally

Getting to the emotional level of your organization's cause is what really resonates with people and gets them to donate. Test this out by asking, "So what?" If someone says, "I'm going to be funding a scholarship program at our school," say, "So what?" That forces her to dig deeper and explain why scholarships are so important for students. What are the end results she is trying to achieve? There are so many different needs.

This exercise is good to bring back to your auction committee. It underscores the inspirational quote attributed to Maya Angelou: "People are going to forget what you said, and they're going to forget what you did, but they're never going to forget how you made them feel."[4] You are underscoring the emotion behind your "ask" and building relationships with your donors.

Characteristics of a Successful Fund-a-Need

It may sound silly, but engaging a lot of people in the decision-making about the fund-a-need item is important. If the decision about what the fund-a-need will benefit is made unilaterally by the president, the board, or your development director, you will miss an important opportunity to generate enthusiasm for the fund-a-need. Involve your committee members in the decision-making process, and you're much more likely to have a successful fund-a-need.

Meeting a Clear Need

Select a fund-a-need item that works. Ask yourself and your team what your organization needs most, right now. Do you need to expand an existing program? Have you been planning a new program or service? Do you have partial funding for a new facility and need more funding? Make sure you choose something that works for everyone involved.

Committee Decision Making

First, facilitate rich discussions about the fund-a-need with committee members. This way you will get the best fund-a-need item. Here's why. Some people will say, "That's great," even though they're not excited. You are waiting for the moment, and it will come, when everyone says, "That's it!" There is an emotional engagement and an exciting connection at that moment, and when you have that as part of a very rich discussion, you know you've got a winner.

Committee Engagement

Because everyone on the committee has participated in the decision-making about the fund-a-need, they feel a sense of ownership, which gives you a built-in base of support. It's likely that your lead gift for the fund-a-need will come from someone who is in the meeting when the fund-a-need item is identified, or from someone who knows someone who can give the lead gift.

An Easy-to-Understand "Ask"

It's important that your guests are able to understand the fund-a-need "ask" in a nanosecond. If it's difficult to explain your project or it's too complex, the fund-a-need probably won't be successful, because there's a short amount of time for giving. People understand emotion. If you want the fund-a-need to be engaging, the "ask" has to touch your guests' hearts. If your need is boring, you'll raise a bit of money, but you won't cross the threshold to huge support.

Fund the Entire Project

You can absolutely fund the entire project during the fund-a-need. If you're thinking, "We're going to add some money to our capital campaign," or "We're going to raise funds for staff pay," your fund-a-need is not going to be successful. Why not? Because guests are going to be thinking, "What difference can I make?" A great fund-a-need creates energy and concern that if guests don't give, the project will not happen. That's the exciting portion of it. Select a fund-a-need project that can absolutely happen. It takes a little bit of forecasting, but make sure guests want to fund the whole project.

For example, if you're going to build a playground, there are a variety of costs (e.g., design, site selection, materials, and maintenance). Make sure you raise enough funds to sustain your project for two to three years, especially if it's a new program. Why? If this is a brand-new activity and you don't get funding the following year, the program will go away. That's the last thing you want to have happen with a fund-a-need.

Showing Donors That Their Gifts Made a Difference

Make sure you can finish the project with the funds you raise that night, because here's the best thing that can happen. Six to eight months after your benefit auction event, send everyone a postcard with a picture of the new stove and commercial-grade fan in the soup kitchen, and in that picture make sure there are people cooking a big, free meal for hungry families. Showing your donors a picture of the results will cause them to say, "Wow, that worked. I wonder what they're going to do next year. I can't wait to be involved and to bring my friends!"

After a fund-a-need to preserve and expand the heritage garden at Strawbery Banke Museum, a 10-acre outdoor American history museum, the auction committee brilliantly mailed a hand-written thank you note to each donor with a photograph of the stunning garden in full bloom. Such gestures make your guests feel good about their contributions. Even guests who gave at a very basic level for the garden felt great about perpetuating this world class garden and understood first hand that without their funds, the garden wouldn't exist. That's part of the amazing energy of collective giving in the fund-a-need.

Why You Need a Professional Benefit Auctioneer

The biggest gift your benefit auctioneer can give is to hold the moment and maintain the emotional undercurrent in the audience throughout the fund-a-need. This is an advanced skill. The benefit auctioneer memorizes the script for the fund-a-need just in case the speaker forgets to make key points. A benefit auctioneer can fill in details. She can remind the audience why they are here and hit other key elements about the cause to make sure that the audience is totally connected to the mission. One of the biggest compliments a guest ever gave me was, "I thought you worked for the organization."

Preparing Your Fund-a-Need Speaker

Practice, run through, and rehearse the fund-a-need. If you tell people you're going to do a rehearsal, you can count on them panicking. Instead, tell them, "We're going to do a run-through." That sounds less threatening. How do you do a run-through? Insist that anyone who is going to hold a microphone must come early and do a sound check. The sound check ensures that the speaker knows where he will stand, and when he will start speaking and exit. The speaker can also practice how he is going to hold the microphone. It's important for your sound specialists to get a level check for the speaker so that they know how to adjust the sound board for him.

The Run-Through Required

Practice never makes perfect. Perfect practice makes perfect. When you're working with a speaker who will tell his story as part of your fund-a-need pitch, remind him that the fund-a-need is the pinnacle fundraising moment of the event. The success of fund-a-need pivots on the outstanding delivery of his story. Now, if you exactly say that to any speaker, some will be encouraged and inspired, but most people will get nervous. Your job is to prepare your speaker.

Ask the speaker to come early, dressed and ready to go. Be specific: "Arrive at 5:30, dressed and ready to go, and meet us on the left side of the stage. We'll review where to go, when to come up, how to use the microphone. We'll be having you go through your remarks on the microphone, which we call a sound check."

Finally, remind your speaker to practice at home and to read though his remarks several times prior to coming for a run-through. One technique that works is to have your speaker practice with you on the phone several times, a week or so prior to the auction. It makes a big difference. As part of my consulting services, I help write the speaker's story and coach the practice sessions, on the phone and in person.

Kathy's Coaching Tips for a Successful "Ask"

Here are my B.E.S.T. techniques for speaking.

B: Breathe. Be brief. Take a breath. Relax.
E: Eat the microphone. It's absolutely imperative that when you're speaking, you hold the microphone really close to your mouth. (When I'm coaching kids as speakers, I remind them that the mic needs to be as close as an ice cream cone.)

S: Slow down. The run-through is the perfect time to make sure that the speaker makes his or her remarks slowly. Getting the pacing right is essential.

T: Take a pause. Sometimes silence is more powerful than a lot of words, especially when we want to hold the moment— when a particularly emotional or inspiring point has been made as part of a story.

First-person testimonial remarks can be powerfully moving. Make sure that if the speaker says something really stirring and inspiring, he or she knows to pause, take a breath, and let the words sink in for the audience. Be sure the remarks are written out based on the structure of a story. Have the speaker read it 10 times before the run-through. Then, have the speaker practice in front of a mirror so it flows naturally. When the speaker comes early to the benefit auction event, the run-through and sound check will raise his or her comfort level even higher.

The Lead Gift

It's crucial to have a presecured lead gift. Let's say you are trying to raise $50,000 for an outreach program for kids to become mentors. First of all, don't tell the audience you're going to raise $50,000. Instead, say, "We're going to raise as much money as we can." If you say a number, it can create a false feeling of limitation. Don't limit yourself. Open up the opportunity for your guests to give as much as possible. To do this, have a lead gift, which is the highest level bid you can presecure. The bids that follow the lead gift go from high to low in predictable increments. If you have a $5,000 lead gift, you could ask everyone to bid at $5,000, $2,500, $1,000, $500, $250, $100, and then $50. Sometimes, you'll want to go as low as $25, because you want to promote the message, "Together we can all do it, whether you can give $25 or $2,500 or $250." This is not the time for public-television-style fundraising, which is incredibly powerful in that arena, but does not apply to a fund-a-need.

There are other presecured gifts, such as matching gifts and incentive matching gifts, that leverage giving at specific levels. It's important to note that the giving levels should always start high and then move down by increments.

Matching gifts are magical to generate excitement and giving. Matching gifts can be for the entire amount raised or for a portion of the funds raised. Be sure to inquire ahead of time exactly how your donor would like to be recognized and incorporate that recognition into your donor recognition for the auction and your follow-up after the event. Additional matching-gift opportunities also come from corporations and small businesses who will match their employees' charitable gifts. Be sure to research, promote, and feature this opportunity for your fundraising event and all aspects of your entire organization's development plan.

Add a new *incentive match* at your lowest level of giving for the fund-a-need. Strategically, you want to leverage even the lowest level of giving to create a spirit of gratitude and excitement and finish with excitement and great goodwill. I can still hear the cheering and feel the joy at the Boys and Girls Club of Greater Lowell as 75 bid cards flew in the air when I announced we had a $5,000 matching gift at our final level of $100, surpassing all expectations.

At the Sonoma Harvest Wine Auction, we knew we had a $50,000 incentive match at the $1,000 level. To our surprise, a well-known local vintner stood up in that moment and doubled their match to $100,000. Dozens and dozens more bid cards skyrocketed us to an astonishing new level of donor engagement.

Visuals during the Fund-a-Need

I recommend that you have a PowerPoint slide behind the speaker during the fund-a-need session. Don't have anything on the screen while the speaker is making the brief inspirational remarks. Everyone needs to be watching and listening to her story. When you are making the "ask," it's a great time to have slides that exemplify your need and why you are raising funds.

No **Envelope, Please …**

There are some practices that just don't work in a fund-a-need. Avoid these missteps:

- Don't lay out envelopes and wait for bids.
- Avoid long speeches right before the fund-a-need.
- Don't show a video, medical slides, or graphics of statistics about a particular disease. They are not inspiring.
- Cancel any remarks that are not emotionally engaging and fall flat.
- Test and fix a bad sound system.
- Make sure the lights are turned up.
- Focus a distracted audience and wait until they're riveted.

A Long-Term Strategy

At a benefit auction event, the fund-a-need is a great technique for raising funds for a specific need and engaging the audience at all levels of bidding. But the fund-a-need is also an essential part of your long-term fundraising strategy. Create a plan to integrate it into your organization's strategy. Include your board, development committee, and auction committee in the plan.

Eight Key Points for a Successful Fund-a-Need

Here are the eight key points to remember for a highly successful fund-a-need:

1. Engage your entire board and committee when you're deciding what could be funded. My experience has shown me time and time again that those who participate in the decision-making process about the fund-a-need become its most generous donors.
2. Make your fund-a-need understandable. Remember, many of your guests may be enjoying adult beverages.

3. Make the fund-a-need's goal achievable.
4. Invest in an experienced professional benefit auctioneer who has successfully conducted fund-a-need appeals.
5. Select a compelling speaker who can make heartfelt, inspiring remarks and tell a compelling story.
6. Keep the pitch brief. Make it about 59 seconds.
7. Create giving levels. Have a lead gift. Start high and go low to create a dynamic climate for giving.
8. Design the fund-a-need so that everything focuses on how people can be involved for long-term giving. Make the fund-a-need a true catalyst for long-term giving. Invite everyone who has participated to become involved in your other events. Ask them to participate again and again. Ask them to be involved on the boards or committees. Figure out unique ways that your organization can leverage their support.

I was consulting with the supporters of a small art museum about their fund-a-need. When I explained how powerful a presecured $5,000 leadership gift would be to generate a culture of giving, the committee said point blank, "No one here has *that* kind of money," and grimly stared at me.

I took a moment and then asked each person why they cared about the museum. As each person shared something they loved about art, history, culture, and the wonderful architectural space, one woman began crying. She said, "I am so upset that we just raised all this money for our new wing, we've filled it with beautiful art and even trained our docents. But just last week, the school district cut funding for bus transportation to field trips, so any hope of bringing our schoolchildren to the museum is lost."

The entire group was deflated. I asked if having extra funds for bus transportation might be a worthwhile need for the fund-a-need. No one said a word for several minutes. Then all at once, the same woman who was so upset, said: "Yes, I love that idea, and I will give the lead gift of $5,000!" She felt great about her gift, leveraging others to be generous, too.

The fund-a-need at the auction raised more than enough to fund buses for every schoolchild to visit the museum and take advantage of its new programs. The lesson here is, involve as many people as possible and always ask for a lead gift.

Conclusion

In the past few years, the fund-a-need portion of auctions has raised more money than live auctions. If you are volunteering with a nonprofit organization or you are an auctioneer working with a group that doesn't have a fund-a-need, add it to your benefit auction event. It's available to everyone. Because you have different levels of giving, it's inclusive, and think about how you can successfully integrate it into your long-term fundraising plans. Guests are giving, but they're giving more strategically. In the words of Sir Winston Churchill, "We make a living by what we get, and we make a life by what we give."

Notes

1. Taylor Robinson, personal communication, May 10, 2014. The name Taylor Robinson is a pseudonym as requested during the communication. The story is true.
2. N. Saffer and K. A. Kingston, "Trends in Fundraising for the Benefit Auctioneer," session presented at the International Auctioneer Conference & Show, Orlando, FL, June 2011.
3. P. Burk, *The Burk Donor Survey: Where Philanthropy Is Headed in 2013* (Chicago: Cygnus Applied Research, 2013).
4. R. L. Evans, *Quote Book by Richard L. Evans* (Salt Lake City, UT: Publishers Press, 1971).

14

Add Strategic Income Streams
(…and Fun)

I'LL NEVER FORGET THE MOMENT—The auction venue full of teachers, and they all leapt up at once when first-grade teacher Courtney's name was drawn to win the Pot of Gold. "You just won a credit of $10,000 to be used tonight at the live auction and fund-a-need." I was the auctioneer for Nashoba Learning Group's annual gala auction.

"But this can't be! I didn't buy a ticket. I couldn't afford the $100 chance," Courtney wondered out loud.

Susan Parziale, a parent, ran over to me and grabbed the microphone. "Courtney, we love how you help our kids, and we bought you a ticket! Enjoy!"

Bidding escalated each time Courtney raised her bid card, her hand, or even her eyebrow. Other guests were "enthusiastically helping" her expend her winnings. Prices rose and fun soared. Determined to win the Tuscany trip for her honeymoon, she had to spend almost double its value, leaving only $3,000 in her Pot of Gold. Parents and alumni drummed on the tables.

Cheering erupted as Courtney took top bid in a fierce battle for a 12-guest stay at the principal's lake home. After she won, Courtney called me over and said, "I won this for our teachers. We're all going together!" The room was buzzing with goodwill and laughter.

With a mere $600 left, her unspent balance would automatically go into the fund-a-need. The final item, a romance weekend package at a luxury hotel with gourmet dinner and breakfast in bed, stalled at $400. Right before I said, "Sold," Courtney jumped up and yelled, "$600! Mr. and Mrs. Parziale, that's for you, and I'll babysit your kids!"

Make Every Minute a Revenue Minute!

Strategically, it's vital to include additional revenue-generating activities to diversify your income streams. The three main revenue streams at fundraising auction events are silent auctions, live auctions, and fund-a-need special appeals. But organizations would *still* be leaving lots of money in the room without pots of gold, raffles, wine pulls, heads and tails, golden tickets, and all the other activities offered in this chapter. These extra revenue generators, sometimes called "auction icebreakers," can become a cherished piece of your auction event. The best part is, they exponentially increase the fun factor!

Planned Spontaneity and Profits

At most fundraising auctions and events, there's a wide socioeconomic mix. Many guests who attend don't want, don't need, or can't afford to bid on a big-ticket auction item. But they do want to contribute and participate, and to have fun, too. By strategically placing a few carefully selected additional revenue activities into the event, an organization can engage everyone at a level that is comfortable for them.

You can't wait for people to create ways to contribute more or to have fun at your event. It's up to you to strategically and intentionally build those interactive revenue generators directly into your show flow. Think about these activities as creative ways to build relationships with your supporters. From an audience engagement perspective, your guests will connect in ways they would not have otherwise. Do you think parents and teachers will ever forget the generosity of the Parziale family or Courtney, their teacher, that night at the school auction? Guests still talk about the fun of helping to break records at that exciting auction more than five years ago.

These are not just lighthearted opportunities to raise funds. You are creating a whole new social dynamic with these activities, stimulating audience interaction while more deeply connecting guests to your cause. Plus, you make it easy for your guests to get to know each other and to share a communal, cathartic experience while raising money for a cause they love. From a donor development standpoint, it's this kind of meaningful, exciting engagement that builds loyalty.

Add More Fun

People spend more money when they're enjoying themselves. And fun is an important factor in the success of your benefit auction events. Why? Recently, the National Auctioneers Association (NAA) commissioned a national study by Morpace, a market research and consulting company, to identify why people attend any type of auction (i.e., benefit, real estate, antique). The results showed that 92 percent of the respondents identified "fun" as their reason for attending auctions.[1] Americans *love* auctions. In this chapter, we'll discuss how you can use income stream strategies to add more of that fun, and increase revenue and audience engagement at the same time. As Katharine Hepburn famously quipped, "If you obey all the rules, you miss all the fun."

Figure 14.1 The Benefit Auction Brain
Source: © 2014 Kathy Kingston. All Rights Reserved.

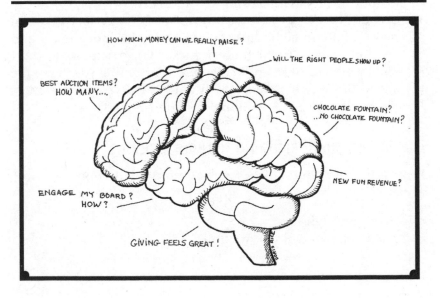

Research shows that play is important throughout a lifetime. Including interactive games in your benefit auction gives guests opportunities to play together, and that will relax them, make them feel closer to each other, enhance their enjoyment of the experience, and encourage greater generosity. According to Stuart Brown, MD, founder of the National Institute for Play, "Nothing lighs up the brain like play. Three-dimensional play fires up the cerebellum, puts a lot of impulses in the frontal lobe—the execution portion—helps contextual memory be developed…"[2] This means that you can have fun, generate revenue, *and* create a meaningful and memorable event that promotes future giving (see Figure 14.1).

Kingston Trio of Benefits

When I'm consulting with a nonprofit or school, I highlight innovative benefits of generating new income streams, using something I call the "Kingston Trio." Here are three significant benefits to your fundraiser auction event. When you're working with your auction committee and they ask, "Why would we add more activities?" you can offer these key reasons.

- First, they're *interactive* because they stir energy, fun, and deepen engagement among the audience.
- Second, they're *inclusive.* They make everyone feel they can make a difference because you're offering a price point and an interest level at which every guest can participate.
- Finally, these games are *income-producing*, lifting your revenue above the grand total from traditional core profit centers (silent auctions, live auctions, and fund-a-need).

Fresh, Fun, and Profitable Income Streams

Here are a few fun activities to consider as additional income streams.

- Heads-and-Tails
- The Grab Bag Balloon Auction

- Premium Dessert Frenzy
- Auction Chicken
- Signup Board
- Gift Card Frenzy
- Centerpiece Auction
- Silent Auction
- Special Line Raffle
- Golden Ticket
- Pot of Gold
- Wild Card Auctions
- Mini-Live Auctions
- Make-It-Mine Boards

The Kathy Kingston Disclaimer: Less is More!

Even though there are countless fun revenue-producing activities you can include in your benefit auction events to maximize fundraising, you cannot do them all in one event. In other words, less is more. Remember, these activities are a sideshow; don't let them swallow up your circus. Do not create "bidder fatigue" in your guests. Be strategic and preserve their energy and generosity for your main fundraising—your live auction and fund-a-need. As you think about additional income producing activities, pick just one or two for your next event. After you use them, let them rest and try a few new ones. By rotating revenue-generating activities each year, you can keep things fresh. Then these interactive activities will continue to grab your guests' attention and produce significant additional revenue.

Heads-and-Tails

Heads-and-Tails is a fun coin-flip game of chance. It's a terrific opportunity for people to have fun and participate at a low price point, such as $20. This is a game of chance. The tickets to play are sold during the silent auction, when volunteers go around to each guest and ask them to pay to play, explaining that the winner of Heads-and-Tails gets a grand prize.

Let's say the grand prize is tickets for two anywhere American Airlines flies in the United States. If you have 200 people in your audience, you might get 50 percent participation in Heads-and-Tails the first time. Every year, that number will increase, because it's so much fun to play. But even if only 100 guests buy tickets to play at $20 each, that totals $2,000. That's pretty good fundraising!

From a strategic perspective, Heads-and-Tails is an excellent way to engage all of your guests, whether they are participating or watching. It's fun and energizing and a great way to involve maximum guests for a modest price and big results. And the shift in mood will carry through the rest of the evening.

The Mystery Grab Bag

The Grab Bag or, as they say in Ireland, the Lucky Dip, is a game of mystery. It's a fixed-price game, using something clever like a balloon, a mystery box, or a glass of champagne. There are countless ways to be creative. At school auctions, for example, they often use chocolate rulers with stickers on the bottom, cleverly titled: "Chocolate Rules."

The advantage of Grab Bag is that you can sell something for a fixed price and have one prize, or you can use the Grab Bag to get 100 percent of the value of one of your silent auction items. When you analyze all of your lower-priced silent auction items, you don't really want items such as a $35 gift certificate to take up valuable space in your silent auction. Instead of including 30 to 50 lower-valued items in the silent auction, get their full value by including them in the Grab Bag. The Grab Bag offers a way to preserve valuable venue real estate in the silent auction for high-value and high-interest auction items, while maximizing the money you raise on lower-value silent auction items.

Premium Dessert Frenzy

Imagine five amazing, scrumptious, sexy, desirable desserts selling in the live auction for ridiculous amounts of money. If your benefit auction event is in a hotel where outside food is prohibited, ask the chef to make three of his favorite and most amazing desserts. Do the Premium Dessert Frenzy in a live auction to keep energy going. Here are some ideas. Consider a 10-layer "death-by-chocolate" cake, or a theme dessert such as a two-foot cake of the Eiffel Tower for the Evening in Paris Gala Auction; or a creatively decorated cake covered with the Autism Speaks logo at the Nashoba Learning Center Auction; or a signature tiramisu made by a beloved volunteer at your gala themed, Under the Tuscan Sun. Mmm. What would you bid to win your weight in chocolate, complete with a wheelbarrow full of beautifully wrapped chocolates? Get super creative!

How Much Dough? More Fundraising Dessert Examples

At the GALE Fund benefit auction in Cape Cod, I sold the most amazing eight-layer coconut cake ever, made by board member Richard Johnson. It was extremely heavy because it was loaded with butter. At the auction, it brought $270, and the table that won it was ecstatic. After it was delivered to their table, they started enjoying it. Then the backup bidder said, "Hey, I'll give you $270 if I can have *just one piece*." The crowd went crazy! It was loads of fun for everyone.

How about $550 for three vials of chocolate foam: white, milk, and dark chocolate. Cha-ching! Oh, what about that five-foot-tall Eiffel Tower cake? Our professional auctioneer June DeLair dropped the hammer at $700 at the Dream Come True Auction in Connecticut—ooh la la!

Everyone Wants Dessert

No worries, everyone still gets dessert. The Premium Dessert Frenzy does not *replace* dessert after the live auction. It's just a way to call attention to everyone's desire for an incredible, special, over-the-top delicious dessert. And that desire builds energy. Imagine raising $550 for three vials of chocolate foam!

The Premium Dessert Frenzy engages people who are not bidding, and its energy carries through the end of the auction, keeping the excitement high. Mostly, it's a lot of fun! Make sure you hide the desserts. Don't leave them on a table in the auction or on a table in the kitchen. Hide them. Otherwise people think it's a dessert buffet! Twice in my experience, desserts were consumed before the Premium Dessert Frenzy. Avoid that disaster by hiding your premium desserts.

Auction Chicken

Auction Chicken is a great interactive revenue-generating activity that can help you power through the live auction. Pick an item that's universally appealing and fun. Use the same criteria for prizes that you use in Heads-and-Tails. From a strategic perspective, you make it easy and fun for 100 percent of your guests to participate at a level that is meaningful to them. Plus, Auction Chicken keeps everybody awake and energized.

Start the bidding on a live auction item at just $1 and ask every single person to participate. Auction Chicken is inclusive, and it's fun for everybody who participates. The important thing is that you engage everyone. Be sure to have a photographer take pictures of your audience playing Auction Chicken. Imagine a photograph of every single guest at your benefit auction event with their bid cards in the air, smiling. This is *the* photo to tweet and post to Facebook during the auction, run in your newsletter, and display on your website.

Party Boards

Party Boards, sometimes called Signup Boards, are fun and lucrative. What if you had someone willing to host a lobster bake for 25 people at their home? What if you had a poker party and scotch tasting for 20 or 50 guests? How about a wine tasting and tour for 50 couples? What about a Ladies Latin Night for 60 moms at the Montessori school, complete with margaritas, Latin dancing, and Mexican food? These are all examples of creative parties you can sell during your cocktail hour and silent auction by using Party Boards. It's a unique and successful way for people who don't know anyone to get involved in the organization. It's also a great way to promote bidding for guests who are looking for an exciting group experience.

How do you decide if the item should go into the live auction or be a Party Board? From a strategic perspective, Party Board experiences involve a large number of participants, so they may be a harder sell in the live auction. Experiences with many guests lend themselves well to a Party Board sales strategy, because even a single guest or one couple can join the group and feel part of your organization.

Gift Card Frenzy

Gift cards waste space in your silent auction and often only yield 30–60 percent of their value. Collect all the gift cards and sell them at the opening of your live auction in a wild froth of happy bidders, all of them competing to be the first and most enthusiastic person to raise his or her bid card to pay 100 percent of the value! Here's another strategic twist on gift cards. Create a Gift Card "Make It Mine" display board. Offer each gift certificate at face value. Be sure to recruit and train gregarious volunteers to promote this board throughout the event for maximum audience engagement.

Centerpiece Auctions

There are many different ways to cash in on centerpieces. Regardless of how you sell centerpieces, it's important that you script your auctioneer so he or she knows to announce what you intend to do with your centerpieces and when you will offer them. There are several ways to raise more money from your centerpieces. Rather than just giving them away, try selling them—at a fixed price or, more creatively, in a mini-auction.

At a "guest centerpiece auction," one designated guest at every table auctions the centerpiece to their tablemates all at once, live auction style. Offer incentive gifts for your highest bidding table and your top centerpiece auctioneer. Sometimes your professional auctioneer can warm up all of your guests in group participation with a favorite tongue twister, like "Rubber baby buggy bumper." Strategically, consider this ice-breaker when you have extra time for fun and excitement and you need unique audience engagement.

Silent Auction Green Line Auction

Incentivize silent auction bidding by creating a raffle for anyone who bids on the green line of the bid sheet. This promotes philanthropic giving by teaching your guests to skip lines and go directly to higher bid increments. Instead of bidding in a traditional manner (e.g., $5, $10, $15, $20), bidders go directly to 80 percent! The green line is typically 80 percent of an item's value. For all who bid at that level, hold a quick raffle for a special prize to be drawn at the end of the event.

Golden Ticket

The Golden Ticket winner can select anything from the live auction. Volunteers sell tickets during your cocktail hour and silent auction. The Golden Ticket is a raffle, so make sure you get your raffle license in order. Because this is a raffle, have great volunteers selling the tickets. This can create a lot of energy, especially if you have a live auction item that's really hot! You'll have to do the math to figure that out. Let's say you are selling the Golden Ticket during the silent auction for $50. If the highest-selling live auction item is $5,000, you have to sell at least 100 tickets. Here's an interesting downside of Golden Ticket. If your winner selects an auction item that everyone wants and thereby removes it from the auction, you may disappoint your guests and introduce a negative element at the beginning of your event. Be sure to weigh all the options.

Pot of Gold

In the Pot of Gold raffle, a limited number of tickets are sold. Most commonly, 100 tickets are sold at $100 apiece, for a total of $10,000. The winner then has up to $10,000 in credit that must be used during the live auction and/or fund-a-need. As they'd do with a Golden Ticket, volunteers sell Pot of Gold tickets during the silent auction. The benefit of the Pot of Gold is that your winning ticket holder is not taking an item out of the live auction. Instead, she is given a credit for the amount sold in Pot of Gold, which she can use in the live auction, fund-a-need, or both. Pot of Gold energizes the audience, is a lot of fun, and gives a guest an immediate cash allowance. (Note: This raffle is for a "credit" and not for cash. Be sure to check your state raffle laws and always secure a raffle or gaming permit.)

Wild Card Auction

Sometimes people come up to me at a benefit auction and say something like, "I wish I knew you needed live auction items. I'll offer a week at my vacation home at the Jersey shore." The Wild Card Auction gives guests an opportunity to offer another live auction item with one of the special Wild Cards waiting on their tables. Extra excitement equals extra funds!

Mini Live Auction

The Mini Live Auction is a special section in the silent auction that includes items that could have gone into the live auction. The Mini Live Auction is the final section to close before guests are seated for the program. It starts out with the last silent bid and then finishes live auction style, right on the spot.

A Word on Raffles

Before all else, check your local and state regulations on raffles and charitable gaming. Be sure to get advice from your legal counsel and tax advisors before you proceed.

Are raffles right for auctions? Most of the time I'd say not so much. Here's my perspective. When your benefit auction guests participate in a raffle, you create a certain mindset: "What can I get? With this, I don't have to pay much, and I can take a chance at winning something." I call this the "raffle mentality," and it has absolutely no connection to your cause. In fact, the raffle mentality is the polar opposite of the "philanthropic mentality" you're shooting for. You want your guests to be so inspired that they're thinking, "How much can I give? How can I make an impact for a cause that I love? How can I make a difference?"

If you're thinking about including a raffle in your auction, there are three ways to make it successful. First, do the math to determine if a raffle will raise enough money to be worth all of your time and effort. Calculate how much you can actually raise before you begin. Second, get organized and train an army of raffle-selling volunteers. The best are gregarious, positive people who know how to positively and consistently engage your guests, and won't be standing in the corner talking to their friends. Third, you must have raffle prizes your guests actually want, not just left-overs from your silent auction.

Great Fundraiser Warm-Ups

Warm-ups are a great way to start a benefit auction by selling nothing, absolutely nothing, and making sure that your guests understand your organization's cause. Warm-ups promote the concept that it's not what you get, but how much you can give. Imagine selling a glass of water. What about selling a $10 bill for $550?

At a benefit auction for the Food Bank, I sold a can of Campbell's tomato soup for over $1,000. Another time, I sold a deflated balloon that floated by my feet during the live auction for $500. Warm-ups are about energizing the audience for good-natured competition and philanthropic bidding. And warm-ups are great ways to remind everybody, "It's not what you get, but what you give that counts to make a difference."

Notes

1. Morpace, National "Auction Industry Holds Strong in 2008 with $268.5 Billion in Sales," auction industry survey, 2008. www.exclusivelyauctions.com/pdfs/naa-2008.pdf.
2. Stuart Brown, *TED TALK: Play Is More Than Just Fun.* Retrieved from www.ted.com/talks/stuart_brown_says_play_is_more_than_fun_it_s_vital?language=en.

Section IV

Leveraging Strategic Benefit Auctions

15

Keep the Money Flowing

THE FUTURE OF AUCTION FUNDRAISING IS BRIGHT. Nonprofit, education, association leaders, development professionals and fundraising auctioneers are becoming more and more savvy about the business, art, psychology, and theater of fundraising auctions.

Now it's time for charitable and educational institutions to leverage the latest innovations in benefit auction strategies and technology. Without those innovations, you're not likely to achieve record-breaking success. With them, you can create a community of champions for your cause, and build momentum that will carry you years into the future (see Figure 15.1).

The Party's Over—See Ya Next Year…Maybe…

In three decades of conducting fundraising auctions and consulting with nonprofits and schools about fundraising, the biggest mistake I've seen is treating an auction event as if it were a one-night, once-a-year deal. That thinking epitomizes the old transaction model of auction fundraising. I've even heard people proclaim, "It's like a retail business, but just a one-day retail business." And when I started my career, I thought that too.

But it's just not true. A benefit auction is part of a whole, a strategic development process that extends far into the future. When you hold a benefit auction, you're not just staging an event. You're developing a philanthropic culture of giving that transcends the event.

Figure 15.1   Community of Champions

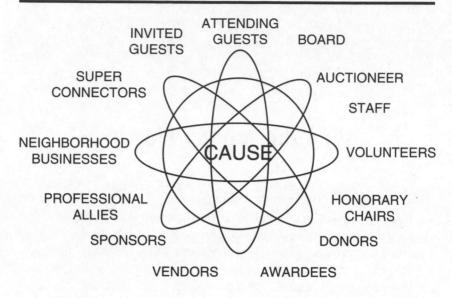

That's why the Philanthropy Model approach extends far beyond your event night. beginning, a golden entry point for continuous donor development. Events, when strategically designed, are a superior way not only to identify new donors, but to cultivate them and continue working with them afterward, showing them what a difference their gift(s) make to the organization.

Penelope Burk of Cygnus Applied Research regularly conducts surveys of the donor environment. She says that of the 95 questions posed to donors in Cygnus's landmark study, none was more revealing than this one: "What would cause you to remain indefinitely loyal to a particular cause, while increasing the value of your contributions over time?"[1] Burk notes that 90 percent of donors who start contributing to a particular cause stop giving by the fifth renewal request, and over 60 percent who make a first contribution never make a second.[2] This disturbing trend limits fundraising growth and forces fundraisers to spend a disproportionate amount of their time and budgets acquiring more donors to replace those one-time supporters.

However, Burk also found that 87 percent of study respondents said they would give again the next time they were asked, 64 percent would make a larger gift, and 74 percent would continue to give indefinitely—if they received the following every time they made a gift:

- Prompt, meaningful acknowledgment of their gifts.
- Reassurance that their gifts will be directed as they intended.
- Meaningful news about their gifts' consequences before they are asked for another contribution.[3]

Stop Inviting Guests and Start Engaging Donors

The critical mind shift is to strategically think of an auction as a golden gateway for year-round connections with donors. Many groups I've worked with, such as STAR, Inc., The Providence Center, the Boys and Girls Club of Greater Lowell, and the Sonoma Harvest Wine Auction, intentionally cultivate donors all year long. They integrate the support of their boards, their vendors, and their key constituents in this expanded effort. And they propel their communities to develop cultures of philanthropy that continue to result in phenomenal success. For example, when Sonoma Harvest Wine Auction made this critical paradigm shift, they shattered their fundraising records by nearly 600 percent, going from $700,000 to $4 million in just two years because they embedded strategies that looked beyond a single-day social event.

Do You Treat Every Guest as a Donor?

One of my most important mentors, Hall of Fame auctioneer Patricia Massart, always said: "Eat a lot of ice cream, but savor more those with whom you enjoy it!" Pat, a beloved national leader in the auction industry, passed away several years ago after a valiant battle with cancer. Her words still ring true for anyone involved in fundraising. The question is, how do you "savor" your donors?

First, treat your auction guests as true donors, not just as event attendees. Be strategic. Design meaningful donor engagement into your auction event and beyond.

We know that giving is up and your donors want to contribute more to your great cause so that they can make a difference.[4] So how can you leverage this exciting donor trend? Give your donors what they really want, which is to continue to support a cause they love, not only at your auction, but for years to come…They'll do this gladly—but only if you get your part right.

Using the Philanthropy Model paradigm shift, communicate the impact of your donors' high bids and contributions not only at your fundraiser event, but also as part of your long-term advancement plan. Engage your board and stakeholders to personally visit with guests during the cocktail hour and silent auction, at the dinner table, and after the auction, so they can share stories, discuss results, and highlight program successes that the guests' gifts support.

Say thank you right away. Assign your board members to call donors within 48 hours to personally thank them for their gifts. This should be a brief, heartfelt message of gratitude; this is not the time to ask for more funds.

Keep donors informed in a meaningful way all year long. After the auction, be sure to send donors specific information on where and how their donations are being used to further your great cause.

Your Auction Items Are Sold, but Are Your Guests?

Will they love you tomorrow? How will they remember you and stay with you? More important than selling items is selling your cause. Show your guests the impact their donations are making for your organization.

Penelope Burk's findings substantiate what I have seen at fundraisers and auctions for many years. It's a fallacy to believe that guests have a spending limit—that they come to an event having already decided the top limit of what they'll spend. Tom Ahern, principal of Ahern Donor Communications and author of *Seeing Through a Donor's Eyes*, asks, "What do your donors care about? From the donors' perspective, if they give you funds, what difference will it make? What good will their donations do?"[5]

Katie Banzhaf, executive director at STAR, Inc., explains how she and her board strategically leverage their auction gala for new board and donor development:

> The gala and benefit auction is a magnet for many more people to become more engaged. Our professional auctioneer/consultant helped us to foster those relationships. While we were sometimes hesitant to ask more of these wonderful donors, Kathy Kingston, our consultant, reminded us that these were charitable individuals who would more than likely want to be involved in other areas of the organization as well. She was correct. A neighbor of a person served by STAR attended the gala as the neighbor's guest. They made a large donation. As Executive Director, I joined our Director of Philanthropy in a private meeting at their home to thank them personally after the event. We learned in that meeting that the donor had a sister with disabilities in another state. We learned she worked at a day care center. We learned that she would be honored to provide sitter services for our families so that they could attend parent meetings. Over time we learned that she would be an active board member with a genuine commitment to the organization. She is now in the middle of her second term on the board.

Cheers! Sonoma Harvest Wine Auction's Stunning $4 Million Success

In 2014, Sonoma Harvest Wine Auction shattered all records to raise over $4 million, a total that more than doubled the record-breaking 2013 total of almost $1.5 million. The year before, I'd been retained as the consultant by executives Maureen Cottingham and Honore Comfort of Sonoma Harvest Wine Auction. I worked with them, their boards of directors, and key vintners to develop strategies to significantly maximize revenue and guest engagement and to continue to position Sonoma as a world class wine region. Let's highlight their success through the Five Pillars of Strategic Benefit Auctions.

Pillar One: Find Out What Matters Most to Your Supporters

Supporting children's literacy was ranked as a top community need in Sonoma. Executive directors and key stakeholders adopted a three-year commitment to support children's literacy as their fund-a-need beneficiary. Additionally, strategies were designed to market Sonoma as a world class wine region. Emphasis was placed on retaining the unique culture of this signature Sonoma charity wine event.

Pillar Two: Invite Your Supporters In

Because the event always sells out, a highly targeted audience development and cultivation strategy was designed to integrate vintners, sponsors, benefactors, winery owners, and growers to target big bidders, major donors, and key auction guests. During the entire year, stakeholders took a personalized active role in developing relationships with guests, sponsors, and prospective donors. Further strategies included a greater outreach and closer connection to community charities, especially groups providing literacy programs.

Pillar Three: Inspire Your Supporters to Fall in Love with You

A well-designed communications plan created inspiration for breakthrough bidding. Sonoma Wine created new messaging with the theme "The Chefs Serve, The Winemakers Pour, and the Proceeds Matter." Most important, a strategically designed approach to the Fund-the-Future included a first-person testimonial story of success, and presecured leadership and matching gifts sparked record giving. And there was a highly orchestrated, fast-paced show flow, integrating music, video, and entertainment into the event and timing the live auction to generate excitement and momentum.

Pillar Four: Give Them Reasons to Stay in Love with You Forever

Sonoma Wine developed a year-round personalized outreach by key vintners, executives, staff, and board members to cultivate big bidders, sponsors, and donors. Greater emphasis was placed on showcasing, year-round, the transformational impact of beneficiary charities, including literacy groups in the community. As a fundraising auction strategist, I provided customized workshops for the vintners, board members, and community leaders about leveraging fundraising and auction trends, and cultivating donors at and after the event.

Pillar Five: Invest in What Counts; Ignore the Rest

Prior to 2013, a transaction model approach dominated Sonoma Wine's event planning. Using the new Philanthropy Model of Fundraising Auctions, we refocused key strategies to maximize revenue and greater guest engagement at the live auction and fund-a-need appeal. An experienced professional auctioneer who specializes in benefit auctions, Scott Robertson, and his team of professional auctioneer bid assistants were retained. We designed a superb guest experience with maximum momentum and a high entertainment production value. Vintner leaders and guests played a key role, not only bidding generously at the auction but contributing auction items beforehand and inspiring others to join the effort. The extraordinary live-auction lots were curated to match the interests of the audience members. For example, the largest grossing auction lot of the day was Hamel Family Wines' "Six Cooks in the Kitchen," featuring a private dinner for 50 at their newly constructed winery. Six top James Beard Award-winning chefs would prepare the meal, which 25 couples bid $10,000 each to experience, bringing the lot total to $250,000. The largest individual lot was the Gallo Family's "Amazing Africa" lot, featuring a luxurious safari to top destinations. The safari sold for a total of $220,000 to two bidders, each bidding

$110,000, generously doubling this trip. The Fund-the-Future, which supported child literacy, received over $1.6 million, more than doubling the previous year's $700,000 total.

"We made history in Sonoma County," Maureen Cottingham said afterward. "Along with our vintners and grape growers, it took the leadership of our incredible honorary chairs, the Ferrer Family and the Klein Family, who led our community this year, to support our kids and our county."

Pick Door Number 3: Take Your Organization to the Next Level

There are three strategic actions you'll want to consider to retain more donors and raise more money. First, create a plan to incorporate your benefit auction into your overall organizational development plan. Second, if you are going to invest the time and effort to produce an event, do it really well. Make sure you get high marks. Third, ask. Be unabashed about inviting your supporters to contribute, then thank people, then ask again when you communicate the impact of their gifts—for the entire year after your event and beyond (see Figure 15.2). That's my special message. People want to give and to give more; they are just waiting to be asked. When you communicate the impact message that connects your donors to your cause, magic happens.

Figure 15.2 Doorways to Greatest Impact

Choose the door that Leads to the greatest IMPACT.

| 1 | 2 | 3 |
| BEFORE EVENT | DURING EVENT | AFTER EVENT |

When you approach fundraising strategically, your supporters and donors will see your organization in a completely different light. An entity that can successfully produce a black-tie gala fundraiser will be looked at differently by the community. Producing a strategic fundraising auction tells foundations and high net worth individuals that you're playing at a different level, that you're taking your donor development seriously.

Robin Godfrey, executive director of GALA Choruses, says, "You must move all the puzzle pieces of fundraising together. If you want to inspire your $50 dollar silent auction bidder to be a $1,000 donor, you have to convince that donor that you'll spend their gift wisely and are worthy and capable of their gift." Additionally, your organization's public persona must reflect that you are worthy and capable of receiving larger gifts. You can't improve your public persona with a silent auction or a bake sale.

Create the Greatest Impact—A Strategic Donor Cultivation Plan

What happens after your doors close and guests go home? Nothing, unless you design intentional strategic actions to show your gratitude, inspire effective communication, invite guests to be further involved, and focus your staff and volunteers on donor engagement and retention. Attracting and retaining fundraising donors is a key priority. Go that extra mile to personally connect with your auction guests, sponsors, donors, and volunteers. It really means the world to them to be part of your nonprofit's future success!

While you're on the phone, brief them with exciting news about your cause and share success stories about programs they love, and services that are meaningful to them. Personally stay involved with your donors and share with them what a difference their wonderful support is making.

The ultimate goal is to inspire your donors to stay with you, now and into the future. There are numerous opportunities along the way for them to connect more deeply with your mission. Here are some meaningful ways that donors can become more engaged: become a volunteer, join your auction leadership team, attend other events and cause-related activities, serve on your board of directors, become a sponsor, participate financially in the annual appeal, invest as a major donor, donate to a capital campaign, give a legacy gift, make a charitable bequest, and most of all, offer their unique gift of influence to introduce others to your great cause.

Development professionals dedicate their lives to this effort, and they've learned the nuanced skills required to develop strategic advancement plans. They know that cultivating donors is a personalized approach that extends far beyond the night of a fundraising auction event and that it can take many years to steward a donor. Be sure to make use of the outstanding experience and other resources offered by your professional fundraising executives. Your auction fundraiser is a springboard for long-term donor engagement and a showcase for your cause. The big idea is to create a strategic plan to engage your bidders and guests after your event—and by that I mean for years, even decades, after your event.

Lynn Sobel of Lynn Sobel & Associates explains,

> Some nonprofits spend the bulk of their efforts getting ready for the gala. It's great to have a good party but that is only the beginning. The gala is your opportunity to introduce guests to your organization and to begin to cultivate their passion for your mission. As Humphrey Bogart says in *Casablanca*, this is the beginning of a beautiful friendship! After the event, call the donors the next day to thank them. Nothing says gratitude like an immediate thank you. Also send an e-mail once you know the financial results of the event. Share those results and thank them again. As the year progresses, keep your donors updated on events and happenings.[6]

Get to the Heart of What Matters

I would like to give you a special gift, my "MIT Strategic Giving Program."

I have created my signature donor impact exercise to get to the heart of why giving matters. This powerful thought exercise can help your staff, volunteers, speakers, donors, event team members, and board members connect with your donors. By telling a true and compelling story, you will quickly communicate the emotional impact of the donors' gifts. When you and your team participate in my "MIT Strategic Giving Program," you'll send off emotional sparks that ignite giving. You can then design a riveting impact story so your donors can deeply feel how their gifts make a difference. And that's what will make them want to stay connected with you, now and well into the future.

Too many organizations pontificate about mission statements, spew out lists of programs, and thrash about with boring statistics. Go deeper. If you want to significantly increase fundraising and donor loyalty, communicate true impact from your donor's perspective. Try this thought exercise with your stakeholders, and see what insights it brings.

Kathy Kingston's "MIT Strategic Giving Program"

MOVES: What moves you personally? Why do you care about our organization?

INSPIRES: What inspires others to give generously? What impassions donors?

TRANSFORMS: What is the key impact on clients that you serve?

If you get stuck, just pretend I'm standing next to you, asking "So what? What does that story mean to you?" You'll be amazed at how much deeper you can go.

The Power of a Story

There's one final story I'd like to share with you. I was teaching my "MIT Strategic Giving Program" at a workshop for nonprofit leaders and corporate sponsors. I was explaining how to personally coach board members, clients, event speakers, and celebrities to powerfully share an emotional story that would inspire generous giving for a fund-a-need appeal.

"Who has a compelling story that shows how your organization really impacted someone's life?" I asked.

Every hand flew up.

"I do!" A gentleman named Dennis stepped right up front, smiling brightly. "Well," he said, "there was this boy about 10 years old who lived in a blue-collar tenement neighborhood. One day on the way home from school, four kids walked at him, pushed him, kicked him, and left him curled in a ball on the ground. When he came home, his father took him over to the local Boys Club. This boy wasn't an athlete, but he found something that he could do—boxing. He loved that there was something for every kid who needed it most. It gave him newfound confidence, and he made a lot more friends from all neighborhoods. Most of all, he felt safe and confident because this was a fun, great place for kids."

I asked my famous question: "So what? What does that story mean to you?"

Dennis became visibly choked up, looked down, and shuffled his feet. After a moment, he looked up again with glistening eyes and said, "That young boy...was me."

He continued:

> Boys and Girls Club changed my life, I felt that I was not alone, I was part of something bigger than me. I felt the camaraderie of caring adults and kids that has grown into lifelong relationships. That's why I believe so deeply in their work. My name is Dennis McCarthy, and today I'm the director of development for this organization. And I'm so proud that for the last 10 years I've been a mentor to a boy, Jio, who doesn't have a dad.... He's like my son.[7]

Just like Dennis, we all have transformational stories that will inspire others. Will you pass yours forward? Will you consider telling your stories with your donors, friends, and colleagues? You'll inspire others to tell why they care, too. That's how to continue to build a community of champions for your cause year-round.

It's an honor and a privilege to raise funds and connect people so they can make an impact for a cause that impassions them. Through the lens of powerful strategic auction fundraising, I invite you to transform your traditional special event into an inspirational culture of giving.

Thank you for reading my book, for sharing your story, and for passing it forward. I wish you unprecedented success. I'm eager to help you transform your fundraising and donor development. Please feel free to write to me and share your ideas at kathy@kingstonauction.com. Please visit www.AHigherBid.com.

I invite you to tell your stories everywhere. Share your passion about your cause, and tell us all why you love what you do. To quote Dr. Seuss, "To the world, you may be one person. But to one person, you may be the world."

Notes

1. P. Burk, *The Burk Donor Survey: Where Philanthropy Is Headed in 2013* (Chicago: Cygnus Applied Research, Inc., 2013).
2. Ibid.
3. Ibid.
4. Ibid.
5. T. Ahern, *Seeing through a Donor's Eyes: How to Make a Persuasive Case for Your Annual Drive to Your Planned Giving Campaign to Your Capital Campaign* (Medfield, MA: Emerson & Church Publishers, 2009).
6. Lynn Sobel, personal communication, October 29, 2014.
7. Dennis McCarthy, personal communication, September 30, 2014.

Acknowledgments

I wish to convey my profound appreciation to my editors at John Wiley and Sons: to Matthew Davis for his ace navigation throughout the publishing process, Maria Sunny Zacharias for her expert guidance, and Alison Hankey for her superb insights and support of strategic benefit auctions.

I wish to express my deepest gratitude to my mentor Alan Weiss, PhD, the Million-Dollar Consultant. Alan's extraordinary insights inspired me to write this book. His compelling coaching helped me expand my mind-set and move beyond auctioneering itself, providing greater value with high-level consulting and, in the process, powerfully transforming my business and my life.

As a first-time author, I am indebted to a dream team of world-class professionals who provided immeasurable support. My astute and generous literary agent, John Willig, expertly guided me though myriad publishing details and writing nuances. I am grateful to writing guru Mark Levy, who helped me crystalize and position big ideas for the book with his astute coaching. I am deeply appreciative of Linda Popky, author, marketing maestro, pianist, and valued colleague. Her excellent suggestions and masterful editing made every word count. I also wish to thank Jeanette Cooperman, PhD, who polished the final manuscript with her keen eye and perceptive pen. Thank you to my sister, Sally Kingston, PhD, an educational consultant, who has unwaveringly supported me since this book's inception with countless readings, research, editing, laughter, dog stories, and savvy recommendations.

I'm indebted to the clients of Kingston Auction Company, who for three decades have offered me the privilege of serving them. Their passion and service inspire me more than words can express. I wish to publicly thank everyone for sharing their stories and success strategies. I am grateful to my colleagues who shared their professional expertise on philanthropy and new technologies. I offer fervent thanks to fundraising consultant and colleague Sharon Danosky, who introduced me to the concept of integrating benefit auctions into long-term development planning. I have the pleasure of acknowledging the vision of Penelope Burk for her research and writing about donor-centered fundraising. I deeply appreciate the leadership and writing of Tom Ahern and Simone Joyaux. I also wish to thank the late Robert B. Parker and Joan Parker, writers and generous philanthropists who unwaveringly supported nonprofit causes, me, and my passion for fundraising auctions.

I'm pleased to publicly express my gratitude to Hannes Combest, chief executive officer, and the entire National Auctioneers Association, as well as the Education Institute Trustees and the National Auctioneers Association Foundation. I am indebted to my auctioneer colleagues around the world, a true family of greathearted and generous professionals. Thank you to our outstanding professional auctioneers and our superb support team at Kingston Auction Company.

I wish to thank my mentors at Saint Louis University, who deeply influenced me to work in the service of others. I am grateful for the 10 years I lived in Anchorage, Alaska; it is where I learned the power of building community. To my loving friends and family, who were a never-ending well of support and laughter during the writing of this book, thank you. Special thanks to artist and friend Doris Rice, whose art beautifully illustrates key ideas for this book.

And, finally, heartfelt thanks to that unknown Easter Seals volunteer over 50 years ago, whose handwritten thank-you note launched me on this incredible journey.

Resources

Associations

Association of Fundraising Professionals (AFP), www.afpnet.org
Association for Healthcare Philanthropy (AHP), www.ahp.org
BoardSource, www.boardsource.org
The Center for Association Leadership (ASAE), www.asaecenter
   .org
Charity Navigator, www.charitynavigator.org
Guidestar, www.guidestar.org
Council for Advancement and Support of Education (CASE),
   www.case.org
Council on Foundations, www.cof.org
International Special Event Society (ISES), www.ises.com
Meeting Professionals International (MPI), www.mpiweb.org
National Association of Independent Schools (NAIS), www.nais
   .org
National Center for Charitable Statistics, www.nccs.urban.org
National Center for Social Entrepreneurs, www.social
   entrepreneurs.org
National School Foundation Association, www.schoolfoundations
   .org

Journals and Media

Auctioneer magazine, www.auctioneers.org/auctioneer
Chronicle of Philanthropy, www.philanthropy.com
Nonprofit About, www.nonprofit.about.com
Nonprofit Quarterly, www.nonprofitquarterly.org

Auctioneers

Benefit Auctioneer Specialist (BAS), www.auctioneers.org/
   designations/bas
Certified Auctioneer Institute (CAI), www.auctioneers.org/
   designations/cai
National Auctioneers Association (NAA), www.auctioneers.org

Books

Ahern, Tom. *Seeing Through a Donor's Eyes.* Medfield, MA: Emerson
   & Church Publishers, 2012.
Ahern Tom, and Simone Joyaux. *Keep Your Donors: The Guide to
   Better Communications and Stronger Relationships.* Hoboken, NJ:
   John Wiley & Sons, 2008.
Allen, Judy. *Event Planning: The Ultimate Guide to Successful Meetings,
   Corporate Events, Fundraising Galas, Conferences, Conventions, Incen-
   tives and other Special Events.* Hoboken, NJ: John Wiley & Sons,
   2008.
Burk, Penelope. *Donor-Centered Fundraising.* Chicago: Burk & Asso-
   ciates, 2003.
Burk, Penelope. *Donor-Centered Leadership.* Chicago: Cygnus
   Applied Research, 2013.
Carr, Eugene, and Michelle Paul. *Breaking the Fifth Wall: Rethinking
   Arts Marketing for the 21st Century.* New York: Patron Publishing,
   2011.
Davis, Karen Eber. *7 Nonprofit Income Streams: Open the Floodgates to
   Sustainability!* Rancho Santa Margarita, CA: Charity Channel
   Press, 2014.
Fiske, J. R., and Colleen A. Fiske. *The Big Book of Benefit Auctions.*
   Hoboken, NJ: John Wiley & Sons, 2009.
Fredricks, Laura. *The Ask.* San Francisco: Jossey-Bass, 2010.
Kihlstedt, Andrea. *Asking Styles: Harness Your Personal Fundraising
   Style.* Rancho Santa Margarita, CA: Charity Channel Press, 2012.
Kihlstedt, Andrea, and Andy Robinson. *Train Your Board (and
   Everyone Else) to Raise Money: A Cookbook of Easy to Use Fundraising
   Exercises.* Medfield, MA: Emerson & Church Publishers, 2014.
Kingston, Kathy. *Record Breaking Fundraising Auction Tips:* Volumes
   1 and 2. Hampton, NH: Kingston Auction Company, 2006.

Klein, Kim. *Fundraising for Social Change*, 6th edition. San Francisco: Jossey-Bass, 2011.

Sargeant, Adrian, and Elaine Jay. *Building Donor Loyalty*. San Francisco: Jossey-Bass, 2004.

Weiss, Alan. *Million Dollar Consulting*. New York: McGraw-Hill, 2009.

Weiss, Alan. *The Consulting Bible*. Hoboken, NJ: John Wiley & Sons, 2011.

Articles and Reports

Association of Fundraising Professionals and the Urban Institute. "2013 Fundraising Effectiveness Survey Report," 2013. www.urban.org/uploadedpdf/412906-2013-fundraising -effectiveness-survey-report.pdf.

Blackbaud. "Charitable Giving Report: How Nonprofit Fundraising Performed in 2013," 2014. www.blackbaud.com/nonprofit-resources/charitablegiving#.VHdsTkv_Rbg.

Burke, Penelope Burk. "The Burk Donor Survey: Where Philanthropy Is Headed in 2014," 2014. http://cygresearch.com/the-burk-donor-survey-2014/.

Danosky, Sharon. The Polishing Touch: Board Members Boost Event Success." *Field Guide, Land Trust Alliance*, Spring 2014. www.landtrustalliance.org.

Giving USA Foundation. *The Annual Report on Philanthropy for the Year 2013*. Indianapolis: Indiana University Lilly Family School of Philanthropy, 2014. www.philanthropy.iupui.edu/news/ article/giving-usa-2014.

Havens, J., and P. Schervish. "A Golden Age of Philanthropy Still Beckons: National Wealth Transfer and Potential for Philanthropy Technical Report," May 28, 2014. Cambridge, MA: Boston College, Center on Wealth and Philanthropy.

National Auctioneers Association. "Auction Industry Holds Strong in 2008 with $268.5 Billion in Sales." Auction industry survey compiled by Morpace, Inc., 2008. www.exclusivelyauctions.com /pdfs/naa-2008.pdf.

Saffer, Neil, and Kathy Kingston. "Trends in Fundraising for the Benefit Auctioneer." Session presented at the International Auctioneer Conference & Show, Orlando, FL, June 2011.

References

Ahern, T. 2012. "The Brain According to Me: Neuroscience Is the Most Important Force at Work in Fundraising Today. Or It Should Be." *Ahern Donor Communications* 12.03. Retrieved from http://ahern comm.com/ss_plugins/content/content.php?content.5093.

Ahern, T. 2010. "Why Gifts Matter: They Buy Impact and Self Esteem." *Ahern Donor Communications* 10.08. Retrieved from http://ahern comm.com/ss_plugins/content/content.php?content.5069.

Ahern, T. 2009. *Seeing Through a Donor's Eyes: How to Make a Persuasive Case for Your Annual Drive to Your Planned Giving Campaign to Your Capital Campaign*. Medfield, MA: Emerson & Church Publishers.

Association of Fundraising Professionals and the Urban Institute. 2013. "2013 Fundraising Effectiveness Survey Report." Fundraising Effectiveness Project, 2013. Retrieved from www.urban.org/ uploadedpdf/412906-2013-fundraising-effectiveness-survey-report .pdf.

Ayyar, R. 2014. "Why a Good Story Is the Most Important Thing You Will Ever Sell." *Fast Company*. Retrieved from www.pauljzak .com/images/documents/fastcompany.com-Why_A_Good_Story _Is_The_Most_Important_Thing_Youll_Ever_Sell.pdf.

Barber, P., and B. Levis. 2013. *Donor Retention Matters*. Washington, DC: The Center on Nonprofits and Philanthropy at the Urban Institute.

Blackbaud. 2012. *The 2012 State of the Nonprofit Sector Report*. Charleston, SC: Blackbaud.

Brown, S. 2008. *TED Talk: Play Is More than Just Fun*. Retrieved from www .ted.com/talks/stuart_brown_says_play_is_more_than_fun_it_s_ vital?language=en.

Burk, P. 2013. *The Burk Donor Survey: Where Philanthropy Is Headed in 2013*. Chicago: Cygnus Applied Research, Inc.

Dixon, J., and D. Keyes. 2013. "The Permanent Disruption of Social Media." *Stanford Social Innovation Review*. Retrieved from www .ssireview.org/pdf/Winter_2013_The_Permanent_Disruption_of_ Social_Media.pdf.

Evans, R. L. 1971. *Richard Evans' Quote Book*. Salt Lake City, UT: Publishers Press.

Gibson, C., and W. Dietel. 2010. "What Do Donors Want?" *Nonprofit Quarterly*. Retrieved from https://nonprofitquarterly.org/index.php? option=com_content&view=article&id=5866:what-d.

Giving USA Foundation. 2014. *The Annual Report on Philanthropy for the Year 2013*. Indianapolis: Indiana University Lilly Family School of Philanthropy.

GuideStar. 2013. "One Web Site Enables Nonprofits to Tell Their Stories, Commit to Transparency, and Define Their Impact" [press release]. Retrieved from www.guidestar.org/rxa/news/news-releases/2013/ 2013-08-14-charting-impact-integrated-into-guidestar-exchange .aspx.

Hanson, D. J. 2014. "How Alcohol Affects Us: The Biphasic Curve." *Alcohol Problems and Solutions*. Retrieved from www2.potsdam.edu/ alcohol/HealthIssues/1100827422.html#.VFBVEPnF91Z.

Klitgaard, R. 2006. "On the Drucker Legacy." Claremont, CA: Claremont Graduate University. Retrieved from www.cgu.edu/PDFFiles/ Presidents%20Office/Drucker_Legacy_May%2006.pdf.

Monarth, H. 2014. "The Irresistible Power of Storytelling as a Strategic Business Tool." *Harvard Business Review*. Retrieved from www .pauljzak.com/images/documents/The%20Irresistible%20Power %20of%20Storytelling%20as%20a%20Strategic%20Business%20 Tool%20-%20Harrison%20Monarth%20-%20Harvard%20Busi ness%20Review.pdf.

Morpace. 2008. "Auction Industry Holds Strong in 2008 with $268.5 Billion in Sales." Auction industry survey. Retrieved from www.exclusivelyauctions.com/pdfs/naa-2008.pdf.

Saffer, N., and K. Kingston. 2011, June. "Trends in Fundraising for the Benefit Auctioneer." Session presented at the International Auctioneer Conference & Show, Orlando, FL.

Scheimann and Lingle. 2005. *Bullseys! Hitting Your Strategic Targets through High Impact*. Florence, MA: Free Press.

Underhill. P. n.d.. "Why People Buy: The Science of Shopping." *Strategic Marketing*. Retrieved from www.etstrategicmarketing.com/ SmJan-Feb3/art10.html.

A Final Call: Giving Back and Passing Forward

The Kingston Fund

I created The Kingston Fund[1] as a memorial tribute to my parents Winifred and William Kingston, and to provide a unique opportunity for my nephew Arley and seven nieces, Megan, Alysha, Molly, Brianna, Erin, Lexi, and Lindsey, to learn how philanthropy works from the inside. All eight comprise our board of advisors. We typically hold our annual Kingston Fund meeting on Thanksgiving between turkey and pumpkin pie. All eight members of our board of advisors discuss the needs of various charities and allocate our annual grant funding to areas that are important to them: helping abused and sick kids, supporting hospice, and strengthening families in need.

A Special Note to Kids

I want to express a deep appreciation to you and to all of the other children who give. We know from research conducted by the Indiana University Lilly Family School of Philanthropy in partnership with the United Nations Foundation that in 2013, 90 percent of children between ages 8 and 19 gave to charity and that boys and girls gave equally.[2,3] Our future is bright and exciting because of you. It's not what you get, it's what you give that counts. Thank you.

Inspire Others and Yourself

How can you give back to your community for something you deeply love? It's really not that difficult. Select a cause that impassions you. Research the cause on the web, call them, and talk to staff and volunteers. Get involved in a way that's meaningful for you. You could volunteer at an event or special program, serve on a committee or the board, or even make a contribution if you are inspired.

You'll meet wonderful like-minded people, make friends, build a network of business allies, learn new things, empower your self-confidence, enjoy yourself, and, most of all, support something that you really care about as you help others. Best of all, you'll feel really good, too. (Hint: When you feel confident and positive, you'll attract more positivity and greatness into your life.)

Notes

1. The Kingston Fund is a donor-designated fund of the Cape Cod Foundation.
2. Giving USA Foundation, *The Annual Report on Philanthropy for the Year 2013*. Indianapolis, IN: Indiana University Lilly Family School of Philanthropy (2014), 76.
3. Indiana University Lilly Family School of Philanthropy, partnered with United Nations Foundation, "Women Give 2013." Retrieved from www.philanthropy.iupui.edu/files/research/women_give_2013-final9-12-2013.pdf.

Index